Recovering Financial Systems

Other books by IDE-JETRO

INDUSTRIAL CLUSTERS IN ASIA
Akifumi Kuchiki and Masatsugu Tsuji (*editors*)

SPATIAL STRUCTURE AND REGIONAL DEVELOPMENT IN CHINA
Nobuhiro Okamoto and Takeo Ihara (*editors*)

GENDER AND DEVELOPMENT
The Japanese Experience in Comparative Perspective
Mayumi Murayama (*editor*)

EAST ASIA'S DE FACTO ECONOMIC INTEGRATION
Daisuke Hiratsuka (*editor*)

Recovering Financial Systems

China and Asian Transition Economies

Edited by Mariko Watanabe

palgrave
macmillan

IDE-JETRO

First published 2006 by
PALGRAVE MACMILLAN
Houndmills, Basingstoke, Hampshire RG21 6XS and
175 Fifth Avenue, New York, N.Y. 10010
Companies and representatives throughout the world

PALGRAVE MACMILLAN is the global academic imprint of the Palgrave Macmillan division of St. Martin's Press, LLC and of Palgrave Macmillan Ltd. Macmillan® is a registered trademark in the United States, United Kingdom and other countries. Palgrave is a registered trademark in the European Union and other countries.

ISBN 13: 978–0–230–00474–0 hardback
ISBN 10: 0–230–00474–1 hardback

This book is printed on paper suitable for recycling and made from fully managed and sustained forest sources.

A catalogue record for this book is available from the British Library.

Library of Congress Cataloging-in-Publication Data
Recovering financial systems : China and Asian transition economies / edited by Mariko Watanabe.
p. cm.
Includes bibliographical references and index.
ISBN 0–230–00474–1 (cloth)
1. China—Economic policy—1976–2000. 2. China–Economic policy—2000– 3. Vietnam—Economic policy—1975– 4. Burma—Economic policy—1988– I. Watanabe, Mariko.

HC427.92.R426 2006
332.095–dc22 2006044787

10 9 8 7 6 5 4 3 2 1
15 14 13 12 11 10 09 08 07 06

Printed and bound in Great Britain by
Antony Rowe Ltd, Chippenham and Eastbourne

Contents

List of Figures

List of Tables

Acknowledgments

This book was brought to publication with the invaluable assistance and hard work of many people. This project, an empirical investigation on financial system development of transitional economies in Asia, was a research program funded by the Institute of Developing Economies under the Government of Japan. We would like to express our appreciation to our colleagues both inside and outside the Institute of Developing Economies for their invaluable contributions to this project.

First of all, all the contributors of this project have worked extensively to build the motivation of the study with the editor. Akio Takahara (University of Tokyo) and Hiroshi Akama (Bank of Japan) gave inspiring lectures on China's political and financial institutions. Koji Nisikimi, Takahiro Fukunishi, Momoe Makino, Futaba Ishizuka, Masayuki Kobayashi, Yurika Suzuki, Rika Nakagawa, colleagues at the IDE, shared stimulating, brain-stormed discussions during the initial stages of the project.

Some members of contributors conducted field interviews and data surveys in China, Vietnam and Myanmar. We would like to thank following institutions for their support of the research activities of this study: the People's Bank of China (PBOC), the State Council Center of Development Research (DRC), Changshu Rural Bank, the Sichuan Academy of Social Science (all in China), that State Bank of Viet Nam, and Myanmar Marketing Research and Development (MMRD).

We have also benefited greatly from the advice of Akira Kohsaka (Osaka University), Hidenobu Okuda (Hitotsubashi University), Liu Deqiang (Tokyo Gakugei University), Kensuke Kubo (Institute of Developing Economies), who took part in the final workshop at IDE, and shared their expertise on empirical research on developing economies, and also the five anonymous referees who were selected from both inside and outside IDE. Their comments have greatly improved the chapters in this book. The diligent and hard work of the editorial staffs at Palgrave Macmillan finally brought this work to publication. Lastly, the views expressed here are the authors' own and do not reflect the views of IDE or any other affiliated organizations. Any remaining errors are ours.

MARIKO WATANABE

Notes on the Contributors

Hisatoshi Hoken is a research fellow at IDE. His research areas include the behavior of households, the rural labor market and agriculture in China.

Seiro Ito holds a Degree in Economics from Brown University. He is currently a research fellow at the Institute of Developing Economies, and teaches microeconomics at the IDE Advanced School. His fields of interest include development economics, applied microeconomics, and applied time series analysis.

Koichiro Kimura is a researcher at the Institute of Developing Economies. He is also currently a visiting researcher at the Institute of Industrial Economics, Chinese Academy of Social Sciences.

Masahiro Kodama is a researcher at the Institute of Developing Economies, Japan. He is also an associate professor in the Institute of Developing Economies Advanced School.

Koji Kubo is Research Fellow at the Institute of Developing Economies (IDE-JETRO). His research interests covers financial sector development in transition economies.

Fumiharu Mieno is an Associate Professor in Economics at Kobe University, Japan. His research areas include corporate finance and the banking sector, rural finance in developing economies, financial systems in transition economies, and Thai and South East Asian economies.

Osamu Takamizawa is a professor at the Institute of Oriental Culture. His published works include *Disputes and Law in Contemporary China* (1998). This work was translated into Chinese in 2003. His other works focus on sources of law in China and modern Chinese legal history.

Mariko Watanabe is a research fellow at the Institute of Developing Economies. She is conducting empirical researches on corporate reform, industrial and financial development in China based on field interviews and econometrics work.

Shinichi Watanabe is a Professor of International Development at the Graduate School of International Relations of the International University of Japan. He received his PhD in Economics from the University of Minnesota in 1983. His research interests include dollarization and the evolution of the international monetary system under globalization.

Noriyuki Yanagawa is Associate Professor at the Faculty of Economics, the University of Tokyo

Jianlong Zhou is a Professor of Law at the Law School, Dokkyo University, Japan. His research interests include corporate governance from a comparative view and modern Chinese law.

Foreword

This book presents the results of a research project on Asian transitional economies, which aimed to empirically document their experiences as much as possible. The project grew out of a concern over the following issues: While the gradual reform strategy from plan to market, which are mainly taken by China and other Asian transition economies, has been perceived to be superior to the shock strategy, what are the conditions that make its transition smooth and efficient? Does the gradual reform strategy have no defects at all? What can be learned from the impacts of the institutional change on individual behaviors?

To answer these questions, the project employed macro, micro, and legal perspectives, and has introduced novel approaches based on the perspective of law, institutions and economics. From these perspectives, the project documented the following findings. The gradual process has succeeded in accomplishing economic growth and stability. However, the domestic integration of financial resource flows and the effectiveness of monetary policy are still limited, even a quarter of century after the reform has initiated. From a microeconomic perspective, we can confirm that the lack of appropriate institutions for market-type transactions was complemented by the government's interventions, although they tended to be arbitrary at times. More recently, this arbitrariness in state intervention over the economy has revealed its inefficient nature. A thorough reform of state intervention will be the main subject in the near future. This book shows some evidence of the limited accomplishments of the state interventions. In addition, this volume will provide readers with insights into the recent astonishing economic growth and unforeseen problems of some Asian transition economies, notably China.

This work was prepared as a project conducted by Development Studies Center at the Institute of Developing Economies (IDE), Japan, between 2003 and 2004. IDE has more than 150 research fellows studying the developing economies of the world, and basing their research on extensive field studies. We are grateful to Palgrave Macmillan for providing us with the opportunity to publish the works by IDE staffs from the field, and are looking forward to seeing many similar works by IDE staffs.

Masashisa Fujita
President, Institute of Developing Economies
and University of Kyoto

1

Introduction: From Government Allocation to Market Adjustment*

Mariko Watanabe

1.1 Motivation

1.1.1 What happened in the Asian transition economies?

It has been about twenty-five years since the beginning of the transition process of the post-planned economies in Asia, Europe and Russia. In the course of this phenomenon, the experiences of the Asian economies, and, in particular China, have been praised as an outstanding success. Some characteristics of China's experiences – such as its gradual reform, and its dual track system – have become well-known concepts. Theoretical studies on this process (for example, Roland, 2000) have also been focused on these aspects.

However, there has been comparatively little empirical documentation of what events have actually occurred during this period of gradual transition. Of the studies that have been undertaken, some have these considered how policies worked in Asian transition economies from the macro perspective. Woo, Parker and Sachs 1997 collected macroeconomic case studies and components of the macro aspect of reforms, such as trade liberalization and macro stabilization policy. Lin, Cai and Zhou 1996 offered a description of the institutional interactions during the transition process in China. However, they did not address the empirical aspect of the subject.

In the case of the CIS, and the Central Asian and East European transition economies, the European Bank of Reconstruction and Development (EBRD) has extensively documented information on the

* I would like to thank all the contributors to this project for their help and Hidenobu Okuda (Hitotsubashi University), Akira Kohsaka (Osaka University), and Liu Deqiang (Tokyo Education University) for their insightful comments.

experiences of the transition process, such as the renowned Transition Reports. By contrast, the Asian transitional economies appear to lack such systematic research accumulation, even though the EBRD studies on the CIS, Central Asian and East European transition economies have used East Asia's development process as a useful reference point. However, this analysis has focused on theoretical studies and simple descriptive statistics, rather than on detailed empirical study. This book aims to fill this gap, focusing in particular on the role of the government, which might have been expected to remove itself from market economic activity.

What actually happened in the Asian economies during the transition process? What role did the government and the state sector play in the developments? What are the merits and limitations of persistent government and state sector control over the economy? Furthermore, has the gradual process really been successful? This is a more current and different question. Those economies which have adopted a policy of gradual transition have progressed with state ownership, preceding it with a process of institution building. However, is the substantial share of state ownership acceptable even after institution building has been completed? There is as yet no clear answer to this question. As we will see later, however, the retention of state ownership may generate another problem. Currently, China and Vietnam have no clear and agreed date for the government to exit from direct control over these countries' economic activity.

1.2 The research question of this book: how are governments replaced by law and institutions?

The main intention of this book is to explain the nature of governments' participation in economic activities during the transition process. In terms of the macroeconomic point of view, we can easily presume that with the progress of transition, the system of resource allocation transformed from one in which fiscal allocation was dominant to one characterized by market adjustment. We need to confirm whether this process actually took place and, if so, when the change occurred. We will first document this point.

The next step is to address the question of whether government and state sector actions during the process of gradualist transition did or did not result in huge economic upheavals that harmed the welfare of people in the economy. Our hypothesis here is the governments have substituted immature institutional infrastructures, such as law, rules and agents that are necessary to efficiently and effectively facilitate market and financial transactions.

Allen *et al.* (2003) make similar arguments: They documented that the non-state sector achieved impressive growth in China, though its legal system is still relatively underdeveloped. They then argued that China's experience runs counter to the proposition, advanced in the law and growth literature, that a good legal system promotes higher levels of growth. However, they did not identify how efficient governance worked in China, simply stating that there might have been some informal and efficient governance system.

We rather suggest that it is the government and the state sector of the economy which has assumed the burden of enforcement and governance, albeit imperfectly, rather than "some informal or private system." In the particular case of China, it is clear that the state sector has managed the transition process and has coexisted with and promoted the informal and private sectors. The governments and state sectors have simultaneously played not only the role of a player who competes with the non-state sector, but also the role of a judge who disciplines all the players from both state and non-state sectors. We are motivated to review and document the experiences of the other Asian transition economies from this point of view.

1.2 How to understand the experiences of China and the other Asian transition economies

1.2.1 Diversified Asian transition economies: data

When considering the Asian transition economies in detail, it is clear that they are characterized by substantial diversity. First of all, let us examine the experience of China, Vietnam and Myanmar based on macroeconomic data and the policies adopted by their respective governments.

In Asia, there are seven former or current socialist economies: the People's Republic of China (hereafter, China), Vietnam, Myanmar, Laos, Cambodia, Mongolia, and the Democratic People's Republic of Korea. Here, we will examine China, Vietnam and Myanmar because of the availability of systematic data and information for these countries.

Even among these three, the transition processes exhibit two contrasting trends: one followed by China and Vietnam, the other by Myanmar. The former adopted the path of "open door policy with state ownership," where the government retains ownership of economic assets, while simultaneously pursuing pro-growth, market-friendly policies, such as an open policy on trade, the encouragement of foreign direct investment and a substantial tax preference policy for expanding sectors of the economy. By contrast, Myanmar pursued a "closed door policy with liberalized ownership," where the state sector shrank drastically and private ownership prevailed. However, in the case of Myanmar the government retains control of the economy by a "closed-door economic policy," involving exchange rate policy, and the regulation of trade and foreign direct investment. The China–Vietnam group and Myanmar had therefore developed contrasting ideas on the nature of ownership and economic policy during the transition process.

1.2.2.1 Government expenditure, revenue and deficit

First, we will consider to what extent governments control the flow of the economy. Figure 1.1 shows the government share in the expenditure side of economy; that is, the share of fiscal expenditure in the economy. In theory, the share of fiscal expenditure to GDP, the total value of economic activity, may be close to 100 per cent in a planned economy, and will decline over the course of the transition to the market economy. Macro data for each economy show different trends for China, Vietnam and Myanmar. Myanmar's share of fiscal expenditure fell drastically from more than 60 per cent to less than 30 per cent by the 10th year of transition (1996). By contrast, China and Vietnam exhibit more gradual developments. The size of their fiscal expenditure size was originally small. China's figure fell from around 30 per cent to 10 per cent between the 17th and 18th years (1995, 1996), but subsequently rose to around 20 per cent. We lack data regarding the first three years after the break-up of Vietnam's planned economy, but we can see that the share has an upward trend between the third year (1989) and the 15th year (2001). Though the two groups have different trends, their levels converge at between 20 and 30 per cent in the latest year.

Next, we consider the degree of government control of the income or revenue side of the economy. Figure 1.2 shows the trend of the share of fiscal revenues, which is more less the same as that observed for expenditure, although China's data show a basically declining trend.

The breaking down of the planned economy may presume to be induced by increasing the fiscal deficit, and the actual data on fiscal deficit size is broadly consistent with this presumption. In the cases of Myanmar and China, the initial years of reforms recorded one of the

Figure 1.1 Fiscal expenditure (as percentage of GDP)

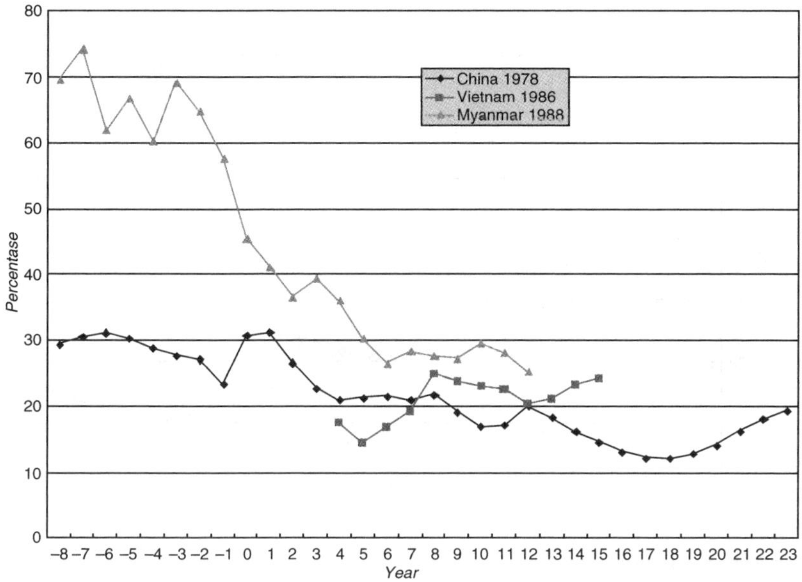

Sources: China: *Comprehensive Statistical Data and Materials on 50 Years of New China*. Beijing: China Statistics Press; *China Statistical Yearbook* (various issues). Beijing: China Statistics Press (in Chinese).
Vietnam: *IMF Economic Reviews 13 Viet Nam*. IMF, 1994; *International Financial Statistics*, December. IMF, 2004; *Statistical Year Book*. Hanoi: Statistical Publishing House (various issues).
Myanmar: *Review of The Financial, Economic and Social Conditions for 1981/82, 1985/86, 1989/90, 1991/92, 1993/94, 1995/96, 1996/97, 1997/98*. Yangon: Ministry of National Planning and Economic Development. *Statistical Yearbook 2002*. Yangon: Central Statistical Organization. *International Financial Statistics*, December. IMF, 2004.

Note: Year is redefined as the initial year of reform as 0; starting year for China = 1978, Vietnam = 1986, Myanmar = 1988.

largest shares of fiscal deficit to GDP of the years examined here (Figure 1.3). Vietnam also shows the largest fiscal deficit in the earliest year available for us. What is interesting is that even after the break down of a planned economy, the fiscal balance records a persistent deficit for all three of the economies. China shows the smallest size of deficit compared to GNP throughout almost the entire period.

Figure 1.2 Fiscal revenue (as percentage of GDP)

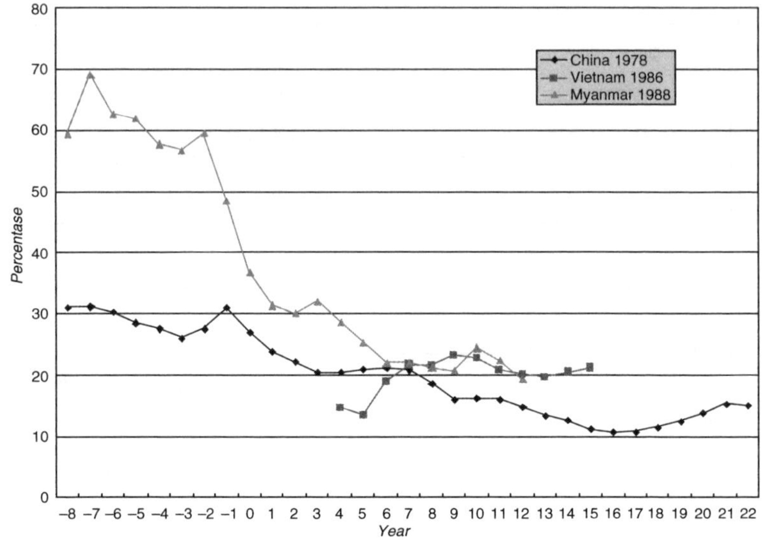

Sources: See Figure 1.1.

Figure 1.3 Fiscal deficit (as a percentage of GDP)

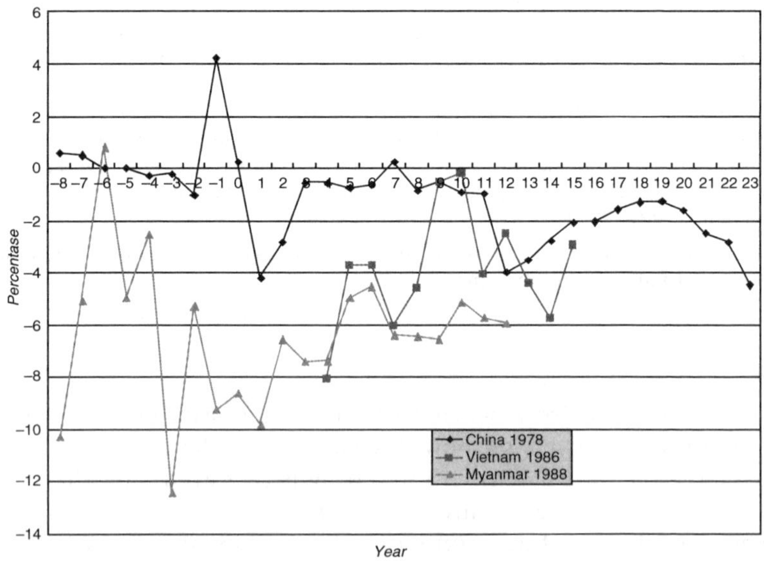

Source: See Figure 1.1.

1.2.2.2 Government control over assets: ownership

Next, we discuss the percentage share of state ownership in the economy. It would be preferable to have figures for the ownership structure of total assets in the economy, but these are not available. Instead, we consider macro data for each of the economies, focusing on investment data by ownership. Figure 1.4 documents that investment by the state sector is still at a much higher level than either collective or individuals' investment even in the 25th year (2003) of transition. Vietnam is also in a similar situation as we can see from Figure 1.5, where non-state ownership investment is slightly higher than the level recorded for foreign investment.

By contrast, the investment share of the private sector is more or less the same as the state sector in Myanmar. This is consistent with the development of fiscal expenditure that documents how the private sector has a substantial share in the whole economy in Myanmar. What we must note here is the low investment to GDP ratio in Myanmar. China and Vietnam both achieved more than 35 per cent of GDP; China, in particular, showed a steadily increasing trend in the share of to GDP. However, Myanmar recorded a ratio as low as 10 to 14 per cent during the first 10 years of the transition process. Though the presence of the private sector has increased rapidly, the investment ratio of the whole economy is particularly low in Myanmar. This

Figure 1.4 Investment by ownership for China (as a percentage of GDP)

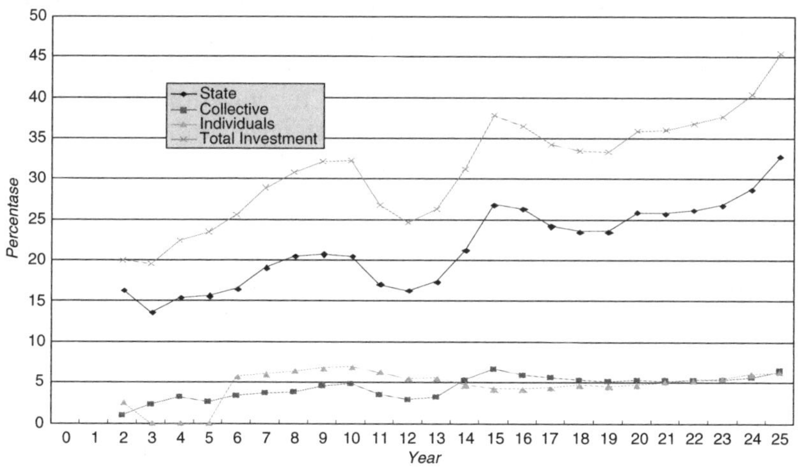

Sources: See Figure 1.1.

Note: 0 is the start year of reform, 1978.

Figure 1.5 Investment by ownership for Vietnam (as a percentage of GDP)

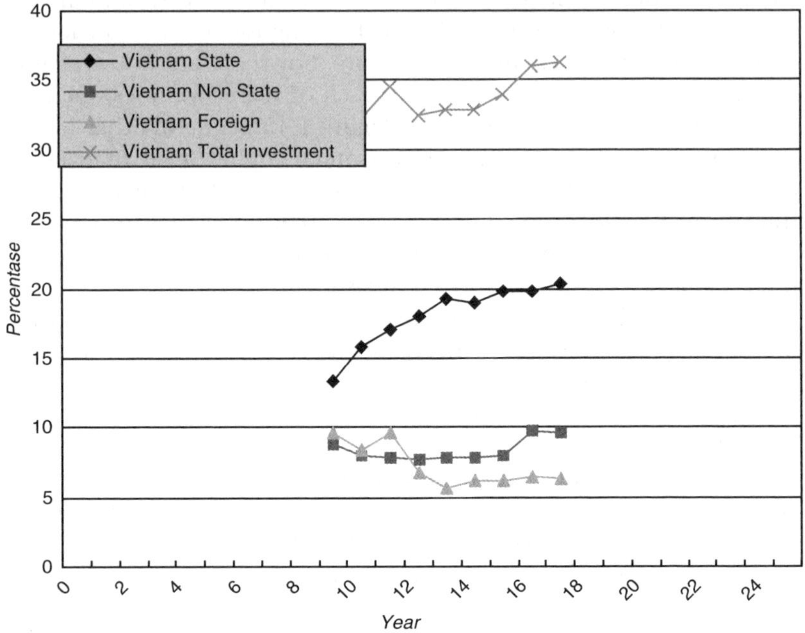

may be due to the peculiar transition path followed by Myanmar. In Myanmar, at the start of the reform process, state-owned enterprises were prohibited from taking loans from commercial banks. Instead, their expenditures were paid directly by the government (Myanmar Budget Law for various years, Part III Interview with former higher officials of Ministry of Finance, 8 September 2004). This is in stark contrast to the path taken by China and Vietnam, where the "financial repression system" was employed. In China and Vietnam, state-owned banks were forced to continue lending to the inefficient or even loss-making state-owned enterprises even after the break-up of the planned economy. As a result, the level of non-performing loans grew significantly.

1.1.2.3 Banking sector reforms

In this section, we will consider what happened in the banking sectors in the Asian transition economies. Table 1.1 tabulates the basic information regarding the banking sector reforms for China, Vietnam,

Figure 1.6 Investment by ownership in Myanmar (as a percentage of GDP)

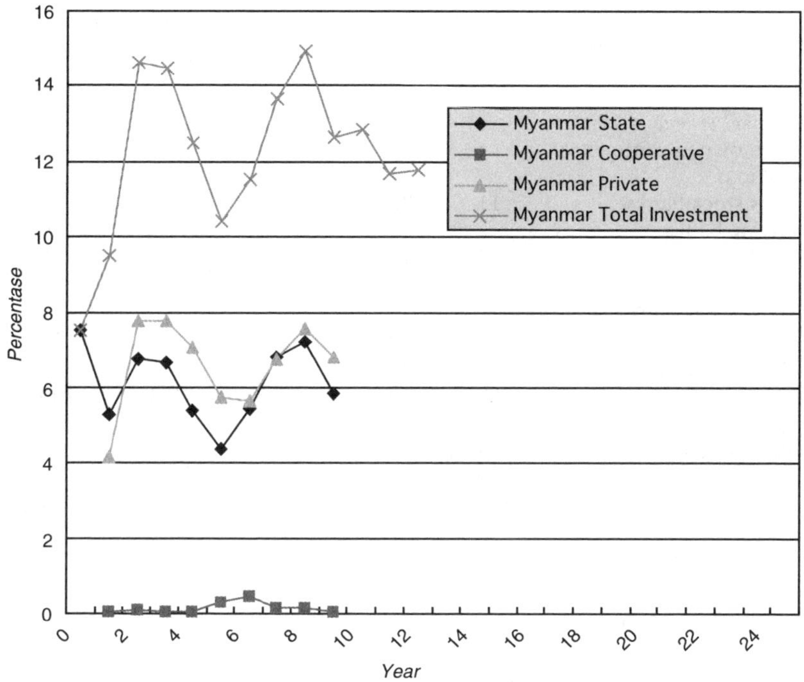

Myanmar, Cambodia and Laos. From this, we can see the following: (i) loans and deposits throughout the entire banking sector in China are remarkably high – as much as 166 or 183 per cent of GDP. By comparison, Myanmar's banking sector is very small – as little as 6 or 14 per cent of GDP. Vietnam is in the middle. (ii) Private banks are more prevalent in Myanmar than in China. By contrast, foreign banks in China and Vietnam account for as much as 13 and 37 per cent of funds, but zero for Myanmar due to the "closed-door" policy. (iii) The share of state-owned commercial banks in Vietnam is very high. China and Laos are similar to Vietnam.

In this section, we have reviewed macro, size of fiscal expenditure and revenue, and share of investment by the state sector, implying that the pattern of financial flows differs across all three countries under consideration – China, Vietnam and Myanmar. China and Vietnam have a substantially larger state sector, and the size of government activity and

Table 1.1 Banking sector reforms for Asian transition economies

	China	*Vietnam*	*Myanmar*	*Cambodia*	*Laos PDR*
Break up of monobank	1984	1989	1976	1989	1989
Number of (end of 2003):					
State-owned commercial banks	4	6	4	1	2
Joint stock banks	11	38	10	3	3
Private banks	1	n.a.	20	n.a.	n.a.
Foreign banks	13	37	0	9	8
Market share of SOCBs as percentage of:					
Credit to the economy	55.8	72.6	n.a.	9.5	53.5
Credit to the SOEs	35.72	91.1	0	0	74.1
Total deposits	58.6	74	57.89	19.3	736
Total presence of bank as percentage of GDP:					
Total deposit	182.8	56	14	14.4	17.2
Credit to the economy	165.5	51.8	6.3	8	11.1
Credit to SOEs	n.a.	17.1	0	0	4.4
Credit to the private sector	n.a.	34.7	6.3	8	6.7
Non-performing loans	20.6	7.8	–	1.1	3

Source: China, Vietnam, Cambodia, Lao from Unteroberdoerster (2004), Table.1; Myanmar: Fukui (2004) in Japanese.

investment share is much larger. By contrast, Myanmar has a relatively large private sector, but the total size of economic flows and investment is much smaller.

The comparison here shows that Vietnam and Myanmar offer useful pointers to understanding China's transition experience. Vietnam follows a process of gradual transition with a similar framework, sustained public ownership and an open door policy. Myanmar follows the other route to gradual transition, characterized by private ownership and a closed-door policy.

1.2.2 How this book evaluates Chinese and Asian experiences

The main purpose of this book is to document both the positive and the negative aspects of the policy of gradual transition. We first documented, from the macro point of view, that the exit of the government from economic activity was now complete – however, it has also been a gradual process. The government has certainly remained. What then are the positive and negative factors of this phenomenon? Positive aspects of the gradual transition process are that the governments substitute law and rules, or an enforcement function, which are necessary for institutions to facilitate market transactions. This conclusion is shared with Allen *et al.* (2003); however, they did not analyse what or who assumed the burden of substituting law and rules. Our book argues that it is the government, or the state sector, that facilitates smooth market transactions, even in the private and informal sector. This phenomenon was confirmed across various aspects of the economy – in relation to trade credit, saving decisions by households, and banking activity.

With regard to trade credits, we extend a hypothesis that the state sector contributed to the expansion of this very private credit activity. Though legal enforcement may be imperfect, the state sector – both government and the state-owned enterprises – could have improved the enforceability regarding market transactions. In this volume, we have addressed this proposition from the point of view of economic theory (Chapter 5), legal institutions (Chapter 6) and econometric tests (Chapter 7). Though it may have been awkward, the state sector remained in market transactions, and the government retains its commitments. This helped to ensure enforceability of contract to some extent. These are our findings about China's case. Furthermore, empirical tests on the trade credit and financing behavior of Myanmar's private companies has also proved illuminating. In Myanmar, privatization prevailed during the very early stages of transition, and, thus government lost its commitment to facilitating market transactions. In this world, not only trade credit, but also credit from bank loans or formal financial institutions become very limited for the financing of the corporate sector. It seems that lack of credibility, or enforcement commitment by the government, reduced the level of available credit.

With regard to banking sector development and household savings decisions, we can draw some positive conclusions. In order to construct a savings mobilization network at the national level, the Chinese government assumed considerable burdens, by subsidizing the rural financial sector's deficit. Faced by this government policy, we have confirmed that households responded positively by increasing their level of savings at the financial institutions. This certainly helps to increase the level of resources available to the national economy, giving the formal banking sector access to large amounts of savings (Chapter 9).

On the other hand, there are some negative aspects to sustained government commitment. With regard to this, we considered two aspects: banking sector and corporate governance. The intervention of bank lending is a legacy of the planned economy, which induced a policy of "financial repression." In the sequences of policies necessary to produce the marketization of the economy, the liberalization of banking behavior is usually given a very low priority. The government often maintains direct control of banking sector activities, particularly in relation to lending decisions (Chapter 10). With regard to corporate governance, the problem is also very clear; in the gradual transition economies, the government retains its commitment to corporate activity as the shareholder. This can all too easily result in abusive behavior on the part of the government against the listed company; governments are often tempted to "expropriate" the resources of a listed company. This issue is also examined both from the legal point of view (Chapter 11) and through econometric tests (Chapter 12).

Before detailing our own findings, we will consider some of the recent literature about the transition process. This will allow our analysis to be seen in its proper context.

1.3 Transition from plan to market: a survey of the literature

1.3.1 From government allocation to market adjustment

More than a quarter of a century has passed since 1978, when China began its transition process from the planned economy to a market-based one. In the late 1980s, the former Soviet, other European planned economies, Vietnam and other Asian socialist economies followed this direction. However, actual routes were diversified into two: the "big bang" approach and the "gradual" approach. The big bang approach, mostly adopted in former Soviet economies in the early 1990s, seems to have terminated around 2000, and embraced political transition as well as this economic transition. By contrast, the Asian transition economies, including China, are still in a process in terms of both economic and political reform. However, it is now possible to review what actually happened in the process of transition.

In this section, we will review what has been argued in the literature in relation to the transition economies, focusing in particular on changes in the function of the "resource allocation" system. Here, we will define two contrasting aspects of the resource allocation system;

one is "government allocation," where economic resources are primarily controled by the government or administrative purpose. The next section will give a precise definition. The other is "market adjustment," where resource allocation is completed by "through market mechanism adjustment."

1.3.2 The planned economy system

1.3.2.1 Institutions constitute the planned economy

The planned economy is a variant of the resource allocation system, which is designed to allow the government to have sole control over the allocation of the economy's resources. Lin, Fang and Zhou (1996) argued that China's planned economy system constituted a "government allocation system," attempting to accelerate the same level of economic development as in the developed western economies, such as the UK or the United States. This strategy aimed to implement a model of industrialization focused on capital-intensive sectors, based on the perception that heavy and chemical industries could secure higher levels of growth in the economy. The strategy was characterized by four main factors:

(1) An artificially strong foreign exchange rate so that they can import inputs for the capital-intensive industries, which are lacking in the domestic market.
(2) Price control over agricultural goods and lower lending interest rates so as to induce investment in the capital-intensive industries.
(3) Higher savings interest rates to induce higher savings by households, which can finance the import of capital goods.
(4) A mono-bank system and the prohibition of direct finance, such as securities, or equity and even trade credit. This is because financial institutions cannot survive in the negative interest margin environment described above, thus government monopolizes the financial intermediation.

On this course, the "government allocation system" which accompanies "financial repression" was formed in China in the 1950s and 1960s, which had the intention of promoting heavy and chemical industries industrialization. "Financial repression" is a resource allocation system which imposes a heavy restriction on financial resource adjustment by financial institutions, including both banking and financial intermediation and securities.

1.3.2.2 Financial repression under the planned economy: McKinnon (1993)

McKinnon (1993) pointed out that "financial repression" emerged in the planned economy or "resource allocation system by the government" because the governments cannot help financing their huge fiscal deficit via money finance or seigniorage revenue. Under the planned economy system the government relies on money printing and charges a high reserve ratio to the banking sector, because no other channel, for example bond issues, is available to the government. McKinnon (1993) identified the cause of "financial repression" as being the absence of a market for government financing, which may be more appropriate in the situation in Latin American economies in the 1980s than transition. "Financial repression" under the planned economy would be attributed to the system, as Lin *et al.* (1996) indicates.

1.3.3 The "big bang" approach versus the "gradualism" approach

So what kind of approach should be taken to conquer these problems? In the early 1990s, this was mainly argued in terms of the framework of "big bang" versus "gradualism."

Lipton and Sachs (1990a, 1990b) advocated that the "big bang" approach is superior to the gradual one.

> Both the economic logic and political situation argue for a rapid and comprehensive process of transition. History in Eastern Europe has taught the profound shortcomings of a piecemeal approach, and economic logic suggests the feasibility of a rapid transition. (Lipton and Sachs, 1990a: 99).
>
> We are advocating the rapid conversion of state enterprises into corporate form and the distribution of tranches of shares to various groups in the population, including workers, commercial banks, pension funds, and mutual funds. ... The free distribution of shares helps to sidestep the difficult, costly, and time-consuming process of enterprise valuation, as well as the scarcity of financial capital in private hands in Eastern Europe. More importantly, corporatization combined with the free distribution of shares can occur quickly. Rapid privatization is needed to combat the inevitable social, political, and economic problems associated with the lack of corporate governance. (1990b: 333)

In opposition to this view, McMillan and Naughton (1992) advocated the superiority of the gradualist over the big bang approach.

> The countries of Eastern Europe and the former Soviet Union have been flooded with advice from the West on how to liberalize their planned economies. This advice is, unfortunately, offered in an empirical vacuum. (McMillan and Naughton, 1992: 130)

> The price, fiscal, monetary, ownership, and legal systems must all be changed. A big-bang transition can indeed cause the interconnected socialist system to collapse. But there is more to moving to a market economy than just removing government controls. New institutions must be created.

In the wake of China's successful transition in the 1990s, a number of papers emerged that advocated the success of "gradualism" rather than the "big bang" approach. Among the most important of these were Wei (1997), Li (1999) and Lau, Qian and Roland (2000).[1]

1.3.4 Focuses on microstructure

However, as the failure of the big bang approaches implemented in the CIS and Russia became more apparent, increased attention was paid to the "microstructure" aspect of reform.

1.3.4.1 Product market deficiency will lead to production decline

One stream of "microstructure explorers" focuses on the efficiency of the product market. Example of this approach include Murphy, Shleifer and Vishny (1992), Blanchard and Kremer (1997) and Li (1999). Blanchard and Kremer (1997) and Li (1999) claim that well-functioning product markets in the transition economies are a (sufficient) condition under which the "big bang" approach reduces output, while gradual approach increases output. Jian and Marukawa (2003) descriptively documented how the domestic market has emerged, taking the home appliance sector as a case study. It also claims that competition at the product market disciplines the firms.

1.3.4.2 "Soft budget constraint" revisited

The other stream of "microstructure explorer" focuses on a concept of "soft budget constraints." Kornai (1986) defines "soft budget constraint" as "a status where redistribution via taxation, continuation of the firm and investment has no relationship with profitability of the firm." Based on this definition, Kornai (1986) claims that to "harden budget constraint" is to link the profitability of the firm with all other related activities of the firm. The channels that related activity to the firm are: (i) subsidy; (ii) taxation; (iii) price; and (iv) credit.

This definition is rather narrow. In addition to the four channels above, current applied microeconomics also pays considerable attention to issues like corporate governance, bankruptcy procedure and related institutions, which all have an influence on softening the "budget constraints" of the firm. Thus, some theorists follow to generalize this concept of "soft budget constraint." Kornai, Maskin and Roland (2003) offer a good survey of this issue.

MacKinnon (1993) takes a similar course to claim that to harden the system of money and credit, banks and liberalized enterprises have to alleviate the extent of "financial repression." Li (2001) presented a possible remedy in the case of China's repression.

1.3.4.3 Discipline and enforcement matter

Regardless of whether the approach adopted is big bang or gradualism, the reconstruction of the disciplinary (enforcement) mechanism is very important for a successful transition. This approach is becoming increasingly popular. More recently, this stream meets "law, finance and growth" literatures by La Porta, Lopez-de-Silanes, Shleifer and Vishny (hereafter LLSV). Berglof, E., and P. Bolton (2002) offer a summary of this development. LLSV argues that a more well-developed law and judiciary system promotes financial intermediation, thus promoting growth. In a series of arguments, LLSV claim that the Anglo Saxon model is a better law system since it offers more protection to investors. Their claim invites much criticism and active debates. Among them, Allen *et al.* (2003) propose that China offers a good counter-example to LLSV's propositions, since it offers a situation where "informal enforcement and governance mechanism" promoted rapid growth. Our chapters on trade credit will investigate this claim in relation to a similar problem.

Recently, Roland and Verdier (2003) also adopt a similar approach in their theoretical work. They suggest that two mechanisms may have functioned to solve the coordination problem in the transition economies; the first one is "dualism," a system adopted in China whereby the government retains direct control of economic resources and a liberalized non-state sector follows market rules; the second is international integration like the European Union, experienced by Poland, which has enjoyed a smooth transition.

As mentioned, our study is inspired by their arguments, and tried to document it is the government who substituted legal institutions.

1.4 Findings in this book

This book is divided into two parts; the first group concerns government's behavior on macro fluctuation. The other focuses on institution building, which provides all the market economy participants – household, firm and financial institutions – with incentive and discipline. In this section we will summarize the main propositions.

1.4.1 Macro performance: from government allocation to market adjustment

Chapter 2 documents comparative studies on macroeconomic performance in two main regions: (i) Eastern Europe and the CIS, and (ii) East Asia. Descriptive data show that East Asian economies rely heavily on seigniorage, which may induce high or hyperinflation, a very common phenomenon during the initial stage of transition. In other words, the relatively long period of transition and the heavy reliance of East Asian governments on seigniorage revenue inflationary expectations. However, East Asia actually experienced relatively low inflation, especially in China, though East Europe and CIS experienced hyperinflation during the early stages of transition. Econometric tests indicate that inflation is mitigated by real GDP growth. While sensitivity of inflation to fiscal deficit is less variable among whole transition economies, the sensitivity of inflation to income growth differs significantly among the group of transition economies. In particular, China shows high negative sensitivity of inflation to income growth, which implies that fiscal revenues were used to fund more productive activities. The two other Asian transition economies considered – Vietnam and Myanmar – showed no significant difference in their sensitivity to income growth compared with the CIS.

Chapter 3 considers the next question: how have the policy tools for macroeconomic adjustment been affected by the transformation of the system? In the planned economy period, naturally, fiscal expenditure substantially affected the total output of the economy. The transition process means that government will lose this direct channel of control over the macroeconomy, and it needs to build a tool and supporting institutions to substitute for these direct control channels. One important tool is monetary policy, exercised through interest rates, and base money controls, which are common in the market economy. The empirical studies here show clearly that the relationship between fiscal expenditure and GDP vanished after the break-up of the planned economy. On the other hand, the money supply, which is also a policy target of the central bank, does not affect trends in output. The results here imply that there may be no effective tools for macro policy in the transition period.

To see how the indirect tools for macro policy become effective, we need to know to what extent the national economy is integrated in terms of capital flows. Chapter 4 focuses on this particular aspect – the degree of spatial integration of financial resources flows during the transition period. The chapter considers the "savings retention ratio" based on the concept developed by Feldstein and Horioka (1980), who reported striking results that the savings retention rate was lower during the planned economy era, and increased following a progress of reform. This chapter claimed that this documents the switch from fiscal expenditure reallocation to market-based financial flows, where the latter development is far behind the retreat of the former. A hypothesis that the transformation of inter-provincial financial flows from a planned economy to market-based one is complete was rejected by our findings. A complementary study by Boyreau-Debray (2003) also supports similar results.

This conclusion, together with the findings in chapter 3 that monetary policy has not yet significantly affected output, suggests that we may claim that a nationwide financial flow was interrupted even in the late 1990s to the early 2000s, and institution building for market-based resource allocation is still in progress.

The empirical studies on macro phenomena in Part I document that the transition process in the East Asian post-planned economies were more growth-oriented and rather deflationary (Chapter 2). However, transformation of resource allocation function itself, which is a gradual and slow transformation from government allocation to market adjustment, has been delayed and is still ongoing even in the late 1990s to early 2000s (Chapter 3, 4).

1.4.2 Micro-agents: transformation of agent's behavior principle

The chapters in Part II of this volume focus on the micro agent's behavior. Under the transition process, fundamental changes took place in the micro agent's principle of behavior. In this book, we will consider the corporate, household and banking sectors. Topics covered include trade credit, savings and loans in the banking sector, and corporate governance issues.

1.4.2.1 Trade credit, financing and institutions

Trade credit issues provide a good example to understand how the enforcement system works or fails to work in the transition economies. Trade credit takes place when there is a difference in the timing of payment and the transfer of products between customer and trader. Whether the customer will make payment to the firm, or the firm will make payment to its supplier, is strongly subject to an enforcement mechanism, as the purchaser is inclined to default on payment as it means retention of cash.

Chapter 5 presents a theoretical economic model of trade credit in an imperfect enforcement environment. It formally analyzed that the higher enforcement technology will expand the trade volume and trade credit, where descriptive data support the point that the role of government in payment is important, although the mechanism is biased one. In the case of China, default of payment had happened to one-third of firms in our survey, and most of them filed lawsuits. Access to the legal system is familiar for China's firms. However, the judgment and its execution exhibit some local favoritism bias.

Chapter 6 describes the legal background in China where defaults on payments are not fully punished by the law. Based on examinations on legal institutions such as procedural and substantive laws, and actual conditions on implementation, this chapter advanced several hypothetical views of the current situation on legal contribution on civil conflicts regarding payment; poor management and enforcement on payment of the firm itself, the "soft budget situation" due to loose lending by banks, loose implementation of bankruptcy law and procedures and arbitrary implementation of legal enforcement.

Chapter 7 implemented econometric tests on the determinants of trade credit lending and borrowing on the original survey data conducted in a middle-income industrialized city Yuban, Sichuan Province. This econometric test shows (i) that state-owned and collectively owned companies borrow significantly more credit than non-state firms, however, (ii) the size of lending is not different from types of ownership, (iii) larger lending is offered to firms which are local, (iv) larger lending is offered by the firms which have higher cash holdings, (v) less borrowing is obtained by the firms with bank lending, etc.

In a similar exercise, Chapter 8 conducted an econometric survey of the funding behavior of Myanmar's private firms, which rapidly replaced state-owned enterprises in the course of the transition process.

As we saw in the previous section, this is a different path from that taken by China and Vietnam. Here, first of all, (i) we found that there is an extremely low dependence on external finance, even including trade credit. This is the case even though access to bank lending itself has no prohibitively high institutional obstacles. (ii) Trade credit is a substitute for lending from bank for working capital. (iii) The younger firms, which need more investment in fixed capital, borrow more from the bank. (iv) Few lawsuits have been filed in the case of default, which is in contrast to China's case. Instead of resorting to the legal system, ending transactions and personal relationships are regarded as more effective responses to payment default. (v) Even though there is a high risk and prevailing experience of default, the firms will not charge punitive rates of interest, something which is also the case in China.

These studies on trade credit, particularly from the viewpoint of law and enforcement literature, are in their infancy. Thus, we cannot draw any final conclusions. However, information on China and Myanmar, though it is still too fragmented to compare systematically, seems to imply that the different path with regard to the retreat of the state seems to have a significant effect on inter-firm trade credit and transaction volumes, which may have substantially affected macroeconomic growth.

1.4.2.2 Saving and lending decisions and state ownership

Part II also contains some studies on household and banking behavior. Households are the ultimate suppliers of savings in a market economy. However, as already mentioned, the planned economy provided a level of wage that did not allow them to save. For households, transition is a transformation process to independently decide about savings. When decentralized decision making by household becomes prevalent, the nature of the institution affecting household decisions becomes important. On this point, Hellman, et al. (1998) argue that a "financial restraint system" where households would be guaranteed positive interest on savings at formal financial institutions, and formal financial institutions, in turn, would be guaranteed positive lending–saving interests margins, as opposed to the "financial repression system" where lending and savings interest margins were repressed to be negative in order to promote investment by the corporate sector. Under certain circumstances, households would prefer to hold their savings as cash in order to save at a financial institution.

To see whether the claim of Hellman et al. (1998) is feasible, it is important to see whether households would really save money at formal financial institutions if a positive real interest rate is guaranteed. Chapter 9 conducted an empirical test of households from four rural villages in Shanxi Province to see whether the households will deposit savings at a formal institution or will just hold cash at hand. In rural China, the state sector committed to build a network of formal financial institutions called Rural Credit Cooperatives (RCCs). This infrastructure building may have induced savings in formal financial institutions. This is an empirical hypothesis which we advance. The results show that households in better-off villages responded to increase savings at financial institution as the deposit-taking infrastructure develops. This chapter documents that the induction of households' savings to the financial institution via infrastructure building and positive real interest was successful.

On the other hand, how has the banking sector been regulated? Chapter 10 conducted a case study on Vietnam's experience, which precedes China in terms of the liberalization of interests and other related issues regarding transformation from a repressive financial system under the planned economy. This chapter describes how the banking sector repression was facilitated through two channels: interest control and policy-directed lending. The former was liberalized in 2001; however, the latter still seems to persist both implicitly and explicitly. The repressive environments made it difficult for banks to develop essential functions such as screening and monitoring. Even after the deregulation of interest controls, banks are in a lending rate dumping competition. This implies that credit risk management capacities of banks remain weak. A simple econometric test also implies the banking sector in Vietnam is not fully responsive to interest rate movement, which implies full transformation from repression was not complete yet.

1.4.2.3 Corporate governance under state dominant ownership

Chapter 11 develops the legal background and analysis based on the legal theory of corporate governance in China, focusing particularly on abuse by the controling shareholder. During a process of "corporatization" of former state-owned enterprises which were owned by the whole nation, the state sector reconfirmed its claim over the former state-owned enterprises, which were formally invested by the state sector. Not only was a related administrative organization, the State Asset Management Companies, established, but also the Chinese company law, enacted in 1993, provided the concept of "state share monopolized company" and the concept of "state share" is also used in the implementation. For historical reasons, the state shareholder is absolutely large at least at the initial stage and becomes a concentrated controling shareholder for an individual company. However, the company law lacked related legislation to prevent this abusive behavior. Thus, the state share has had a tendency to abuse their position at the costs of profits of the company and minority shareholders' interests. This chapter suggested possible future legislation to prevent this problem.

Relating to the legal analysis in Chapter 11, Chapter 12 conducted an econometric study. It implemented a test to see whether the current asset level has deviated from an efficient and profit-maximizing level. If actual asset size deviates from the efficient level, this implies the existence of "expropriation" by the ultimate owners via some accounting items on the balance sheet of the listed company. This chapter documents (i) that deviation from the profit maximization level of asset is confirmed via "account receivable" and "account payable." (ii) the state-owned company showed existence of "expropriation." (iii) Among "state owned listed company," a group of companies under a few local and municipality governments such as Shanghai shows evidence of "expropriation."

Thus, even under a more modern or market-based company law system, state ownership may generate a different type of problem – the violation of distributive fairness by an abuse of the company's profit and minority shareholder's interests, from what was criticized at the planned economy era as "low efficiency under soft budget problem." However, this might be a rather new problem. We cannot unilaterally condemn the state sector's involvement in economic activity as negative for economic development during the transition period. State sector involvement may produce a substitutive function of law, which has provided some agents of economic activity with regulations or perform the role of a referee on the conflicts in business activity during the period when the legal framework was relatively underdeveloped.

1.5 Concluding remarks

The transition process from a planned economy to a market economy has been regarded a process of exit of the government. However, this has not occurred fully in the gradual transition economies, which implies that it has both advantages and disadvantages. Among the positive aspects are that the government can substitute for an incomplete legal framework; the government's commitment to financial infrastructure building and confidence by the public induced led to high levels of deposits at financial institutions. This is a micro mechanism that is consistent with a positive evaluation of Asian "gradualism" reforms. However, retained state ownership may induce wasteful and expropriative behavior on thc part of the government. When should the government exit? This is still an unanswered question.

Notes

1 Woo, who also advocated the "big bang" with Sachs, still claims that the "gradualism versus big bang" framework can help to explain China's success. Woo (1999), rearranged the "gradualism versus big-bang" framework as an "Experiment school" versus "Convergence school". Woo (1999), who classifies the former supports "gradualism" in market reforms as the key to China's rapid growth, and where non-capitalist institutions proved to be successful in town and village enterprises, and state-owned enterprises. The latter, the convergence school, holds that China's success is due to the consequences of its institutions being allowed to converge with those of non-socialist market economies, and that China's economic structure (comparative advantages; author's note) at the start of reforms is a major explanation for the country's rapid growth (Woo, 1999: 117). However, E-school and C-school classification seems rather arbitrary.

References

Allen, Flanklin, Jun Qian and Meijun Qian (2003) "Law, Finance and Economic Growth in China," *Research Paper* No. 03-21, University of Pennsylvania Law School.

Berglof, E. and P. Bolton (2002) "The Great Divide and Beyond: Financial Architecture in Transition," *Journal of Economic Perspectives* 16(1), 77–100.

Blanchard, O.J. and M. Kremer (1997) "Disorganization," *Quarterly Journal of Economics* 112, 1091–1126.

Boyreau-Debray, Genevieve (2003) "Financial Intermediation and Growth: Chinese Style," *World Bank Working Paper*, 3027.

Fukui, Ryu (2004) "Development and Current Situation of Financial Sector in Myanmar" in Koichi Fujita (ed.), *Myanmar under the Transition – its Development and Current Situation*, Tokyo: Institute of Developing Economies.

Jian Shaojuan and Marukawa Tomoo (2003) "Transformation and Industrial Development – Implication to Transition Economy," in T. Tajima, S. Jian and T. Marukawa (eds), *China's Transformation and Industrial Development*. Tokyo: Institute of Social Science, University of Tokyo.

Kornai, Janos (1986) "Soft Budget Constraint" based on speech at University of Pittsburgh in 1985, in Janos Korinai (ed.), *Economic Reforms in Hungary*. Tokyo: Iwanami Shoten (in Japanese).

Kornai, Janos, Eric Maskin and Gerard Roland (2003) "Understanding the Soft Budget Constraint," *Journal of Economic Literature* 41(4), 1095–1136.

Murphy, Kevin M., Andrei Shleifer and Robert W. Vishny (1992) "The Transition to a Market Economy: Pitfalls of Partial Reform," *Quarterly Journal of Economics* 107(3), 889–906.

Lau, Lawrence, Y. Qian and Robert W. Vishny (1997) "Legal Determinants of External Finance," *Journal of Finance* 52, 1131–1150.

La Porta, Rafael, Florencio Lopez-de-Silanes, Andrei Shleifer and Robert W. Vishny (1998) "Law and Finance," *Journal of Political Economy* 106, 1113–1155.

La Porta, Rafael, Florencio Lopez-de-Silanes, Andrei Shleifer and Robert W. Vishny (2000) "Investor Protection and Corporate Governance," *Journal of Financial Economics* 58 (1–2), pp. 3–27.

Lau, Lawrence, Y. Qian and G. Roland (2000) "Reform without Losers: An Interpretation of China's Dual-Track Approach to Transition," *Journal of Political Economy* 108(6), 1121–61.

Li, D.D. (2001) "Beating the Trap of Financial Repression in China," *Cato Journal* 21(1), 77–90.

Li, Wei (1999) "A tale of Two Reform," *RAND Journal of Economics* 30(1), 120–36.

Lipton, David and Jeffery Sachs (1990a) "Creating a Market Economy in Eastern Europe: The Case of Poland," *Brookings Papers on Economic Activity* 1, 75–133.

Lipton, David and Jeffery Sachs (1990b) "Privatization in Eastern Europe: The Case of Poland," *Brookings Papers on Economic Activity* 2, 293–333.

Lin, Justin Yi-fu, Cai Fang and Li Zhou (1996) *The China Miracle: Development Strategy and Economic Reform*. Beijing: The Chinese University Press.

McKinnon, Ronald I. (1993) *The Order of Economic Liberalization: Financial Control in the Transition to a Market Economy*. Baltimore, MD: The Johns Hopkins University Press.

McMillan John and Barry Naughton (1992) "How to Reform a Planned Economy: Lessons from China," *Oxford Review of Economic Policy* 8(1), 130–43.

Roland, Gerald (2000) *Transition and Economics*. Cambridge, MA: MIT Press.

Unteroberdoerster, Olaf (2004) *Banking Reform in the Lower Mekong Countries*, Policy Discussion Paper No. 04/5. Washington, DC: International Monetary Fund.

Wei, S.J. (1997) "Gradualism Versus Big Bang: Speed and Sustainability of Reforms," *Canadian Journal of Economics*, 30, 1234–1247.

Woo, W.T., S. Parker and J. Sachs (1997) *Economies in Transition*. Cambridge, MA: The MIT Press.

Part I

Macro Performance: How Has the Government Affected Macro Performance?

2

Macroeconomic Stability and Seigniorage for Fiscal Revenue: East Asia versus Eastern Europe and the CIS*

Koichiro Kimura

2.1 Introduction

This chapter discusses the progress of transition in financial systems and economic stabilities in East Asian countries in comparison with those of Eastern Europe and the CIS. One of the purposes of transition is to raise the general economic level by transforming the social system from a planned economy to a market-based one. Clearly, the financial sphere will not be exempt from any such historic change.

Many countries have initiated such transitions, especially in the aftermath of the Cold War. As it turned out, various patterns of transition were demonstrated in these countries. De Melo *et al.* (2001), Falcetti *et al.* (2002), Nakagane (2002), and others compared the macroeconomic circumstances of countries in transition. The former two studies examined the relations between growth, initial conditions, and reforms. Using cluster analysis, Nakagane classified transition countries, including East Asian countries, into groups. Based on the results of this comprehensive analysis, this chapter concentrates in particular on the comparison of financial phenomena.[1]

* The author wishes to thank Prof. Akira Kosaka (Osaka University), Prof. Hidenobu Okuda (Hitotsubashi University), and Prof. Shinichi Watanabe (International University of Japan); Professor Watanabe commented at a workshop held at IDE on December 18, 2004), and all members of the "Reconstruction of Financial Systems in Transition Economies in Asia" seminar conducted by Ms. Mariko Watanabe.

In order to make such comparisons, this chapter first describes economic performance and the progress of the transition process. Economic performance, in particular macroeconomic stability and the progress of reforms, are essential aspects of the transition process. Even when progress of reform is maintained, the stability of economy is also important for the whole process. Progress of the reform is characterized by a simultaneous process that involves the fading-out of an old system to coordinate financial resources and the introduction of a new system. The old system of financial flows is a fiscal system, and the new one a financial market. In a planned economy, a fiscal system is run by a centralized administration, and a financial market is characterized by decentralized decision making. In this chapter, we will analyze this trade-off between progress and the stability of the transition process based on selected indicators used in McKinnon (1993).[2]

When a government takes a long time to abandon the power of distribution mechanisms to market principles, it can still remain capable of manipulating the financial system in order to raise funds. Since a government in transition requires fiscal expenditure to establish a market economy under a new and undeveloped system for tax collection, the government may experience persistent revenue shortfalls. If the government does not have the ability to collect sufficient tax revenues, it may be tempted to finance its deficits by seigniorage, and will then suffer from hyperinflation. The next section will show that East Asia, in contrast to other transitional economies, has not suffered from terrible inflation.[3] In this chapter, we will analyze this relationship between inflation and fiscal performance and determinants of inflation, based on a model first developed by Cagan (1956).

The rest of this chapter is organized as follows: section 2.2 describes macroeconomic performance and progress in transition; countries treated are listed at the beginning. Based on facts clarified in the previous section, section 2.3 includes an estimate of the relationship between inflation and its factors. Finally, section 2.4 contains conclusions and a discussion of problems that remain to be solved in future.

2.2 Performance and progress in transition

Beginning with a review of macroeconomic circumstances in transition, the features in each area or country can be described through an analysis of selected indicators. Transition projects are only one way of moving from plan to market, and the diversity of transitional phenomena across areas or countries can also be seen.

Table 2.1 A list of transition countries

Country	*Year*	*Ground*
EA (East Asia)		
China	1979	Economic reform was manifest at the third Plenum of the 11th Chinese Communist Party Central Committee meeting in December 1978.
Vietnam	1987	The *Doimoi* was manifest at a conference of the party in December 1986.
Myanmar	1989	SLORC established a military administration, renounced Burmese socialism, and executed marketization in September 1988.
CEB (Central Eastern Europe and the Baltic States)		
Croatia	1992	Croatia was independent in June 1991. Although an internal war broke out, a cease-fire agreement was concluded with the federal army in January 1992. It joined the UN in May
Czech Republic	1991	Communism was terminated by the democratic Velvet Revolution, and liberalization occurred after January, 1991. It seceded from former Czechoslovakia in 1993.
Estonia	1992	The national council of the former Soviet Union approved the independence of three Baltic countries in September, 1991.
Hungary	1990	Making the regime a republic in October, 1989, a democratic government was established the next April. Consequently, marketization was launched in earnest.
Latvia	1992	Same as Estonia.
Lithuania	1992	Same as Estonia.
Poland	1990	After the social system was discussed at a round-table conference in 1989, the Plan Balcerowicza, a kind of shock therapy, was executed after January of the following.
Slovak Republic	1991	Same as Czech Republic.
Slovenia	1992	Independent in June 1991. Although it became belligerent with the former Yugoslavian federal army, that army withdrew in October of that year.
SEE (South Eastern Europe)		
Albania	1991	Democratization was executed under the influence of revolution in Eastern Europe and accompanied with plural party politics after 1990.
Bulgaria	1990	After revolution in Eastern Europe, Bulgaria started economic reforms for transition to a market economy.

Table 2.1 A list of transition countries – *continued*

Country	*Year*	*Ground*
FYR Macedonia	1992	A stabilization program was introduced in December 1989, and it became independent from the former Yugoslavia in June, 1991.
Romania	1997	A government unrelated to the communist party was established in November 1996, and economic reform was launched under an agreement with the IMF and others
CIS (The Commonwealth of Independent States)		
Armenia	1992	The CIS was inaugurated in December, 1991, and the former Soviet Union was formally dissolved at the end of year.
Azerbaijan	1992	Same as Armenia.
Belarus	1992	Same as Armenia.
Georgia	1991	A Declaration of Independence was announced in April, 1991. Legal reform for marketization was executed in 1991 and 1992. It joined the CIS in 1993.
Kazakh	1992	Same as Armenia.
Kyrgyz Republic	1992	Same as Armenia.
Moldova	1992	Same as Armenia.
Russia	1992	Same as Armenia.
Tajikistan	1992	Same as Armenia.
Turkmenistan	1992	Same as Armenia.
Ukraine	1992	Same as Armenia.
Uzbekistan	1992	Same as Armenia.

Note: Annual data are used, and the "Year" was rounded off up to "before June" and "after July", respectively.

Sources: EBRD, *Transition Report*, various years. London: EBRD. Morita, Tsuneo (1994). *Taisei tenkan no Keizaigaku* (*Economics of System Transformation* (in Japanese), Tokyo: Shinsei-sha. Kimura, Takeo (1998). *Keizai taisei to Keizai seisaku* (*Economic Structure and Economic Policy* (in Japanese), Tokyo: Soseisha. Lavigne (1999). Koyama, Yoji (1999). *Tohoh Keizai* (*Eastern European Economy* (in Japanese), Kyoto: Sekaishisosha. MOFA official website (at http://www.mofa.go.jp in October 2003).

2.2.1 A list of transition countries

First, the geographical and historical scope of transition must be defined. Geographically, this section covers 28 countries located in East Asia, Eastern Europe, and the CIS, as listed in Table 2.1.[4] The next section covers 26 countries and does not include Turkmenistan and Uzbekistan, because insufficient data are available for these two countries. The countries in this table are classified into four areas: East Asia (hereafter EA), Central Eastern Europe and the Baltic States (hereafter

CEB), South Eastern Europe (hereafter SEE), and the CIS (Commonwealth of Independent States).

EA contains China, Vietnam, and Myanmar – countries that are studied in later chapters in this volume. The classification of the countries of East Europe and the CIS follows that adopted in EBRD (2003). Transitional countries are categorized by comprehensive analysis in terms of their initial conditions, foreign trade, political conditions, and other such factors. The CEB is characterized as having good performance during transition. As a result, eight countries from the CEB region were able to join the EU in 2004. In addition, new members in our list have come only from the CEB.[5] SEE is intermediate in terms of economic performance and resides between the CEB and the CIS, as mentioned below. However, Bosnia and Herzegovina as well as Serbia and Montenegro are excluded from the list due to the fact that they had war regimes for considerable periods during the period under consideration. This is one aspect of the SEE region. Bulgaria also experienced economic instability owing to its frequent changes of government. The CIS has been distinguished by painful transition, which has been the result of the collapse of former CMEA markets, the adoption of inconsistent policies, and other factors.

While features of each area in Eastern Europe and the CIS are introduced to show that they are coherent groups, any definitive conclusion is difficult because the process of transition is still ongoing in this region.

The historical perspective for each country is also shown in Table 2.1. The year given for each country in the table represents an inaugural year of transition. Here, China has the longest experience, 24 years since 1979. Romania, by contrast, has the shortest experience – six years since 1997. Since the transition process covers many aspects of society, it is certainly difficult to establish clear criteria for determining each turning point. For example, it is well known that Hungary underwent a course of liberalization of some societal aspects from the late 1960s. In this section, however, overall economic structural changes are considered as the basis for determining turning points. The changes are explained briefly in the table.

2.2.2 Economic performance during transition

First, economic performance as a result of transition can be observed. Performance consists of economic growth and stability. Table 2.2 shows the rates of real changes in GDP over previous years. Elapsed years, from each starting year to 2002, are shown in columns using ordinal numbers. As an example, the first column for China relates to the year 1979, and the first for Vietnam relates to 1987.

Table 2.2 Rate of real GDP change over previous years (%)

Country\ Elapsed Years	*1*	*2*	*3*	*4*	*5*	*6*	*7*	*8*	*9*	*10*	*11*	*12*	*13*	*14*	*15*	*16*	*17*	*18*	*19*	*20*	*21*	*22*	*23*	*24*
EA																								
China	7.6	7.8	4.5	8.3	10.4	14.6	16.2	8.9	11.6	11.3	4.1	3.8	9.2	14.2	13.5	12.7	10.5	9.6	8.8	7.8	7.1	8.0	n.a.	n.a.
Vietnam	3.6	6.0	4.7	5.1	5.8	8.7	8.1	8.8	9.5	9.3	8.2	5.8	4.8	6.8	6.9	7.0								
Myanmar	3.7	2.8	–0.7	9.7	6.0	7.5	6.9	6.4	5.7	5.8	10.9	n.a.	n.a.	n.a.										
CEB																								
Croatia	–11.7	–8.0	5.9	6.8	6.0	6.5	2.5	–0.9	2.9	3.8	5.2													
Czech Republic	–11.6	–0.5	0.1	2.2	5.9	4.3	–0.8	–1.0	0.5	3.3	3.1	2.0												
Estonia	–14.2	–8.8	–2.0	4.3	3.9	9.8	4.6	–0.6	7.1	5.0	5.8													
Hungary	–3.5	–11.9	–3.1	–0.6	2.9	1.5	1.3	4.6	4.9	4.2	5.2	3.7	3.3											
Latvia	–34.9	–14.9	2.2	–0.9	3.7	8.4	4.8	2.8	6.8	7.9	6.1													
Lithuania	–21.3	–16.2	–9.8	3.3	4.7	7.0	7.3	–1.8	4.0	6.5	6.7													
Poland	–11.6	–7.0	2.6	3.8	5.2	7.0	6.0	6.8	4.8	4.1	4.0	1.0	1.0											
Slovak Republic	–14.6	–6.5	–3.7	4.9	6.7	6.2	6.2	4.1	1.9	2.2	3.3	4.4												
Slovenia	–5.5	2.8	5.3	4.1	3.5	4.6	3.8	5.2	4.6	3.0	2.9													
SEE																								
Albania	–28.0	–7.2	9.6	8.3	13.3	9.1	–7.0	8.0	7.3	7.8	6.5	4.7												
Bulgaria	–9.1	–11.7	–7.3	–1.5	1.8	2.9	–9.4	–5.6	4.0	2.3	5.4	4.0	4.5											
FYR Macedonia	–8.0	–9.1	–1.8	–1.2	1.2	1.4	3.4	4.3	4.6	–4.1	0.0													
Romania	–6.1	–4.8	–1.2	1.8	5.3	4.9																		

Table 2.2 Rate of real GDP change over previous years (%) – *continued*

Country\ Elapsed Years	*1*	*2*	*3*	*4*	*5*	*6*	*7*	*8*	*9*	*10*	*11*	*12*	*13*	*14*	*15*	*16*	*17*	*18*	*19*	*20*	*21*	*22*	*23*	*24*
CIS																								
Armenia	–41.8	–8.8	5.4	6.9	5.9	3.3	7.3	3.3	6.0	9.6	12.9													
Azerbaijan	–22.6	–23.1	–19.7	–11.8	0.8	6.0	10.0	9.5	11.1	9.9	10.6													
Belarus	–9.6	–7.6	–12.6	–10.4	2.8	11.4	8.4	3.4	5.8	4.1	4.7													
Georgia	–20.6	–44.8	–25.4	–11.4	2.4	10.5	10.8	2.9	3.0	1.9	4.5	5.4												
Kazakh	–5.3	–9.3	–12.6	–8.2	0.5	1.7	–1.9	2.7	9.8	13.5	9.5													
Kyrgyz Republic	–19.0	–15.5	–20.1	–5.4	7.1	9.9	2.1	3.7	5.4	5.3	–0.5													
Moldova	–29.1	–1.2	–31.2	–1.4	–5.9	1.6	–6.5	–3.4	2.1	6.1	7.2													
Russia	–18.6	–13.0	–13.5	–4.1	–3.4	0.9	–4.9	5.4	9.0	5.0	4.3													
Tajikistan	–29.0	–11.0	–18.9	–12.5	–4.4	1.7	5.3	3.7	8.3	10.3	9.1													
Turkmenistan	–5.3	–10.0	–17.3	–7.2	–6.7	–11.3	7.0	16.5	17.6	11.8	5.1													
Ukraine	–9.7	–14.2	–22.9	–12.2	–10.0	–3.0	–1.9	–0.2	5.9	9.1	4.6													
Uzbekistan	–11.1	–2.3	–4.2	–0.9	1.6	2.5	4.3	4.3	3.8	4.2	4.2													

Sources: China and Myanmar: IMF, *International Financial Statistics August 2003* (Washington, DC: IMF, 2003). Vietnam: ADB, *Key Indicators 2002*, and *2003* (Philippines: ADB). Eastern Europe and the CIS: For 1990, EBRD, *Transition Report, 2002* (London: EBRD, 2002). After 1991, EBRD, *Transition Report Update May 2003* (London: EBRD, 2003).

Table 2.2 indicates that while Eastern Europe and the CIS started transitions with declines, EA achieved growth from the earliest stages of its transition. While transition is just a one-way process, a difference

Table 2.3 GNP per capita, 1991 (US dollars)

Country	*Value*	*Class*
EA		
China	370	L
Vietnam*	170	L
Myanmar	n.a.	L
CEB		
Croatia	n.a.	
Czech Republic*	2,710	LM
Estonia	3,830	UM
Hungary	2,720	UM
Latvia	3,410	UM
Lithuania	2,710	UM
Poland	1,790	LM
Slovak Republic*	1,950	LM
Slovenia	n.a.	
SEE		
Albania	n.a.	
Bulgaria	1,840	LM
FYR Macedonia	n.a.	
Romania	1,390	LM
CIS		
Armenia	n.a.	
Azerbaijan	1,670	LM
Belarus	3,110	UM
Georgia	1,640	LM
Kazakh	2,470	LM
Kyrgyz Republic	1,550	LM
Moldova	2,170	LM
Russia	3,220	UM
Tajikistan	1,050	LM
Turkmenistan	1,700	LM
Ukraine	2,340	LM
Uzbekistan	1,350	LM

Notes 1. Values in Vietnam, Czech Republic, and Slovak Republic with * represent 1993.
2. "L" stands for "Low-Income," "LM" stands for "Lower-Middle-Income," the "UM" stands for "Upper-Middle-Income."

Sources: World Bank (1993, 1995) *World Development Report 1993 and 1995*. Washington, DC: World Bank.

in growth between EA and the other countries can be observed. Basically, only EA has not had to pay costs or experience great pain in the course of its transition.

In addition to the presence of costs in Eastern Europe and the CIS, there is also a quantity difference between them. Eastern Europe, specifically CEB and SEE, experienced a period of positive growth between years three and five. By contrast, the CIS continued to experience negative rates until years five to nine. The CIS has also had larger costs than other areas. At the time the table was compiled many CIS countries had not yet recovered to their pre-transition GDP levels.

The difference in the levels of economic pain experienced by EA and the other regions is related to their initial economic level. Table 2.3 shows the GDP per capita in 1991, as well as classes of income levels. To simplify the comparison of countries as much as possible, levels in 1991 are presented here as an indicator of initial conditions. Most countries in the list started their transition immediately after 1991. The table shows that while EA countries experienced longer transitions with good performance, they still were ranked at low-income (L) levels. This indicates that there are very large differences in the initial levels of income in transition countries. The initial level is not the only factor, however. Other initial differences, such as in institutions, geographical location, and length of period spent under planned economies, must also be taken into account.[6] However, the initial level is one of the principal factors indicating the feature in EA because only EA countries are classified into L, although they started transition earlier than the other areas.

Next, we review inflation as an indicator of economic stability. The indicator here is the rate of CPI changes over previous years, and these can be seen in Table 2.4.[7] The table shows that EA countries have all remained stable – with the single exception of Myanmar. Myanmar has not suffered serious inflation compared with Eastern Europe and the CIS, but its CPI has fluctuated relative to other EA nations.[8] On the other hand, Eastern Europe, and in particular the CIS, experienced severe inflation in the early years of transition. Below, an attempt is made to explain this CPI change.

2.2.3 Fiscal function for financial systems

In describing the fiscal function, it is possible to apply a concept proposed by McKinnon (1993). This concept treats revenues extracted from financial systems as a means of manipulating them by centralized governments. Revenues are confirmed here.

Table 2.4 Rate of CPI change over previous year (%)

Country\ Elapsed Years	*1*	*2*	*3*	*4*	*5*	*6*	*7*	*8*	*9*	*10*	*11*	*12*	*13*	*14*	*15*	*16*	*17*	*18*	*19*	*20*	*21*	*22*	*23*	*24*
EA																								
China	n.a.	n.a.	n.a.	n.a.	n.a.	n.a.	n.a.	n.a.	7.2	18.7	18.3	3.1	3.5	6.3	14.6	24.2	16.9	8.3	2.8	−0.8	−1.4	0.3	0.5	n.a.
Vietnam	n.a.	n.a.	n.a.	n.a.	n.a.	n.a.	n.a.	n.a.	n.a.	5.7	3.2	7.3	4.1	−1.7	−0.4	3.8								
Myanmar	27.2	17.6	32.3	21.9	31.8	24.1	25.2	16.3	29.7	51.5	18.4	−0.1	21.1	57.1										
CEB																								
Croatia	665.5	1,517.5	97.6	2.0	3.5	3.6	5.7	4.2	6.2	4.9	2.4													
Czech Republic	52.0	11.1	20.8	9.9	9.1	8.8	8.5	10.7	2.1	3.9	4.7	1.8												
Estonia	1,076.0	89.8	47.7	29.0	23.1	11.2	8.1	3.3	4.0	5.8	3.6													
Hungary	28.9	35.0	23.0	22.5	18.8	28.2	23.6	18.3	14.3	10.0	9.8	9.2	4.8											
Latvia	951.2	109.2	35.9	25.0	17.6	8.4	4.7	2.4	2.6	2.5	1.9													
Lithuania	1,020.5	410.4	72.1	39.6	24.6	8.9	5.1	0.8	1.0	1.3	0.3													
Poland	585.8	70.3	43.0	35.3	32.2	27.8	19.9	14.9	11.8	7.3	10.1	5.5	1.7											
Slovak Republic	61.2	10.0	23.2	13.4	9.9	5.8	6.1	6.7	10.6	12.0	7.3	3.3												
Slovenia	207.3	32.9	21.0	13.5	9.9	8.4	7.9	6.1	8.9	8.4	7.5													
SEE																								
Albania	35.5	226.0	85.0	22.6	7.8	12.7	33.2	20.6	0.4	0.1	3.1	5.4												
Bulgaria	26.3	333.5	82.0	73.0	96.3	62.0	123.0	1,082.0	22.2	0.7	9.9	7.4	5.9											
FYR Macedonia	1,664.4	338.4	126.5	16.4	2.5	0.8	2.3	−1.3	6.5	5.3	2.4													
Romania	154.8	59.1	45.8	45.7	34.5	22.5																		
CIS																								
Armenia	1,346.0	1,822.0	4,962.0	175.8	18.7	14.0	8.7	0.7	−0.8	3.2	1.2													
Azerbaijan	912.0	1,129.0	1,664.0	412.0	19.7	3.5	−0.8	−8.5	1.8	1.5	−2.8													
Belarus	970.8	1,190.2	2,221.0	709.3	52.7	63.8	73.2	293.8	168.9	61.4	42.6													
Georgia	79.0	887.4	3,125.4	15,606.5	162.7	39.4	7.1	3.6	19.2	4.1	4.6	5.6												
Kazakh	1,381.0	1,662.3	1,892.0	176.3	39.1	17.4	7.3	8.3	13.2	8.4	5.9													
Kyrgyz Republic	855.0	722.4	180.7	43.5	31.9	23.4	10.5	35.9	18.7	6.9	2.1													
Moldova	1,276.4	788.5	329.7	30.2	23.5	11.8	7.7	39.3	31.3	9.8	5.3													
Russia	1,526.0	875.0	311.4	197.7	47.8	14.7	27.6	86.1	20.8	21.6	15.7													
Tajikistan	1,157.0	2,195.0	350.0	609.0	418.0	88.0	43.2	27.6	32.9	38.6	12.2													
Turkmenistan	493.0	3,102.0	1,748.0	1,005.3	992.4	83.7	16.8	24.2	8.3	11.6	10.6													
Ukraine	1,210.0	4,734.0	891.0	377.0	80.0	15.9	10.5	22.7	28.2	12.0	0.8													
Uzbekistan	645.2	534.2	1,568.3	304.6	54.0	70.9	29.0	29.1	25.0	27.2	27.6													

Sources: (1) East Asia: IMF (2003), *International Financial Statitics August 2003*. Washington, DC: IMF.
(2) Eastern Europe and the CIS: For 1990, EBRD (2002), *Transition Report 2002*. London: EBRD, After 1991, EBRD (2003), *Transition Report Update May 2003*. London: EBRD.

Table 2.5 Ratio of fiscal surplus to GDP (%)

Country\ Elapsed Years:	*1*	*2*	*3*	*4*	*5*	*6*	*7*	*8*	*9*	*10*	*11*	*12*	*13*	*14*	*15*	*16*	*17*	*18*	*19*	*20*	*21*	*22*	*23*	*24*
EA																								
China	–4.2	–2.8	–0.5	–0.5	–0.7	–0.6	0.2	–0.8	–0.5	–0.9	–1.0	–4.0	–3.5	–2.7	–2.0	–2.0	–1.6	–1.3	–1.2	–1.6	–2.5	–2.8	–4.4	n.a.
Vietnam	n.a.	n.a.	n.a.	n.a.	n.a.	–1.8	–4.3	–1.4	–0.5	–0.2	–1.7	–0.1	–1.6	–2.8	–2.9	n.a								
Myanmar	–4.2	–5.1	–4.8	–2.8	–2.2	–3.3	–4.1	–3.2	–1.8	0.5	–0.1	n.a.	n.a.	n.a.										
CEB																								
Croatia	–3.9	–0.8	1.2	–1.4	–1.0	–1.9	–1.0	–6.5	–6.9	–6.8	–6.2													
Czech Republic	–1.9	–3.1	0.5	–1.2	–1.1	–1.7	–2.1	–2.4	–2.8	–4.4	–5.1	–7.3												
Estonia	n.a.	n.a.	1.3	–1.3	–1.5	2.2	–0.3	–4.6	–0.7	0.4	1.2													
Hungary	0.0	–2.9	–6.1	–6.0	–7.5	–6.7	–5.0	–4.8	–4.8	–3.4	–3.4	–4.7	–9.9											
Latvia	n.a.	n.a.	–4.4	–4.0	–1.8	0.3	–0.8	–3.9	–3.3	–1.9	–2.5													
Lithuania	n.a.	–5.3	–4.8	–4.4	–4.5	–1.8	–5.8	–8.5	–2.8	–2.0	–1.2													
Poland	3.1	–2.1	–4.9	–2.4	–2.2	–3.1	–3.3	–3.1	–3.2	–3.7	–3.2	–5.4	–5.7											
Slovak Republic	n.a.	–11.9	–6.0	–1.5	0.4	–1.3	–5.2	–5.0	–3.6	–3.6	–3.9	–5.5												
Slovenia	0.3	0.6	–0.2	–0.3	–0.2	–1.7	–1.4	–0.9	–1.3	–1.2	–2.9													
SEE																								
Albania	–20.7	–23.1	–15.5	–12.6	–10.1	–12.1	–12.6	–10.4	–11.4	–9.1	–8.5	–7.5												
Bulgaria	–8.1	–4.5	–2.9	–8.7	–3.9	–5.7	–10.3	–2.0	1.3	0.2	–0.6	–0.6	–0.8											
FYR Macedonia	–9.8	–13.4	–2.7	–1.0	–1.4	–0.4	–1.7	0.0	2.5	–5.9	–3.5													
Romania	–4.6	–5.0	–3.5	–3.7	–3.5	–2.7																		
CIS																								
Armenia	–13.9	–54.7	–16.5	–9.0	–8.5	–5.8	–4.9	–7.4	–6.3	–3.8	–0.6													
Azerbaijan	2.7	–15.3	–11.2	–3.1	–2.4	–4.0	–4.9	–4.7	–0.6	1.4	1.5													
Belarus	–2.0	–5.5	–3.5	–2.7	–1.6	–0.7	–0.3	–2.2	–0.6	–1.4	–0.4													
Georgia	–3.0	–25.4	–26.2	–7.4	–5.3	–7.3	–6.7	–5.4	–6.7	–4.0	–2.0	–1.9												
Kazakh	–7.3	–4.1	–7.4	–3.4	–5.3	–7.0	–8.0	–5.2	–1.0	–0.9	0.0													
Kyrgyz Republic	n.a.	–14.4	–11.6	–17.3	–9.5	–9.2	–9.5	–11.9	–9.6	–5.1	–5.8													
Moldova	–26.6	–7.5	–19.2	–13.1	–15.2	–14.1	–5.7	–5.4	–2.6	–0.5	–1.3													
Russia	–18.9	–7.3	–10.4	–6.1	–8.9	–8.0	–8.0	–3.3	3.0	2.9	1.4													
Tajikistan	–31.2	–22.3	–10.1	–6.1	–5.8	–3.3	–2.7	–2.3	–1.6	–1.1	–0.6													
Turkmenistan	–9.4	–4.1	1.7	0.4	0.3	–0.2	–2.6	0.0	0.3	1.0	–2.7													
Ukraine	–25.4	–16.2	–8.7	–6.1	–3.2	–5.4	–2.8	–2.4	–1.3	–1.6	0.8													
Uzbekistan	n.a.	–18.3	–4.4	–4.1	–7.3	–2.2	–3.3	–2.6	–2.2	–2.3	–0.8													

Sources: Same as those in Table 2.4.

Table 2.6 Reserve ratio (%)

Country\ Elapsed Years	*1*	*2*	*3*	*4*	*5*	*6*	*7*	*8*	*9*	*10*	*11*	*12*	*13*	*14*	*15*	*16*	*17*	*18*	*19*	*20*	*21*	*22*	*23*	*24*
EA																								
China	n.a.	n.a.	n.a.	n.a.	n.a.	n.a.	41.6	36.9	30.1	28.6	39.0	46.6	47.8	35.4	22.5	22.1	21.6	23.0	22.2	17.8	16.5	14.8	14.4	13.7
Vietnam	n.a.	n.a.	n.a.	n.a.	n.a.	44.3	46.1	n.a.	44.9	41.1	31.6	25.9	26.7	23.6	17.3	15.7								
Myanmar	215.0	174.4	38.5	4.7	17.8	–26.4	–26.6	–12.5	11.3	22.6	19.8	15.5	15.2	n.a.										
CEB																								
Croatia	n.a.	10.0	13.8	16.6	14.2	11.2	11.5	17.9	16.1	15.4	19.2													
Czech Republic	n.a.	n.a.	11.3	11.0	17.6	16.2	20.4	26.6	27.3	24.4	23.4	4.0												
Estonia	27.3	35.2	22.6	18.4	18.2	24.6	26.9	28.1	25.4	14.5	12.2													
Hungary	17.0	25.1	20.5	14.9	10.7	12.1	5.5	8.6	9.4	10.1	12.7	8.8	6.7											
Latvia	n.a.	22.2	11.8	18.9	18.5	19.0	21.0	22.0	15.2	14.0	15.8													
Lithuania	n.a.	24.9	15.4	14.3	16.7	15.8	26.3	21.6	16.5	13.8	12.6													
Poland	27.1	24.1	18.1	13.2	11.3	10.4	9.4	10.3	12.2	6.6	5.6	7.2	6.9											
Slovak Republic	n.a.	n.a.	1.5	1.3	2.4	3.0	3.2	2.5	2.6	9.6	7.6	7.9												
Slovenia	3.2	3.2	5.4	5.1	5.1	5.5	5.4	5.1	4.6	5.6	4.7													
SEE																								
Albania	n.a.	n.a.	n.a.	40.0	22.7	17.7	18.4	16.5	17.8	18.3	18.2	16.5												
Bulgaria	n.a.	23.3	20.4	12.0	11.7	13.2	10.6	18.8	14.4	14.9	10.1	10.7	11.6											
FYR Macedonia	n.a.	1.7	9.9	13.1	8.3	12.1	11.4	13.6	17.6	10.3	11.8													
Romania	15.6	26.2	53.8	61.9	74.9	81.4																		
CIS																								
Armenia	11.9	26.1	23.4	26.6	31.4	42.3	22.2	16.7	13.7	15.8	18.0													
Azerbaijan	14.9	15.6	5.7	42.9	36.3	31.0	23.6	17.1	15.7	16.2	16.0													
Belarus	n.a.	n.a.	15.5	20.3	27.3	26.4	18.9	22.3	11.6	15.9	11.9													
Georgia	n.a.	n.a.	n.a.	n.a.	64.9	36.8	29.7	28.7	27.8	24.9	21.3	26.4												
Kazakh	n.a.	n.a.	n.a.	n.a.	n.a.	27.9	15.3	13.0	8.5	10.0	8.1													
Kyrgyz Republic	n.a.	n.a.	n.a.	13.5	14.2	24.8	21.1	24.3	21.2	10.7	19.1													
Moldova	14.4	21.5	13.0	9.0	5.2	5.5	22.1	25.8	22.1	21.6	22.1													
Russia	n.a.	26.7	25.8	18.9	18.7	22.7	15.6	22.7	26.8	22.6	22.8													
Tajikistan	n.a.	n.a.	n.a.	n.a.	n.a.	n.a.	52.2	50.6	59.3	58.1	37.8													
Turkmenistan																								
Ukraine	81.0	52.0	31.6	22.4	16.5	14.6	17.4	21.3	25.3	21.7	12.0													
Uzbekistan																								

Note: The reserve ratio is based on reserves/(demand + time + savings Deposits)*100.

Sources: 1. Except for Vietnam: IMF, *International Financial Statistics August 2003* (Washington, DC: IMF, 2003). 2. Vietnam: ADB, *Key Indicators 2002, and 2003* (Philippines: ADB, 2002, 2003).

First, the potential to manipulate the financial system can be viewed. The indicator for this is the ratio of fiscal surplus to GDP, as shown in Table 2.5. Potentiality refers to the assumption that governments finance deficits by using revenues from financial systems, due to the presence of undeveloped government bond markets. This assumption is substantially appropriate because countries are on the way to becoming market economies. Deficits are normalized to each GDP economic level so that clear comparisons can be made. Table 2.5 indicates that every country has posted a deficit during the transition process. However, the quantity of the deficit differs from region to region. EA has run relatively low deficits while the CIS has shown large deficits, especially in the first years of the process. It is expected that the CIS will suffer inflation as a result of financing its deficits.

Indicators for revenue from financial systems may now be confirmed. The reserve ratio in Table 2.6 may be viewed first. This ratio is calculated as a percentage of reserves over savings. This is calculated in order to determine whether or not governments acquire revenues through bank reserves. The table shows that in the EA region China and Vietnam have both extracted relatively large revenues from banks. However, this interpretation is somewhat complicated due to fluctuations in Myanmar and the fact that the central bank of China pays interests on reserves. Consequently, it was impossible to confirm the net volume of reliance on seigniorage revenue. Compared with the ratios for CEB and SEE (with the exception of Romania), the CIS shows relatively high ratios, especially during the first years of transition. Comparing trends and periods underlying ratios, Vietnam (and China) appears to have relied on revenues for relatively long periods during the process of transition.

The indicator of seigniorage is shown in Table 2.7. Here, this ratio is defined as a percentage of increased amounts of base money over GDP due to the availability of data. EA has relatively high ratios for long periods. China has especially high rates in the early 1990s (for example, 11.4 per cent in 1993). After scoring higher rates, CEE and the CIS appear to have converged at a range of 0 to 5 per cent since the third year.

Next, a comparison can be made between deficit ratios and two kinds of revenues, EA and the CIS for our analysis. While EA has relied on relatively large gross revenues for the long term, the area has low fiscal deficit ratios. By contrast, the CIS showed especially high rates in the first years of transition.

Table 2.7 Seigniorage

Country\ Elapsed Years	*1*	*2*	*3*	*4*	*5*	*6*	*7*	*8*	*9*	*10*	*11*	*12*	*13*	*14*	*15*	*16*	*17*	*18*	*19*	*20*	*21*	*22*	*23*	*24*
EA																								
China	n.a.	n.a.	n.a.	n.a.	n.a.	n.a.	n.a.	5.3	3.1	5.5	5.6	8.1	7.3	5.0	11.4	8.7	6.1	9.0	6.1	1.1	3.0	3.5	3.9	n.a.
Vietnam	n.a.	n.a.	n.a.	n.a.	n.a.	n.a.	2.8	n.a.	n.a.	1.9	1.3	0.9	4.9	3.3	2.5	n.a								
Myanmar	21.6	5.9	–0.4	6.2	3.8	3.9	4.5	5.0	4.3	3.5	2.3	n.a.	n.a.	n.a										
CEB																								
Croatia	6.5	4.9	2.8	2.1	1.9	1.3	–0.3	0.2	0.9	3.7	n.a.													
Czech Republic	n.a.	n.a.	n.a.	4.8	8.7	0.1	0.0	4.2	2.0	1.6	1.1	–11.2												
Estonia	8.8	8.8	1.5	2.1	2.1	3.6	0.7	3.2	2.0	–1.3	–0.2													
Hungary	–1.0	6.5	3.6	0.5	–0.2	1.9	–0.9	2.3	1.8	2.4	1.7	0.2	n.a											
Latvia	n.a.	n.a.	2.1	0.2	2.2	3.2	0.8	1.4	0.9	1.6	2.3													
Lithuania	n.a.	n.a.	3.3	2.6	0.2	2.1	2.2	–0.4	–0.3	0.7	1.8													
Poland	9.4	3.0	3.4	0.7	1.6	2.9	1.5	2.5	1.4	–0.1	–0.6	2.0	–0.2											
Slovak Republic	n.a.	n.a.	n.a.	1.9	2.6	2.9	2.1	–0.7	2.2	0.5	2.6	0.2												
Slovenia	2.1	1.0	1.6	0.9	0.6	0.9	0.9	1.0	0.1	1.6	–0.1													
SEE																								
Albania																								
Bulgaria	n.a.	n.a.	7.5	3.3	5.8	5.0	7.9	11.6	1.0	1.9	1.2	3.0	1.3											
FYR Macedonia	n.a.	n.a.	1.8	1.1	–0.1	1.0	0.3	1.6	n.a.	n.a.	n.a.													
Romania	4.9	1.2	4.4	3.4	3.9	n.a.																		
CIS																								
Armenia	n.a.	n.a.	7.2	2.6	1.9	1.3	0.3	0.0	1.8	0.7	2.3													
Azerbaijan																								
Belarus	n.a.	n.a.	n.a.	4.2	2.8	3.6	5.9	3.9	2.5	2.5	1.1													
Georgia																								
Kazakh	n.a.	n.a.	1.5	0.6	0.2	0.3	–0.6	0.5	0.1	0.6	n.a.													
Kyrgyz Republic	n.a.	n.a.	n.a.	n.a.	2.1	1.7	0.7	2.1	0.8	0.7	3.1													
Moldova	21.5	10.5	6.6	3.5	1.0	3.2	–0.8	3.6	3.0	2.7	n.a.													
Russia	n.a.	n.a.	6.8	4.4	1.6	1.8	1.9	3.7	4.1	2.3	2.9													
Tajikistan																								
Turkmenistan																								
Ukraine	n.a.	19.1	10.2	3.7	1.7	2.6	1.2	2.8	n.a.	n.a.	n.a.													
Uzbekistan																								

Note: The seigniorage is based on (base money t – base Money t–l)/GDP t*100.

Sources: Same as for Table 2.6. "Base Money" is "Reserve Money" in IMF, *IFS*.

Country\ Elapsed years	*1*	*2*	*3*	*4*	*5*	*6*	*7*	*8*	*9*	*10*	*11*	*12*	*13*	*14*	*15*	*16*	*17*	*18*	*19*	*20*	*21*	*22*	*23*	*24*
EA																								
China	n.a.	–0.4	–0.4	1.4	1.4	1.4	0.7	0.7	0.7	0.4	0.0	0.7	1.1	1.1	0.0	0.0	1.1	2.6	3.0	2.6	3.6	3.6	3.6	3.3
Vietnam	n.a.	n.a.	n.a.	n.a.	n.a.	n.a.	10.1	n.a.	n.a.	n.a.	5.9	5.2	5.3	6.9	4.1	2.6								
Myanmar	6.5	2.1	n.a.	–1.0	n.a.	7.5	6.8	4.0	4.0	4.0	5.1	5.5	5.5	5.5										
CEB																								
Croatia	1898.4	31.6	10.4	16.2	14.3	9.7	12.0	9.2	7.1	6.7	n.a.													
Czech Republic	n.a.	7.0	7.1	5.9	5.8	5.7	5.5	4.8	4.2	3.8	4.0	4.0												
Estonia	n.a.	n.a.	8.7	7.1	3.4	0.4	7.4	–0.3	2.1	5.6	2.7													
Hungary	3.6	2.5	11.2	8.4	6.1	7.8	5.4	4.5	4.4	7.5	2.9	2.6	2.7											
Latvia	n.a.	42.4	17.9	16.1	10.3	6.8	9.9	8.3	7.6	4.2	2.2													
Lithuania	77.9	68.5	22.2	3.0	10.4	9.0	7.1	8.5	9.7	7.3	5.8													
Poland	8.0	4.0	7.0	10.0	5.0	4.5	3.5	4.5	7.6	7.4	7.2	8.3	8.5											
Slovak Republic	n.a.	n.a.	5.4	5.2	6.6	7.0	7.5	5.8	3.6	5.2	5.0	5.3												
Slovenia	23.9	12.4	10.6	7.2	7.1	6.4	5.3	5.6	5.4	5.2	5.0													
SEE																								
Albania	3.0	7.0	7.0	3.5	7.3	9.7	14.5	8.5	16.7	16.0	16.3	6.0												
Bulgaria	n.a.	26.2	19.3	30.1	45.5	26.1	269.0	10.9	10.0	10.8	8.4	8.2	5.8											
FYR Macedonia	665.0	45.0	42.2	21.9	8.8	9.8	9.3	8.7	8.3	9.2	8.5													
Romania	12.1	18.6	20.5	20.8	17.2	16.1																		
CIS																								
Armenia	n.a.	n.a.	n.a.	48.7	34.2	28.1	23.6	11.5	13.5	11.8	11.6													
Azerbaijan	50.0	223.0	0.0	17.0	20.0	10.0	16.8	17.6	15.0	16.1	n.a.													
Belarus	n.a.	6.5	58.9	74.2	30.0	16.2	12.7	27.2	30.1	12.8	n.a.													
Georgia	n.a.	n.a.	n.a.	n.a.	51.9	27.1	36.9	29.0	23.0	20.8	23.0	25.0												
Kazakh	n.a.	n.a.	n.a.	13.9	24.3	10.8	3.9	7.8	4.3	4.4	n.a.													
Kyrgyz Republic	n.a.	n.a.	n.a.	n.a.	28.3	9.8	37.6	25.3	33.5	24.8	18.9													
Moldova	n.a.	n.a.	n.a.	9.4	11.3	9.8	9.1	n.a.	8.0	n.a.	7.8													
Russia	n.a.	n.a.	n.a.	218.0	91.7	15.2	24.6	28.9	13.0	11.3	n.a.													
Tajikistan	0.0	0.0	0.0	400.0	13.0	–15.0	34.0	19.2	–23.0	–4.2	0.0													
Turkmenistan	n.a.	58.0	94.0	–10.0	70.0	11.5	34.4	14.7	n.a.	n.a.	n.a.													
Ukraine	–5.0	35.0	41.0	53.0	46.0	31.0	33.0	34.0	28.0	18.8	12.5													
Uzbekistan	n.a.	n.a.	40.0	15.0	21.7	13.2	20.0	19.2	3.9	4.4	n.a.													

Sources: 1. East Asia: IMF, *International Financial Statistics August 2003*. (Washington, DC: IMF, 2003). Eastern Europe and the CIS: EBRD. *Transition Report* London: EBRD, various years.

Table 2.9 Real deposit interest rates (%)

Country\ Elapsed Years	*1*	*2*	*3*	*4*	*5*	*6*	*7*	*8*	*9*	*10*	*11*	*12*	*13*	*14*	*15*	*16*	*17*	*18*	*19*	*20*	*21*	*22*	*23*	*24*
EA																								
China	n.a.	n.a.	n.a.	n.a.	n.a.	n.a.	n.a.	n.a.	0.0	–10.1	–7.0	5.6	4.0	1.2	–3.6	–13.3	–5.9	–0.9	2.9	4.6	3.7	2.0	1.8	n.a.
Vietnam	n.a.	n.a.	n.a.	n.a.	n.a.	n.a.	n.a.	n.a.	n.a.	n.a.	5.3	2.0	3.3	5.4	5.7	2.6								
Myanmar	–25.7	–11.8	–23.3	–12.9	–22.8	–15.1	–15.4	–3.8	–17.2	–39.0	–7.4	9.9	–11.6	–47.6										
CEB																								
Croatia	–231.0	–1490.1	–92.6	4.1	0.7	0.8	–1.6	0.1	–2.8	–2.1	n.a.													
Czech Republic	n.a.	–4.8	–13.8	–3.0	–2.1	–2.0	–0.8	–2.6	2.4	–0.5	–1.7	0.2												
Estonia	n.a.	n.a.	–38.9	–20.3	–12.6	–0.4	0.8	5.6	2.8	–1.3	0.1													
Hungary	–0.4	–2.0	–5.4	–5.3	–4.8	–3.8	–5.0	–2.0	0.1	1.9	0.1	0.2	2.8											
Latvia	n.a.	–80.8	–17.1	–10.0	–7.6	–3.1	1.8	1.8	1.6	3.2	3.3													
Lithuania	–978.2	–390.7	–64.5	–32.2	–20.3	–7.0	–2.7	0.8	0.0	–0.5	0.0													
Poland	–532.8	–34.3	–11.0	–10.3	–6.2	–8.3	–2.9	3.1	1.0	5.6	4.2	2.4	2.6											
Slovak Republic	n.a.	n.a.	–14.5	–4.2	–1.7	0.4	2.6	3.7	–0.7	–6.4	–2.5	0.2												
Slovenia	–159.0	–2.7	6.9	7.3	1.3	5.5	–0.9	3.5	2.0	0.1	0.7													
SEE																								
Albania	–30.5	–194.0	–62.0	–6.1	5.9	6.4	–4.7	–4.1	8.7	7.6	4.6	3.1												
Bulgaria	n.a.	–275.8	–36.7	–19.4	–24.0	–36.7	88.8	–1079.0	–18.9	2.6	–6.8	–4.5	–3.0											
FYR Macedonia	–1229.0	–16.4	–8.9	7.7	10.3	10.8	9.4	12.6	4.2	4.7	6.8													
Romania	–103.2	–20.8	–0.4	–13.0	–11.1	–9.7																		
CIS																								
Armenia	n.a.	n.a.	n.a.	–112.6	13.5	12.1	16.2	26.7	18.9	11.7	8.3													
Azerbaijan	–902.0	–1095.0	–1258.0	–322.0	–6.7	8.0	11.7	18.4	10.4	10.5	n.a.													
Belarus	n.a.	–1124.9	–2131.4	–608.5	–20.4	–48.2	–58.9	–270.0	–131.3	–27.2	n.a													
Georgia	n.a.	n.a.	n.a.	n.a.	–144.8	–8.3	6.6	13.4	–7.2	7.9	7.4	4.3												
Kazakh	n.a.	n.a.	n.a.	–131.9	–9.8	–5.4	7.2	5.2	2.4	2.6	n.a													
Kyrgyz Republic	n.a.	n.a.	n.a.	n.a.	4.8	16.2	25.3	–0.3	–0.3	5.6	3.8													
Moldova	n.a.	n.a.	n.a.	2.3	1.9	11.7	14.0	n.a.	–3.8	n.a.	15.6													
Russia	n.a.	n.a.	n.a.	–95.7	7.3	2.1	–10.5	–76.7	–15.8	–16.3	n.a.													
Tajikistan	–1127.0	–2165.0	–320.0	–509.0	–309.0	1.0	–27.5	–16.2	8.4	–13.1	–0.1													
Turkmenistan	n.a.	–3052.0	–1542.0	–925.3	–862.4	–42.6	7.4	2.9	n.a.	n.a.	n.a.													
Ukraine	–1128.0	–4594.0	–682.0	–307.0	–46.0	2.1	11.5	–1.7	–14.2	–1.2	6.2													
Uzbekistan	–635.0	–504.0	–1508.0	–214.6	–26.0	–56.1	–15.9	–15.6	–3.1	–5.4	n.a.													

Note: The rates are derived by subtracting the rates of CPI change from nominal deposit interest rates. Notice that, because depreciation by inflation can not exceed deposit, the rates do not be below –100 per cent in practice.

Sources: Same as those in Table 2.9.

2.2.4 Financial institutions

Finally, the conditions for the construction of financial markets may be confirmed. Based on the concept of financial repression, interest rates are utilized as indicators. These show the concrete conditions that determine whether or not financial institutions (in this instance banks) can be operated as business units.

First, the interest rates spread between loans and deposits is given in Table 2.8. This is shown in order to understand the conditions of secure financial intermediation function relative to positive spread. Of course, if complete competition among banks is considered, the spread might be small. However, if the possibility of a financial restraint situation arises, then banks must have a positive and sufficient spread. Most transition countries have maintained positive spreads throughout their transitions, though these spreads have fluctuated due to inflation (as seen in Table 2.4). Focusing on China, this country started real financial reform in the middle 1990s; from this time, positive spreads appeared. Before the reforms, however, the existence of positive spreads is not clear. It seems evident that after reform, banks in China secured profits in terms of interest.

Another indicator for consideration is the real deposit rate, shown in Table 2.9. This indicator shows conditions that attract depositors. Unlike the spreads seen above, negative values are observed for long periods in many countries. It is clear that negative interest depends upon the rates of inflation shown in Table 2.4. Due to a lack of data, the first years in Vietnam cannot be judged, but EA marked negative rates for substantial periods in this area's transition. Although EA has not suffered severe inflation, as seen previously, the area has continued to receive negative marks. For example, only recently has China shown positive marks – no doubt as a result of the reforms mentioned earlier.

2.2.5 Summary

Compared to the other transition countries considered in our study, countries in the EA region have experienced stable economic performance. Myanmar, however, has experienced relatively high levels of instability compared to other countries in the EA region. The progress of transition of the financial systems in EA is relatively slow when compared with others. Looking at interest and again comparing with other transition economies, conditions for the reconstruction of market mechanisms in EA have not been developed for a long time.[9]

From the descriptive data to date, it can be assumed that the economic growth experienced in the first few years of transition is not caused by the progress of transitions in financial systems. Low initial conditions that allow for room to grow are just one explanation for the achievement of economic performance.

Next, we consider the CEB. Since similar trends are shown in the selected indicators of the above areas, features in the areas as a variation for progress of development or transition are dealt with here. U-shaped economic growth is a feature of CEB as well as the other East European and CIS countries. The economic level in CEB recovered after a decline during the first years of transition.

2.3 Inflation and its factors

This section analyses the relation between inflation and its determinants. As discussed in the previous section, the EA region seems to have maintained a dependency on the fiscal function from Tables 2.5 to 2.8. However, high inflation rates in this area do not seem to be caused by seigniorage. The reasons for this are investigated in the following sub-sections.

2.3.1 Fiscal function and seigniorage

Excess dependency of the fiscal revenue on seigniorage has the potential to produce inflation, which is caused by revenues being acquired from financial systems to finance fiscal deficits. Average revenues during transition can be confirmed and are shown in Table 2.10. This table shows the revenue in transition countries compared with developed and developing countries. Indicators and data for non-transitional countries in the table are obtained from McKinnon (1993) who based them on work by Brock (1984). In the table, "Total Revenue" is (base money$_t$ – base money$_{t-1}$)/GDP$_t$, "Currency Component" is (currency$_t$ – currency$_{t-1}$)/GDP$_t$ and "Required Reserve Component" is (required reserves$_t$ – required reserves$_{t-1}$)/GDP$_t$. To compare transition countries with some Latin American countries that extract seigniorage and developed countries, data for the non-transitional countries are based on the averages from 1972 to 1980.

Generally, the total revenues in transition countries are larger than those in either industrial countries or developing countries. Further, the ratios of revenue from financial systems in transition countries, with the exception of CEB, are higher than the rates for South and Central American countries. Table 2.10 clearly shows that on average EA gained larger gross revenues than other areas. As elements of the total, revenues from currency components are greater that those of the required reserve component.

Table 2.10 Revenue from financial system (% of GDP)

Country	*Total revenue*	*Currency component*	*Required reserve component*
Industrial countries (average from 1972 to 1980)			
United States	0.46	0.39	0.07
West Germany	0.74	0.43	0.31
United Kingdom	0.85	0.62	0.23
Developing countries (in average from 1972 to 1980)			
Mexico	4.3	1.2	3.1
Colombia	2.7	1.2	1.5
Brazil	2.3	0.9	1.4
Transitional countries (average from each inaugural year to 2002)			
EA			
China	4.98	2.47	2.51
Vietnam	2.42	1.97	0.46
Myanmar	5.06	4.27	0.80
CEB			
Croatia	2.09	0.75	1.34
Czech Republic	1.36	0.92	0.44
Estonia	2.76	1.87	0.89
Hungary	1.56	1.16	0.41
Latvia	1.67	1.29	0.38
Lithuania	1.33	1.08	0.25
Poland	2.09	1.40	0.69
Slovak Republic	1.45	0.85	0.60
Slovenia	0.92	0.54	0.39
SEE			
Albania	n.a.	n.a.	n.a.
Bulgaria	4.29	2.81	1.48
FYR Macedonia	0.95	0.65	0.30
Romania	3.39	1.02	2.37
CIS			
Armenia	1.94	1.56	0.38
Azerbaijan	n.a.	n.a.	n.a.
Belarus	3.21	1.72	1.49
Georgia	n.a.	n.a.	n.a.
Kazakh	2.87	2.49	0.38
Kyrgyz Republic	1.58	1.34	0.25
Moldova	3.99	2.84	1.15
Russia	3.25	2.11	1.14
Tajikistan	n.a.	n.a.	n.a.
Turkmenistan	n.a.	n.a.	n.a.
Ukraine	5.99	3.45	2.54
Uzbekistan	n.a.	n.a.	n.a.

Notes 1. Refer to McKinnon (1993), Table 5.3, who introduced it from work by Brock (1984).
2. Data of "Developing Countries" are truncated to two decimal places by Brock.

Sources: 1. Industrial and Developing Countries: McKinnon (1993).
2. Transition Countries: IMF (2003). *International Financial Statistics*. Washington, DC: IMF.

It is quite likely that inflation is connected with a heavy dependency on seigniorage revenue by government to finance fiscal deficits, or, in other words, an implicit tax. EA has relied on large gross revenues, as shown in Table 2.10, and this seems to imply a higher rate of inflation. On the other hand, if deficits are normalized by GDP, EA ratios of fiscal deficit to revenue-based finance are not high. Hence, it may be possible to advance a hypothesis that inflation was caused by a reliance on seigniorage revenue under conditions of slow transitional progress, particularly in the case of East Asia. Or, alternatively, it might be that high dependence on seigniorage have been mitigated by high and stable economic growth. To test this hypothesis, we build an estimation model of the relation between inflation and money supply and demand as follows.

2.3.2 Model building

To specify the abovementioned relation in a formula, a model developed by Cagan (1956) may be applied. Romer (1996) introduced this model, and seigniorage is a major factor causing inflation in developing economies. As mentioned in the previous section, transition economies also need large expenditures in order to execute historic projects when there is a lack of means for finance.

Desired real money holdings, m^*_{it}, may be expressed as:

$$M^*_{it} = c_{it} \exp(-a\pi_{it}), \tag{2.1}$$

where subscript i indexes countries and t indexes time. This means that the higher the change rate of prices, π_{it}, the greater the decrease in m^*_{it}. Here, m^*_{it} equals the constant c_{it}, multiplied by $-a\pi_{it}$ (of the exponential function). Further, c_{it} includes real output and real interest rates that are assumed to be constant. The power, a, is an elasticity of money demand. It is assumed that the adjustment from actual money holdings, m_{it}, to m^*_{it} takes the form:

$$\ln m_{it} = \alpha(\ln m^*_{it} - \ln m_{it}),$$

where α indicates an adjustment speed. Using Equation (2.1),

$$\frac{\dot{m}_{it}}{m_{it}} = \alpha(\ln c_{it} - a\pi_{it} - \ln m_{it}). \tag{2.2}$$

On the other hand, if the revenue from money supply is seigniorage, S_{it}, to finance fiscal deficit, then the following may be expressed:

$$S_{it} = g_{it}\, m_{it} - f_{it}, \tag{2.3}$$

where g_{it} is the rate of change in the money supply and f_{it} is the difference in net foreign assets. Originally, the equation of money supply did not contain a variable of net foreign assets. In that version, increased base money was considered to be the same as seigniorage. However, increased base money includes domestic assets and increased net foreign assets. Particularly in the case of EA, it would be expected that increased net foreign assets have an effect on base money. Therefore, the variable is included in Equation (2.3). Using nominal money amounts, m_{it}, g_{it} is expressed as M^{*}_{it}/M_{it}. Equation (2.3) means that revenue equals change in the rate of money supply, g_{it} (as a tax rate) times money demand, m_{it} (as a taxable base).

Combining demand and supply, an equilibrium equation may be given as follows:

$$G_{it} = \pi_{it} + \frac{\dot{m}_{it}}{m_{it}}.$$

Rearranging terms and using Equation (2.3),

$$\pi_{it} = \frac{s_{it}}{m_{it}} + \frac{f_{it}}{m_{it}} - \frac{\dot{m}_{it}}{m_{it}}, \tag{2.4}$$

Substitute Equation (2.2) into Equation (2.4),

$$\pi_{it} = \beta_1 \frac{s_{it}}{m_{it}} + \beta_1 \frac{f_{it}}{m_{it}} - \beta_2 \ln c_{it} + \beta_2 \ln m_{it},$$

where $\beta_1 = 1/(1 - a\alpha)$ and $\beta_2 = \alpha/(1 - a\alpha)$. It may be assumed that s_{it} equals the fiscal deficit, z_{it}. This assumption means that the whole of the fiscal deficit is financed by seigniorage. As mentioned in the previous section, this would be appropriate when there is a lack of financial means for the government. In addition, let c_{it} equal real GDP, y_{it}. This assumes that the expansion of economic activities calls for higher levels of money demand. In this case, the relation between the independent and dependent variables is:

$$\pi = \pi(\overset{+}{z/m}, \overset{+}{f/m}, \overset{-}{\ln y}, \overset{+}{\ln m}).$$

An estimation formula may be specified as follows:

$$\pi_{it} = \gamma_{0i} + \gamma_1 \frac{z_{it}}{m_{it}} + \gamma_2 \frac{f_{it}}{m_{it}} + \gamma_3 \ln y_{it} + \gamma_4 \ln m_{it} + u_{it},$$

where u_{it} is the error term.

There are four determinant factors of inflation. The first variable is the amount of the real fiscal deficit normalized by the amount of real money holdings. This is the primary parameter used to measure the first causal factor of inflation. The next factor is the increased amount of net foreign assets normalized by the amount of real money holdings. This represents base money supply due to international transactions. The third is the logarithm of real GDP. This represents the demand factor of money that restrains inflation. As such, the sign of this factor is negative. The final factor is the logarithm of real money holdings. This index expresses contributions to the inflation rate when the money supply increases under a given price.

2.3.3 Data and empirical results

An estimate of the parameters mentioned above can be made using a panel dataset.[10] The set consists of both cross-country and annual time series. The dataset is prepared with statistics used in section 2.2 to compose the indicators. Sources for each of the variables are listed at the bottom of Table 2.11. A summary of the data is also shown in Table 2.11.

EViews 5.0 statistical software was used to estimate all models. Table 2.12 shows results for the estimation of Model 1. It is more appropriate to eliminate individual effects; thus, a least squares dummy variable model, LSDV, was used. Results of the Wu–Hausman test are shown at

Table 2.11 Summary of data

Series	*Arithmetic mean*	*Median*	*Maximum*	*Minimum*	*Standard deviation*	*No. of Observations*
π	2.779	0.207	156.065	–0.085	10.683	294
z/m	0.313	0.088	35.065	–0.140	2.158	265
f/m	0.066	0.049	0.704	–0.768	0.150	248
In y	12.162	12.456	17.535	6.364	2.702	289
In m	10.680	10.938	16.364	3.902	2.881	262

Note: Real values are computed by dividing each nominal value by prices in 1997.

Sources: Prepared by the author with the following:

(1) π, z, and y:

For East Asia, IMF (2003), *International Financial Statistics August 2003*. Washington, DC: IMF.

For 1990 in the Eastern Europe and the CIS, EBRD (2002), *Transition Report 2002*. London: EBRD.

For after 1991, EBRD (2003), *Transition Report Update May 2003*. London: EBRD.

(2) f and m:

IMF (2003), *International Financial Statistics August 2003*. Washington, DC: IMF.

Table 2.12 Determinants of inflation with a model of fixed effects by country

	Model 1	
Independent variable	*Coefficient*	*t-statistic*
Fiscal deficit ratio	9.868	5.31***
Net foreign asset ratio	4.369	1.99**
Income	–9.681	–3.94***
Money supply	6.449	5.73***
Constant	45.624	2.04**
Fixed effects		
China	–18.008	
Vietnam	2.519	
Myanmar	6.118	
Croatia	–1.076	
Czech Republic	2.458	
Estonia	–2.810	
Hungary	9.609	
Latvia	–12.131	
Lithuania	–3.821	
Poland	2.235	
Slovak Republic	–0.352	
Slovenia	7.911	
Albania	–1.469	
Bulgaria	–8.215	
FYR Macedonia	4.116	
Romania	1.973	
Armenia	–11.040	
Azerbaijan	20.856	
Belarus	8.469	
Georgia	–7.602	
Kazakh	9.616	
Kyrgyz Republic	–5.463	
Moldova	–8.391	
Russia	10.296	
Tajikistan	–8.888	
Ukraine	6.364	
Sample size	240	
Adjusted r-squared	0.220	

Note: *significant at the 0.1 level, **at the 0.05 level, and *** at the 0.01 level.

Source: Author.

the bottom of the table, and the null hypothesis that coefficients of random effect estimator and fixed effect estimator are consistent was rejected.

The table shows the following results: first, a fiscal deficit increases the change rate of price, as theory predicts. It can be seen that real GDP absorbs the inflation factor. The coefficient of real money shows that inflation may be increased by nominal money holdings to a price. Fiscal deficits increase inflation through a factor related to money supply.

Next, area dummy variables are applied as shown in Table 2.13. The following estimations from here are applied using plain panel OLS due to a singular matrix with dummy variables. Model 2 has EA, CEB, and SEE dummy variables. In addition to CEB and SEE area dummy variables, Model 3 has the dummy variables of China, Vietnam, and Myanmar as EA components, by which it shows the country- and area-wide differences in intercept terms. These models show that each area has negative effects against inflation when compared with the CIS area. In addition to these comparative negative levels, the order also reflects the levels of severe inflation as discussed in section 2.2.

Based on the area dummy variables shown in the previous table, the effects of coefficient dummy variables for each explanatory variable may be considered. These coefficient variables distinguish the effects of each explanatory variable among areas and countries. The coefficient dummy variable shows a synergy effect relative to explanatory and area variables.

Table 2.13 Determinants of inflation with area dummy variables

	Model 2		*Model 3*	
Independent variable	*Coefficient*	*t-statistic*	*Coefficient*	*t-statistic*
Fiscal deficit ratio	6.555	4.24***	6.315	4.10***
Net foreign asset ratio	2.876	1.38	3.206	1.54
Income	–2.472	–3.72***	–3.556	–4.38***
Money supply	2.435	3.78***	3.376	4.44***
EA dummy	–3.280	–2.52**		
China dummy			–7.091	–3.37***
Vietnam dummy			–2.654	–1.29
Myanmar dummy			–2.085	–1.31
CEB dummy	–2.605	–2.64***	–3.399	–3.27***
SEE dummy	–2.276	–2.07**	–2.999	–2.64***
Constant	4.998	2.39**	8.462	3.29***
Sample size	240		240	
Adjusted R–squared	0.124		0.136	

Note: *significant at the 0.1 level, **at the 0.05 level, and ***at the 0.01 level.

Table 2.14 Determinants of inflation with coefficient dummy variables for the four areas

	Model 4 (z/m)		*Model 5 (f/m)*		*Model 6 (ln y)*		*Model 7 (ln m)*	
Independent variable	*Coefficient*	*t-statistic*	*Coefficient*	*t-statistic*	*Coefficient*	*t-statistic*	*Coefficient*	*t-statistic*
Fiscal deficit ratio	7.221	4.43***	6.404	4.13***	6.806	4.22***	7.436	4.59***
Net foreign asset ratio	3.032	1.45	0.568	0.22	3.152	1.52	3.045	1.47
Income	–2.607	–3.73***	–2.597	–3.89***	–3.437	–4.15***	–3.383	–4.37***
Money supply	2.569	3.82***	2.564	3.96***	3.385	4.33***	3.441	4.57***
Constant dummy								
EA	–3.818	–2.18**	–3.519	–2.47**	–13.698	–2.41**	–13.063	–2.06**
CEB	–2.013	–1.71*	–3.565	–3.18***	0.364	0.10	1.559	0.53
SEE	–1.036	–0.68	–2.811	–2.22**	0.153	0.02	9.364	1.20
Coefficient dummy								
EA	18.789	1.12	–1.360	–0.05	–2.601	–3.81***	4.283	3.92***
CEB	–0.145	–0.02	12.033	1.99**	–3.734	–4.21***	3.020	4.20***
SEE	–2.502	–0.32	5.161	1.16	–3.700	–3.94***	2.284	2.25**
Constant	4.993	2.21**	5.362	4.65***	6.842	2.37**	5.460	2.07**
Sample size	240		240		240		240	
Adjusted R-squared	0.125		0.126		0.135		0.143	

Note: *significant at the 0.1 level, **at the 0.05 level, and ***at the 0.01 level.

First, the coefficient dummy variables in the four areas are considered. Table 2.14 shows the results for Models 4 to 7. In addition to estimates of the coefficient dummy variables, each independent variable is also reported. The explanatory variables satisfy each sign condition. However, the estimates of the net foreign assets ratio are statistically insignificant. Considering coefficient dummy variables, neither of the estimates on the fiscal deficit ratio is statistically insignificant. This implies that the fiscal deficit has an average and constant degree of effect, which is included in intercept, on the inflation among all the transition countries, and less variation between individual countries. Regarding net foreign assets, the coefficient dummy for CEB in Model 5 is statistically significant. It would appear that foreign assets are a significantly different degree of factor in bringing inflation to CEB. Regarding a positive demand from real GDP, all the coefficient dummies of $\ln y$ are statistically significant, as shown in Model 6. This shows sensitivity of GDP growth on inflation is a significantly different factor in each of these four areas. In comparing the levels of the coefficient dummy, it would appear that the inflation rates in CEB and SEE are more sensitive to GDP growth than those in EA; around –3.7 for both CEB and SEE and –2.6 for EA. Finally, coefficients dummies for all the areas on the money supply were statistically significant, as were the estimates of $\ln y$. In comparing coefficients, it would appear that the EA's inflation is more sensitive to the money supply than other areas: around 4.3 for EA, 3.0 and 2.3 for CEB and SEE, respectively.

Next, we will consider the individual effects of Asian economies on coefficient dummy variables. Table 2.15 shows the results for Models 8 to 11. No statistically significant estimates were obtained, except for the coefficient dummy of Model 10 in China. It would appear that only the GDP of China in EA is sensitive to inflation. Otherwise, there were similar results.

As expected from the discussion offered in section 2.2, the fiscal deficit ratio is a factor that leads to inflation. In addition, EA has a relatively lower sensitivity of inflation to rates of real growth. Therefore, as EA showed higher dependence on seigniorage in fiscal revenue it has also paid inflation costs under the gradual transition process. Thanks to the constituent economic growth, however, the inflationary impact has been saved by real demand for money.

By contrast, China has a relatively high sensitivity of inflation to real growth. This result implies the possibility that in China fiscal revenue through seigniorage was utilized in a productive way in order to promote further economic growth. Thanks to this mechanism, in con-

Table 2.15 Determinants of inflation using coefficient dummy variables for the six areas

	Model 8 (z/m)		*Model 9 (f/m)*		*Model 10 (ln y)*		*Model 11 (ln m)*	
Independent variable	*Coefficient*	*t-statistic*	*Coefficient*	*t-statistic*	*Coefficient*	*t-statistic*	*Coefficient*	*t-statistic*
Fiscal deficit ratio	7.114	4.37***	6.137	3.96***	6.902	4.25***	7.546	4.64***
Net foreign asset ratio	3.312	1.58	0.667	0.26	3.197	1.53	3.161	1.52
Income	–3.525	–4.30***	–3.748	–4.57***	–3.761	–4.33***	–3.965	–4.72***
Money supply	3.372	4.38***	3.566	4.64***	3.698	4.50***	3.993	4.90***
Constant dummy								
China	–6.662	–2.17**	–7.544	–2.98***	17.742	0.60	8.600	0.52
Vietnam	–1.197	–0.33	–3.218	–0.96	108.169	0.66	31.765	0.71
Myanmar	–1.031	–0.37	–2.374	–1.48	–32.968	–0.31	–17.489	–0.19
CEB	–2.707	–2.22**	–4.470	–3.80***	0.375	0.11	1.454	0.49
SEE	–1.692	–1.09	–3.644	–2.79***	–0.700	–0.08	8.998	1.15
Coefficient dummy								
China	4.116	0.04	–1.817	–0.03	–6.640	–1.81*	2.165	1.12
Vietnam	–21.952	–0.31	7.725	0.16	–12.453	–0.96	1.002	0.26
Myanmar	–1.876	–0.08	–7.723	–0.05	–1.531	–0.19	5.189	0.69
CEB	0.293	0.04	12.909	2.14**	–4.080	–4.39***	3.541	4.56***
SEE	–2.094	–0.27	5.881	1.32	–3.968	–4.11***	2.835	2.67***
Constant	7.843	2.99***	9.034	3.48***	7.509	2.55**	6.794	2.48**
Sample size	240		240		240		240	
Adjusted R-squared	0.127		0.133		0.127		0.140	

Note: *significant at the 0.1 level, **at the 0.05 level, and ***at the 0.01 level.

trast to other areas, China experienced lower inflationary pressures. The Opposite direction of a similar mechanism in the CIS seems to explain the especially strong impact of inflation in that region. This result here allows us to interpret as to suggest the following conclusion: the governments in China, who retained substantial control over the economy for a longer period than was the case in other areas, directed revenue from money printing towards productive investment, instead of consumption, against a negative prediction by McKinnon (1993).

2.4 Concluding remarks

This chapter has documented a relationship between economic performance and the progress of financial systems in EA as compared with other transitional areas. Section 2.2 included an examination of the features of financial transition. During the period of transition, EA has maintained a fiscal system run by centralized administrations. A slow shift in transition and high reliance of seigniorage in fiscal revenue was observed in EA.

In order to test whether this high level of seigniorage induced instability in the macro economy, an inflation function was estimated with the supply-demand of money in section 2.3. While EA has relied on relative large gross revenues from the financial system, under paying costs of inflation along with the other transitional areas, higher economic growth has helped to restrain inflation by increasing the demand for money, especially in China. This implies that the usage of seigniorage revenue generated higher rates of growth in the economy, with the exception of Myanmar, which experienced instability. Therefore, it may be necessary to distinguish Myanmar from China and Vietnam in any discussion of EA.

In EA, especially in China and Vietnam, economic growth seems to have been achieved not so much by a shift in financial systems, but rather by maintaining dependence on the fiscal function for a long period of time in transition. This is drastically different from the position in the CIS. Many areas extracted revenues that led to inflation. However, the CIS suffered serious instability of prices due to a lack of money demand, as indicated in its GDP figures. Of course, conditions for the presence of financial markets have recently emerged. Thus, the conclusions stated above may only be appropriate for periods in which there is little change in financial systems.

Several issues still merit future research. One concerns the relation between recent changes in the financial systems of EA and the impact of these changes on economic performance. Another concern whether or not unsustainable fiscal deficits can lead to hyperinflation. Finally, this chapter considered the relation between fiscal deficits and inflation. Of particular importance for future studies is the issue of how excessive deficits may relate to more severe forms of inflation.

Notes

1 World Bank (1996), EBRD (1998), Lavigne (1999), and others described financial institutional changes in transition countries.

2 McKinnon discusses a procedure of policies in the context of economic liberalization that is not only in transition. However, there are similar processes that construct economies: (a) from financial systems controlled by administrative means and (b) from systems controlled by market principle. In this chapter, the idea is utilized as an adequate combination.

3 Among studies on China, Fry (1998) examined the financial system in terms of inflation and seigniorage.

4 Many countries in transition are not dealt with here. In the East Asia, these include the Kingdom of Cambodia, Laos People's Democratic Republic, and Mongolia. Many countries throughout the world have adopted planned economies in their process of modernization. Thus, the list reported here is incomplete. To make general conclusions about transition, wider experiences must be included.

5 These include the Czech Republic, Estonia, Hungary, Latvia, Lithuania, Poland, Slovakia and Slovenia.

6 For example, see EBRD (1999), de Melo *et al.* (2001), and others.

7 Although the GDP deflator is a more suitable index for comparison across countries, limited availability of data makes use of the CPI necessary.

8 Although price controls affect the level of CPI, we utilize CPI as the indicator of price changes because consumers face prices presented by CPI for expenditures, and price controls, for example, in China had now tended to be eased to some degree.

9 An argument concerning so-called "gradualism" and "shock therapy" must be recalled at this point. Although this is not dealt with here, it may reflect differences in the progress of all transition factors, including the financial system.

10 Panel unit root tests against five series data show (1) π_{it} and $fi_t/m_{it} \sim I(0)$ and (2) z_{it}/m_{it}, $\ln y_{it}$ and $\ln m_{it} \sim I(1)$ respectively. However, $\gamma_1 (z_{it}/m_{it}) + \gamma_3 \ln y_{it} + \gamma_4 \ln m_{it} \sim I(0)$, so all of π_{it}, $\gamma_2 (f_{it}/m_{it})$, and $\gamma_1(z_{it}/m_{it}) + \gamma_3 \ln y_{it} + \gamma_4 \ln m_{it}\, z_{it}/m_{it} \sim I(0)$. Therefore, $u_{it} \sim I(0)$ can be obtained.

References

Brock, Phillip L. (1984) "Inflationary Finance in an Open Economy," *Journal of Monetary Economics* 14(1), 37–54.

Cagan, Phillip (1956) "The Monetary Dynamics of Hyperinflation," in Milton Friedman (ed.), *Studies in the Quantity Theory of Money*. Chicago: The University of Chicago Press.

De Melo, Martha, Cevdet Denizer, Alan Gelb, and Stoyan Tenev (2001) "Circumstances and Choice: The Role of Initial Conditions and Policies in Transition Economies," *World Bank Economic Review* 15(1), 1–31.

European Bank for Reconstruction and Development (EBRD) (1998) *Transition Report 1998: Financial Sector in Transition*. London: European Bank for Reconstruction and Development.

European Bank for Reconstruction and Development (EBRD) (1999) *Transition Report 1999: Ten Years of Transition*. London: European Bank for Reconstruction and Development.

European Bank for Reconstruction and Development (EBRD) (2003) *Transition Report Update May 2003*. London: European Bank for Reconstruction and Development.

Falcetti, Elisabetta, Martin Raiser, and Peter Stanfey (2002) "Defying the Odds: Initial Conditions, Reforms, and Growth in the First Decade of Transition," *Journal of Comparative Economics* 30(2), 229–50.

Fry, Maxwell J. (1998) "Can Seigniorage Revenue Keep China's Financial System Afloat?" in Donald J.S. Brean (ed.), *Taxation in Modern China*. New York: Routledge.

Lavigne, Marie (1999) *The Economics of Transition: from Socialist Economy to Market Economy*, 2nd edn. Basingstoke: Macmillan Press.

McKinnon, Ronald I. (1993) *The Order of Economic Liberalization*, 2nd edn. Baltimore: Johns Hopkins University Press.

Nakagane, Katsuji (2002) *Keizai hatten to Taisei ikoh* (*Economic Development and Structural Transition*). Nagoya: Nagoya University Press (in Japanese).

Romer, David (1996) *Advanced Macroeconomics*. New York: McGraw-Hill Companies, Inc.

World Bank (1996) *World Development Report, 1996: From Plan to Market*. Washington, DC: World Bank.

3

The Effects of Changes of Policy Tool during the Transition Period in China

Masahiro Kodama

3.1 Introduction

One aspect of the transition from a planned economy to a market economy can be seen in changes in how firms finance themselves. In a planned economy, the central government distributes funds, while in a market economy, funds are acquired through banks or other financial mechanisms. In terms of policy tools, with the transition, the government loses some of the policy effects of government expenditures on national output, while it gains control of a new economic policy tool – monetary policy.

We will take China as a case study on this issue, since it is a representative of the gradual transition economies, and also experienced a gradual financial transition. After the economic reforms which began in 1979, the Chinese central government began to offer less direct support to the production sectors of the economy, and instead began to encourage these firms to use financial markets.

In our examination of the actual transition process in China, we can pose some empirical questions. Did the influence of government expenditures on GDP decrease? In place of fiscal policy, has monetary policy been effective in influencing the output of the economy? This chapter will consider these questions.

In this chapter, we will consider these questions separately using different datasets. In order to test the fiscal policy effect, we use an annual dataset for the period between 1952 and 2003. For the test of the effects of monetary policy, we use a monthly dataset between December 1996 and December 2003. The reason for the use of different datasets for the examination of the two policy tools stems from the availability of data. Fiscal policy data on government expenditures are not available over a long period on a "monthly" basis. Conversely, monetary policy data are not available over a long period on an "annual" basis. Because of this, it is not possible to use a single dataset that includes a long series of data on both money supply and government expenditures.

In summary, we find that government expenditures have had a smaller effect on GDP in the period after the economic reform than before it. We also find that the money supply does not have a large influence on output in the sample period between December 1996 and December 2003, that is, in a period after the economic reforms.

3.2 Events during the sample period and test methodology

In this section, we give an overview of events during the sample period related to policy tool effects and the test methodology used in this study.

3.2.1 Events during the sample period

In this subsection, we briefly review when and how the distribution system of funds for production in China changed. In 1953, the first five-year plan was issued. One of the goals of the plan was to stimulate the development of the industrial sector. In 1958, all of the banks in China were merged into the People's Bank of China (PBOC), beginning a banking system that is termed a mono-bank system. In addition, a credit rationing system was introduced in China. All capital was concentrated in the mono bank, and, since this was under the direct control of the government, the government could determine which firms would receive concentrated capital investments. In accordance with the goals of the first five-year plan, it gave priority to investment in the industrial sector.

In 1979, the year in which a series of economic reforms began, the mono-bank system ended, and three banks were given independence from the PBOC. These new banks began to lend to creditors, while the PBOC also maintained its own lending department. In 1984, the first financial reforms were announced. Under its provision, the PBOC became specialized as the central bank, and the department conducting lending to the non-financial sector was made completely independent. These four banks are referred as the four largest state-owned commercial banks (SOCBs). In the late 1980s other commercial banks were also established.

Then, in 1994, the upper limit on lending by commercial banks other than the four largest state-owned commercial banks was abolished. With this change, the banks gained the ability to run their businesses more independently. In 1998 the upper limit on lending by the four largest national banks was also abolished.

As is clear from this account of events, 1979 was a turning point for the capital distribution system in China. Before that time, capital was distributed under a credit rationing system. Afterwards, it began to be distributed more in accordance with market principles.

3.2.2 Test methodology

As mentioned in the Introduction, this research considers two empirical questions. First, did the influence of government expenditures on GDP decrease? Secondly, in the place of fiscal policy, did monetary policy begin to affect the output of the economy? We attempt to answer these questions through the use of two types of empirical tests. One is the multivariate Granger causality test developed by Toda and Yamamoto (1995). Since that test uses a VAR model with additional lags, we call it a lag-augmented VAR test (LA-VAR test). The other test is the cointegration test developed by Johansen and Juselius (1990), which is also based on a VAR model.

To date, there have been very few previous researches examining the Chinese economy with VAR models. Among those that have been published are Chen (1989), Summers and Zhang (2001), Shan (2002) and Chang (2002). Of these studies, Chen (1989) and Chang (2002) are relatively close to this study in terms of their examination of monetary policy effects, but they do not examine fiscal policy effects and do not use the LA-VAR test. To our knowledge, there is no previous research examining Chinese policy tool effects using the LA-VAR test.

The LA-VAR test is implemented as follows. We assume that we have *n* variables, and we want to determine the relationship between them. First, we check the order of integration of the variables, using ADF tests. If we find that a variable is integrated without taking any order difference, we call it I(0). If the variable is integrated with a difference of order d, we call it I(d), and we call d the "order of integration." We use d_{max} to denote the largest "order of integration" in our n-variable dataset. Secondly, we make a VAR model with n variables. We set the length of the lags by picking a model which minimizes AIC's. For the explanation, suppose the lag length to be k. Thirdly, we make a VAR model with $k + d_{max}$ lags. Toda and Yamamoto (1995) find that regardless of whether the variables have unit roots or cointegration, a usual chi-squared test statistic on coefficient restrictions in the VAR model follows a chi-squared distribution with the degree of freedom of the number of the coefficient restrictions. Toda and Yamamoto show that this is always true when d_{max} is equal to 1. They also show that it is true as long as k is greater than 2, even if d_{max} is equal to 2.

One of the advantages of the LA-VAR test is that it is simple. Conventionally, if we have cointegrations in our dataset, and if we want to know a Granger causality, we often perform a Granger-causality-type test based on an error correction model (ECM). To construct an ECM, two prerequisite tests must be performed: ADF tests and cointegration tests. However, it is known that these two prerequisite tests are not robust, and that if they contain errors, a Granger causality test based on them will also have problems. The LA-VAR test is somewhat simpler than the Granger causality test based on the ECM. In the above procedure for the LA-VAR test, we do not have to perform cointegration tests, which are needed in an ECM.

We also run cointegration tests. As usual, we interpret the existence of cointegration as the presence of a long-run relationship between the variables. First, we implement ADF tests to check the orders of integration. Secondly, if, as a result of the ADF tests, we find non-I(0) variables in the dataset, we examine whether these variables can be cointegrated. When performing the cointegration test, we follow some rules regarding the combination of the integration order of the variables. For example, to have a cointegration with an $I(d_{max})$ variable in our dataset, we need to have at least one more $I(d_{max})$ variable. If the variables satisfy these rules, we check for the existence of cointegrations using Johansen tests. The existence of cointegration implies that the variables have a long-run relationship. It is possible that even if we find a short-run relationship in a dataset, such as a relationship of a Granger causality, we still do not find a long-run relationship.

3.3 Government expenditures and GDP

In this section, we examine the relationships between government expenditures and GDP in China. The main purpose of this section is to examine whether the influence of government expenditures on GDP decreased after the economic reforms were launched in 1979. We attempt to answer the question by comparing the effects in two periods, i.e., before 1979 and after 1979. For this purpose, we construct a VAR model with only two variables – government expenditures and GDP.

This is because of the limited amount of data available. In order to prevent a reduction of the degree of freedom of the estimation, in this study, we limit the number of variables in the VAR model.

In acquiring data on government expenditures, it is difficult to use the SNA data as a source, since these data include government investment within total national investment. Thus, one available data source is the expenditure section of the government's budget balance sheet. In the budget balance sheet data, monthly data are only available for a short period. Because of this we make use of annual base data, which is available for the entire period between 1952 and 2003. The government expenditure data record the expenditures of all government, including both central and local governments. The data exclude the problem of double counting which can occur in the event of subsidies between the central government and local government. Having 52 annual datasets, we split the period into two discrete sections – before and after the economic reforms.

3.3.1 ADF tests and VAR lag length

Here, we examine whether real GDP (Y) and real government expenditures (G) are stationary, with ADF tests. Before performing the tests, both variables are transformed into logarithmic forms. When examining the variables, we split the period from 1952 to 2003 into two parts, namely 1952–78 (hereafter, the first period) and the 1979–2003 (hereafter, the second period). There are several types of the ADF tests corresponding to different assumptions of error terms and numbers of differences used for the variables. Here we use regular models, with and without a time trend. The lags are determined in reference to AIC's.

In the ADF tests of G in the first period, the AIC of the model with trend is smaller than the AIC of the model without trend, and the ADF test statistic in the model with trend is significant at the 10 per cent level (see Table 3.1). Therefore, G in the period is I(0). In the ADF tests of Y in the first period, we find a smaller AIC in the model with trend than in the model without trend, and the ADF statistic in the model with trend is significant at the 10 per cent level. Therefore, Y is also I(0) in the first period. In the second period, the ADF tests for G at the zero and first difference are not significant. In the test of the second difference, the AIC in the model with trend is smaller, and the ADF test statistic in the model is significant at the 5 per cent level. This implies that G in the second period is I(2). The ADF statistics of Y at the zero difference in the second period are not significant. The AIC of Y in the first difference in the model with trend is smaller, and the ADF statistic

Table 3.1 ADF tests for G and Y

Period	*Variable*	*Lags*	*Without trend*	*Lag*	*With trend*
1952–1978	G	1	–1.368	1	–3.544*
	Y	2	–0.541	2	–3.356*
1979–2003	G	3	1.410	3	–0.820
	ΔG	2	–1.346	2	–2.908
	$\Delta^2 G$	1	–3.459**	1	–3.293**
	Y	2	–1.510	4	–2.512
	ΔY	1	–4.012***	5	–3.473*

Note: * stands for 10 per cent significance, ** stands for 5 per cent significance, and *** stands for 1 per cent significance.

in the model is significant at the 10 per cent level. Therefore, Y in the second period is I(1).

As for the lag length of VAR, for the first period a lag length of 2 minimizes the AIC, and for the second period a lag length of 3 minimizes it.

3.3.2 LA-VAR test

From the results of the ADF tests and the determination of lag lengths, we can say that for the first period, we need to construct a LA-VAR model with a lag length of 2, and for the second period we need to construct one with a lag length of 5. In the regressions, we examine

Table 3.2 LA-VAR tests

Period	*Dependent variable*	*Cause Variable*	
		Y	*G*
		Chi-squared	*Chi-squared*
1952–1978	Y	—	28.394 (1.0×10^{-6})
	G	20.354 (3.8×10^{-5})	—
1979–2003	Y	—	1.489 (0.684)
	G	0.506 (0.917)	—

Note:
P values in parentheses.

Granger causalities. The results can be seen in Table 3.2, which tells us that in the first period, Y and G have very close relationships in both directions – from Y to G *and* from G to Y. In the second period, we can no longer see any relationship, *and* neither Y nor G are causes of the other.

3.3.3 Cointegration

From the ADF tests, we find that both G and Y in the first period are I(0), while Y in the second period is I(1), and G in the second period is I(2). This means that Y and G in the first period have cointegrations. Since econometric theories assure that a linear combination of I(0) variables makes an I(0) variable, we do not need to run a cointegration test in this case. In other words, Y and G have a long-run relationship in the period. On the other hand, in the second period, the variables cannot be cointegrated. Econometric theories say that the linear combination of two variables with different integration orders cannot make an I(0) variable. Thus, Y and G do not have a long-run relationship in the second period.

In summary, in this section we discover the following: The direct control over the output via the fiscal expenditure vanished for the period between 1979 and 2003, while in the period between 1952 and 1978 the clear relationships between the output and the fiscal expenditure exist in both the long term and the short term.

3.4 Money supply and GDP

In this section we examine the relationship between money supply (M) and GDP in China. After the economic reforms in 1979, the government began to encourage firms to finance themselves by borrowing from financial intermediaries. As a result, firms became more financially dependent on the financial sector. Considering this, it is significant to ask whether control over the money supply has large effects on output in the period after the reform. We consider this question in this section.

Annual data for the money supply (M2) are available only for a short period, i.e. the period between 1977 and the present, for which the sample size is rather small for a three-variable VAR analysis. Monthly data are available from December 1996 to December 2003, so we use the monthly M2. Since we do not have monthly data for GDP, however, we use data on industrial value added (y) as a proxy. For the price index, we use CPI (P). M and y are seasonally adjusted, and all three variables in the test are used in logarithmic form.

A number of previous studies have analysed the relationship between the economy and money supply based on a VAR model. The simplest model in the research is one with M2 (M), output (y), prices (P), and call rates. We use this type of model here, since our sample size is small and we cannot include many variables. However, our model does not include the call rate, for the following reasons. Call rates are used in other studies since in the countries examined, the call rate is the policy control variable used by the central bank. Consequently, researchers assume that the central bank can change the call rate. However, the call rate is not a policy variable in China. Kojima (1988) points out that the Chinese government controls money supply mainly through administrative guidance, even after the first financial reforms were introduced in 1984. Under administrative guidance, if a firm does not follow the guidance, the government pressures commercial banks to stop lending to the firm as a punishment. It is difficult to find a proxy of the administrative guidance, for an empirical study. Thus, in this research, we construct a VAR model with only three variables – money supply, output and price levels – and we observe effects of money supply change on the other two variables, even though the central bank can control only a part of the money supply.

3.4.1 ADF tests and VAR lag length

In this section, we examine the orders of integration of the three variables, M, y and P. For this purpose we run ADF tests. The results are presented in Table 3.3.

Adopting the same procedure with the AIC's and the ADF statistics as in subsection 3.3.1, we determine the numbers of integrations of the variables. Table 3.3 shows us that all the variables are I(1).

Table 3.3 ADF tests for M, y and P

Period	*Variables*	*Lags*	*Without trend*	*Lags*	*With trend*
Dec. 1997–Dec. 2003	M	1	0.749	1	–1.039
	ΔM	1	–7.800***	1	–7.881***
	y	6	4.700	6	0.316
	Δy	2	–7.017***	5	–6.829**
	P	12	–1.890	12	–2.185
	ΔP	8	–1.822	3	–4.274***

Note:
* stands for 10 per cent significance, ** stands for 5 per cent significance, and *** stands for 1 per cent significance.

Table 3.4 LA-VAR tests

Period	*Dependent variables*	*Cause variables*		
		M	*y*	*P*
		Chi-squared	*Chi-squared*	*Chi-squared*
Dec. 1996– Dec. 2003	M	—	4.875 (0.181)	3.804 (0.283)
	y	2.697 (0.440)	—	4.220 (0.238)
	P	3.988 (0.262)	11.047 (0.011)	—

Note:
P values are shown in parentheses.

In this section, we also check the appropriate lag length in a VAR model with three variables – M, y and P. In order to determine the lag length, we check the AIC. A lag length of 3 minimizes the AIC.

3.4.2 LA-VAR test

Based on the results of the ADF test and the determination of the lag length, we can say that we need to construct a LA-VAR model with a lag length of 4.

In these models, we examine Granger causalities. The results can be seen in Table 3.4. As the table clearly shows, only in the direction of "y to P" does significant causality exist. The causalities related to monetary policy effects, i.e., "M to y" and "M to P," are insignificant. Therefore, we do not find significant monetary policy effects, at least in the short run.

3.4.3 Cointegration

From the ADF tests, we find that during the period, M, y and P are all I(1). This means that they can all be cointegrated in the period, so we examine the presence of cointegration. For the examination, we use a Johansen test. Johansen and Juselius (1990) shows five possibilities for the test model. We run all the tests for the data, and, based on the AIC's, choose the test with "a quadratic trend in the data and an intercept and a trend in a cointegration equation." The results are presented in Table 3.5. r denotes the number of ranks, which is equal to the number of cointegrations. Because the test is based on a VAR model,

Table 3.5 Cointegration among M, y and P

Period	*Null*	*Trace statistics*	*Critical value*	
			5%	*1%*
Dec. 1996–Dec. 2003	r = 0	25.566	34.55	40.49
	r ≤ 1	10.147	18.17	23.46
	r ≤ 2	0.204	3.74	6.40

we need to determine the lag length. Here we use 3 as the lag length based on the AIC of the VAR with the level variables. In Table 3.5 we find that there is no cointegration among M, y and P. In other words, we do not find a long-run relationship among the variables.

As a result, this section produces the following conclusions. In the period between December 1996 and December 2003, the money supply control does not significantly affect either the output or the price level, although the production sector would be more dependent on the financial sector than had previously been the case.

3.5 Conclusion

One characteristic of a transition economy, in terms of policy tools, is that the government loses the direct controling power via fiscal policy on output, while simultaneously establishing a new economic policy tool, monetary policy. In this study, from this point of view, we examined the effects of China's economic policy tools: Did the effect of government expenditures on GDP become smaller? In the place of fiscal policy, did monetary policy come to affect the output of the economy?

We find that before the reforms in 1979, there was a close short-run cause-and-effect relationship between output and government expenditure. Our test results tell us that the two variables also have a stable relationship in the long run. By contrast, after the reforms, the close relationships can no longer be observed in either the short run or the long run. From the results, we conclude that in China, government expenditure has a smaller effect on GDP in the period after the economic reform than it did before it.

In respect of the monetary policy effects, we do not observe causalities in either of the directions of influence of our interest, "M to y" or "M to P." In addition, we do not find any cointegration among the variables. Hence, we conclude that in China, the money supply does not have a large influence on output even in the period after the economic reform, in either the long run or the short run.

The empirical results of the influence of government expenditure are relatively easy to understand, since the results are expected. On the other hand, the results of the money supply effect are unexpected. The reason why control over money supply does not affect output is not immediately apparent. One possible explanation is based on the characteristics of the sample period. Banks were in very bad shape during the period, since the financial conditions of their main customers, the state-owned enterprises, worsened. This led to a deterioration in the banks' balance sheets, since the banks were forced to lend to the enterprises by the government, and they held large levels of non-performing loans. It is said that small- and medium-sized companies could not borrow because of a credit squeeze during the period. Thus, even when the central bank expanded the money supply, commercial banks did not make substantial loans to firms. As a consequence, monetary expansion did not lead to greater output.

There is another possible explanation as to why the money supply did not affect the output. Before the economic reforms, funds were distributed by the government, and the distribution covered the whole country. By contrast, after the economic reforms, funds had to be distributed by the financial sector. It is possible that the financial sector was not well integrated immediately after the economic reforms, as Chapter 4 in this book implies. Suppose that there are two areas. In one of them people need more liquidity, while in the other people do not need it. If the financial market is well integrated, there will be a flow of liquidity from the second area to where it is required. As a result, liquidity is used efficiently in a well-integrated financial market, and this would stimulate an increase in output. In China's case, the country might be experiencing the opposite situation, a poorly integrated financial market, which might explain reason why the money supply did not stimulate the output well.

There are some possible areas for further research. If the first explanation is correct, the period we selected is, in a sense, unique. If we want to answer the question of how monetary control in China affects output in a "normal" period, we must consider another sample period. For empirical research on the monthly money supply, we have already used all the data for this study. We also tried to construct a VAR model using annual money supply data, though it is not shown in this research. Money supply data is available for the period after 1977. Because our VAR model was constructed using limited data, we cannot minimize AIC when determining the lag length of the model. Before minimizing the AIC with a longer lag length, we had used all our available data. Therefore, in order to carry out the same type of research as this study using another period, we need to wait for the production of datasets with both annual and monthly data.

Another interesting question that emerges from this research is whether similar results can be observed in other transition economies. The situation where national banks suffer from non-performing loans from poorly performing national companies (state-owned companies) does not seem to be specific to China – at least in terms of the mechanism of events. It seems that this could also happen in other transition economies. Thus, it would be interesting to examine whether we can actually see such events in other countries. In addition, with such a broad panel dataset, it would be meaningful to examine what we can say regarding policy tool effects immediately after the transition. These subjects are possible extensions of this research.

References

Chang, Tsangyao (2002) "Financial Development and Economic Growth in Mainland China," *Applied Economics Letters* 9, 869–73.

Chen, Chien-Hsun (1989) "Monetary Aggregates and Macroeconomic Performance in Mainland China," *Journal of Comparative Economics* 13, 314–24.

Hamilton, James D. (1994) *Time Series Analysis*. Princeton: Princeton University Press.

Jordan, Shan (2002) "A Macroeconometric Model of Income Disparity," *International Economic Journal* 16(2), 47–63.

Jordan, Shan, Alan G. Morris, and Fiona Sun (2001) "Financial Development and Economic Growth," *Review of International Economics* 9(3), 443–54.

Johansen, Soren, and Katarina Juselius (1990) "Maximum Likelihood Estimation and Inference on Cointegration," *Oxford Bulletin of Economics and Statistics* 52, 169–210.

Kojima, Rei-itus (1988) *Chu-goku no Keizai Kaikaku* (*The Economic Reform in China*). Tokyo: Keisoh Shobo (in Japanese).

Nakagane, Katsuji (2002) *Keizai hatten to Taisei iko* (*Economic Development and Structural Transition*). Nagoya: Nagoya University Press (in Japanese)

Summers, Peter, and Siqi Zhang (2001) "A Bayesian VAR Forecasting Model of the Chinese Economy," in Peter, Lloyd and Xiao-guang Zhang (eds), *Models of the Chinese Economy*, Cheltenham: Edward Elgar Publishing.

Shan, Jordan (2002) "A Macroeconomic Model of Income Disparity in China," *International Economic Journal* 16(2), 47–63.

Teruyama, Hiroshi (2001) "VAR ni yoru kin-yu seisaku no bunseki (VAR Analysis on Monetary Policy," *Financial Review* September, 74–140 (in Japanese)

Toda, Hiro Y., and Taku Yamamoto (1995) "Statistical Inference in Vector Autoregressions with Possibly Integrated Processes," *Journal of Econometrics* 66, 225–50.

4

The Inter-Provincial Capital Flows in China Before and After the Transition to a Market Economy

Shinichi Watanabe

4.1 Introduction

One of the central characteristics of the transition process from a centrally planned economy to a market economy is the transformation of the mechanism of capital accumulation – how savings are made and allocated among potential investment projects in an economy. In a centrally planned economy it is the state planning and its administrative mechanism that coordinate the decisions of savings and investment for the nation as a whole. By contrast, in a market economy it is the financial markets and financial intermediaries that coordinate the decisions of savers and investors. To the extent that market institutions evolve over time, one should expect that during the initial stages of the transition process the functions performed by financial markets and intermediaries fall short of those observed in well-developed market economies, and that they improve only gradually in line with the progress of institution building. A natural question is whether it is possible to test empirically the hypothesis that financial institutions evolve gradually and that their functions are imperfect at the beginning of the transition.[1]

This chapter attempts to answer this question by focusing on inter-provincial capital flows in China. Before the beginning of the transition to a market economy, the state planning and its administrative mechanism determined the allocation of investment and savings among provinces. The surplus funds of the provinces in which savings exceeded investment were reallocated by the state plan to the deficit provinces in which investment exceeded saving.

Kojima (1997, pp. 61–9) argues that the political factors determined the inter-provincial allocation of savings under state planning. In the military confrontation with the USA and the Soviet Union, China built the armaments industry in those inland provinces that had low saving rates, such as Yunnan, Guizhou, Sichuan, west Hubei, and Gansu from the mid-1960s to the end of the 1970s. For that purpose the government accumulated the financial surplus of farmers and state-owned firms from across the nation by controling prices. Furthermore, it chose to invest very little in those municipalities where the saving rate was high. The state planning and its administrative mechanism served as "a financial center" to coordinate saving and investment among the provinces before the transition started. For this reason Kojima labels the state planning system an "integrated socialist market for funds."

At the start of the transition to a market economy, two interrelated processes have been in progress. One is the process of administrative reforms which weaken the function of state planning and its administrative mechanism as "a financial center" to coordinate savings and investment among provinces. The other is the development of nationwide capital markets, which control capital flows across provinces. These two processes have opposite effects on the degree of integration of capital flows. On the one hand, removing the function of "a financial center" from the state planning and administrative mechanism is essentially a political process and can happen quickly once an agreement is reached to do so. But it weakens the ability of an economy to support capital flows across provinces. On the other hand, the development of capital markets enhances capital flows across provinces. But the development process of capital markets depends not only upon the political factor, but also upon the social and economic factors that change only gradually. That is, it depends on the level of development of a market economy as a whole, which further depends on the degree of division of labor, the level of physical infrastructure, and the existence of laws and institutions for economic transactions.[2]

This chapter aims to quantify the development process of capital markets in China by using *the savings retention coefficient* (SRC) of the Feldstein and Horioka model as a measure of hindrances of free capital flows across provinces.

Feldstein and Horioka (1980) developed a simple regression model of the investment rate on the savings rate for the purpose of measuring the degree of integration of the capital markets of OECD countries. They call the estimate of the coefficient of the savings rate the "savings retention coefficient" and interpret its value as a measure of the hindrances of free capital flows across countries. If capital markets are highly integrated, then an increase in savings in one country will be channeled through the capital market to the users of the additional funds according to the expected returns and risks of their investment without regard to their nationalities. As a result, the fraction of savings retained in a country will be small or close to zero if the number of countries is large. That is, the value of the savings retention coefficient will be close to zero.

Somewhat surprisingly, however, their estimate is 0.887, significantly different from zero. This is termed the Feldstein–Horioka puzzle.[3] But, in contrast to the findings of Feldstein and Horioka, the estimates of the savings retention coefficient turn out to be close to zero or negative for regional data within one country with highly integrated domestic capital markets. For instance, Sinn (1992) finds the estimate being –0.1115 (–1.47) for the USA in 1957; Helliwell and McKitrick (1998) –0.069 (0.82) for Canada, 1961–93; Dekle (1996) –0.36 (–4.52) for Japan, 1975–88; Yamori (1995) –0.291 (–5.94) for Japan, 1980–85; Bayoumi and Rose (1993) –0.99 (1.87) for the UK, 1971–75, where the numerical values in parentheses are t-values. The estimates except Dekle and Yamori obtained for Japan are consistent with the hypothesis that the value of the saving retention coefficient is zero among the regions in one country with highly integrated domestic capital markets. The estimates of Dekle (1996) and Yamori (1995) are obtained from the macroeconomic data of Japanese prefectures and are negative and statistically significant. But they also find that the estimates become zero when investment is limited to private investment. They attribute the negative coefficient to the government policy which allocates a larger amount of public investment to the regions with lower savings rates.

Thus, we ask the following questions concerning the value of the savings retention coefficient (SRC): (i) What is the value of the SRC under the state planning mechanism? (ii) What is the value of the SRC for the period after the transition started? (iii) What has happened to the value of SRC during the transition period?

In section 4.2 we first estimate and compare the values of the SRC for the period under the state planning and for the period after the transition to a market. We then estimate the changes in the value of SRC during the transition period and evaluate their implications for the development of capital markets in China. Section 4.3 provides short concluding remarks.

4.2 Empirical evidence

We use the provincial macroeconomic data, which are available from 1952 to 2002.[4] In order to evaluate the development process of capital markets accurately after the start of the transition it is necessary and desirable to decompose the investment data of each province into public investment and private investment. But it turns out to be impossible to do so at the time of writing. The data about how the central government investment is allocated among provinces are not currently available. In addition, current and capital expenditures are not reported separately for each province. The separate figures are available only for the sum of local government expenditures as a whole. Thus, the empirical evidence presented below should be seen only as a very rough approximation to the reality.

It is necessary to locate the time when the transition from a centrally planned economy to a market economy began. We choose 1985 as the beginning of the period in which market institutions become the dominant mechanism for capital accumulation in comparison with the state planning mechanism. In October 1984 the Chinese communist party abandoned the "bird cage" view which assigned the roles of "cage" and "bird" to the state planning and markets respectively. In doing so, it acknowledged for the first time that the Chinese economy was a market economy, but under the conditions of state planning. At about the same time two important changes were made in the institutions that governed the capital accumulation process. From 1983 to 1984 a fiscal reform started that fundamentally changed the financial relationship between the state and state-owned enterprises (SOEs). The obligation of SOEs to submit their profits to the state was replaced by an income tax on profits.[5] The financial system also experienced a fundamental change from 1983 to 1984. The decision was made in 1983 to separate the functions of commercial banking from the People's Bank of China and establish Industrial and Commercial Bank of China, which started its operation from the beginning of 1984.

In this section we first estimate the SRC for the period under the state planning and then for the period after the transition. Finally we evaluate the development process of capital markets by estimating SRCs for each year.

4.2.1 1952–1984: "capital flows" under the state plan

The time series data are available for 28 provinces: from 1952 to 1984 for 18 provinces, three autonomous regions and three municipalities under the central government;[6] and from 1978 to 1984 for four provinces. We present two estimates – one by a cross-section analysis and the other by a fixed effect model of the panel data analysis.

Cross-section analysis

The average values of the investment rate and the savings rate are computed for each of the 28 regions. Figure 4.1 is the scatter diagram of the averages. A weak negative correlation exists between the investment rate and the savings rate. The regression result is given by

$$\text{Investment rate} = 0.354 - 0.198 \times \text{Savings rate} \qquad (4.1)$$

$$(9.020) \; (-1.74)$$

(The values in the parentheses are t-values. Adjusted $R^2 = 0.071$.)

The estimate of SRC shown in the regression equation (4.1) is surprisingly similar to that found in an economy with highly integrated capital markets. It suggests that state planning performed the function to pool savings from all the regions and reallocate it among the regions to finance investment to achieve national goals.[7]

Figure 4.1 Investment rate vs savings rate, 28 regions, 1952–1984

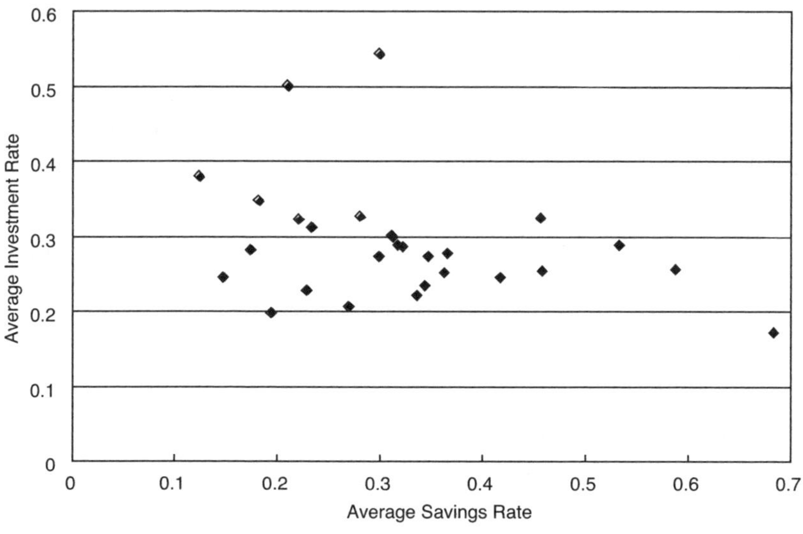

Source: Author.

Panel data analysis

We divide the period from 1952 to 1984 into seven subperiods of five years in length (1952–54, 1955–59, 1960–64, 1965–69, 1970–74, 1975–79 and 1980–84)[8] and apply the fixed effects model of the panel data analysis. We find that

$$\text{Investment rate} = \text{region-specific constant} + \underset{(3.507)}{0.295} \times \text{Savings rate} \qquad (4.2)$$

(The value in a parenthesis is a t-value. Adjusted $R^2 = 0.504$.)

In contrast to the estimate obtained in the cross-section analysis, the value of the SRC is positive and statistically significant. Yet the value of the coefficient is 0.295, which is rather small.[9]

Thus, we may conclude that the investment rate of each province was largely independent of its own savings rate and was determined by the national policies how to collect the funds from the entire nation and reallocate them among different provinces.[10]

4.2.2 1985–2002: "capital flows" in the market economy under the state plan

In this section we study the correlation between the investment rate and the savings rate for the entire 31 provinces.

Cross-section analysis

The average values of the investment rate and the savings rate are computed for each region over 18 years from 1985 to 2002. Figure 4.2 plots their values. A positive correlation exists between them. The regression result is given by

$$\text{Investment rate} = \underset{(5.178)}{0.307} + \underset{(2.104)}{0.304} \times \text{Savings rate} \qquad (4.3)$$

(The values in the parentheses are t-values. Adjusted $R^2 = 0.102$.)

The estimate of the SRC of Equation (4.3) is larger than that of Equation (4.1) by 0.502. The saving rate of each region has become a much more important determinant of its investment rate.

Figure 4.2 Investment rate vs savings rate, 31 regions, 1985–2002

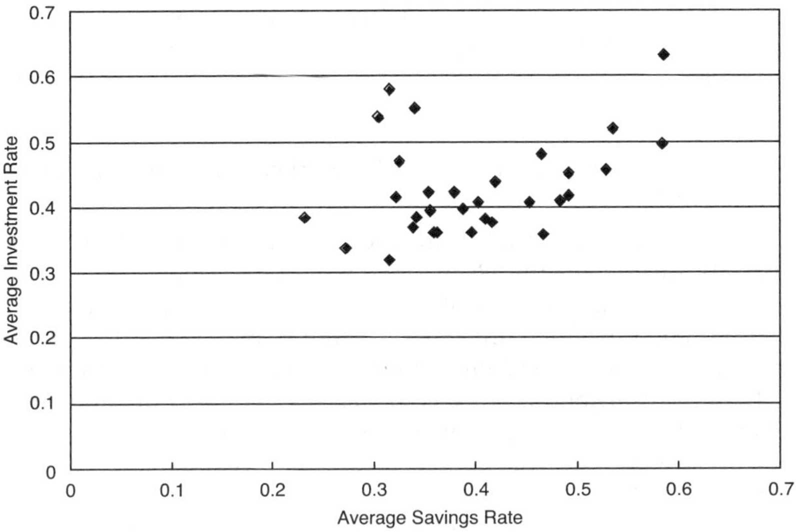

Source: Author.

Panel data analysis

We divide the period from 1985 to 2002 into four sub-periods, each five years in duration (1985–89, 1990–94, 1995–99, 2000–02[11]) and apply the fixed effects model of the panel data analysis. We find that

$$\text{Investment rate} = \text{region-specific constant} + \underset{(5.680)}{0.488} \times \text{savings rate} \quad (4.4)$$

(The value in a parenthesis is a t-value. Adjusted $R^2 = 0.772$.)

The difference between Equations (4.4) and (4.2) is not as significant as that observed in the cross-section analysis, but the SRC has increased from 0.295 in Equation (4.2) to 0.488 in Equation (4.4), showing that the investment rate of a province depends more heavily upon its own savings rate. In other words, the capital accumulation process has become more fragmented after the transition to a market economy.[12]

Neither of the estimates obtained in Equations (4.3) and (4.4) are close to zero, which should be the case if the Chinese economy resembles an economy with highly integrated capital markets. In other words, the capital accumulation process of the Chinese economy is much more fragmented than the one observed in a matured market economy.

4.2.3 The development of capital markets and changes in the annual SRC

In order to gain an insight into the development process of capital markets, we estimate the SRC for each year of the sample period. Figure 4.3 plots the results of this analysis. The solid line is the estimates of the SRC and the dotted lines are the bands of two standard deviations from the estimates. The figure reveals a few interesting observations.

First, the value of the SRC was stabilized around –0.2 under the state plan after 1963. It was extremely volatile from 1952 to 1962, which might have distorted the estimate obtained in section 4.2.1.

Secondly, the value of the SRC increased from 0.124 in 1985 to 0.553 in 1995 and then remained at around the same level until 1997. The

Figure 4.3 Savings retention coefficient

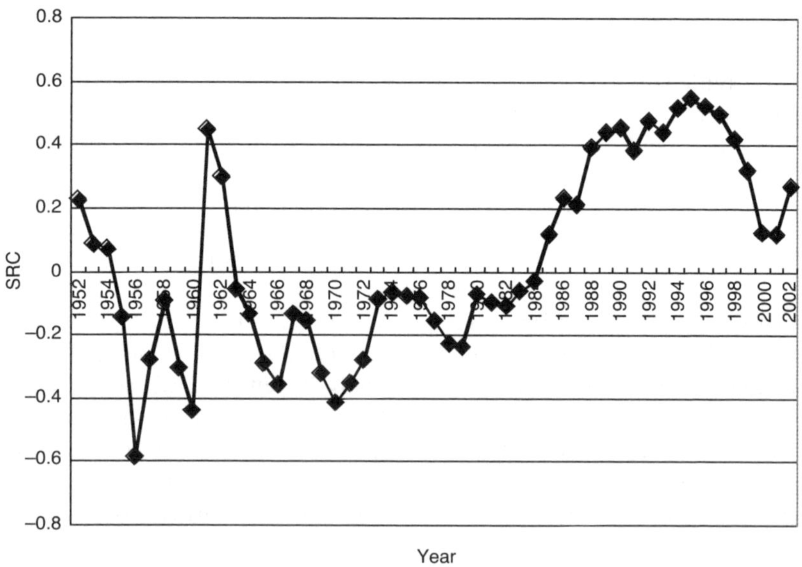

Source: Author.

increase indicates that the negative effects of fiscal reform on capital flows dominated the positive effect of the capital markets development in terms of financial integration. That is, the development of the capital markets was quite limited until around 1997.

Thirdly, the value of SRC declined rapidly – from 0.422 in 1998 to 0.121 in 2001. This indicates that the negative effect of the fiscal reforms was mostly complete and that the positive effect of developments in the capital market was becoming dominant by the end of the 1990s. But the fact that the value of the SRC then rose again to 0.270 in 2002 may show that this process is unstable.

Finally, the period from 1988 to 1998 was the only period in which the band of two standard deviations exceeded the value of zero for longer than two years. This is strong evidence that indicates the imperfection of capital markets in terms of the degree of their integration.[13]

4.3 Concluding remarks

During the period from 1952 to 1984, the state plan and its administrative mechanism served as a highly integrated financial center to coordinate savings and investment. However, the transition toward a market economy has revealed that the capital markets remained underdeveloped under the conditions of state planning. The evidence indicates that the negative effect of fiscal reforms on capital flows was almost complete by this time and that the capital markets had begun to support the capital flows across provinces by the end of the 1990s. But the level of inter-provincial capital flows is still short of the level to be observed in a developed market economy.

Because of the limitation of the available data, this chapter is unable to separate private investment from public investment and so it cannot estimate the net outcome of the negative effects of fiscal reforms and the positive effects of capital markets development. Given the importance of public investment and fiscal savings in China, the value of the SRC obtained in the previous section may underestimate the degree of fragmentation of its capital markets.[14]

Notes

1 The most convincing statement of the hypothesis is found in Ishikawa (1990).

2 Ishikawa (1990), pp. 167–8.

3 Feldstein and Horioka find

$$\text{Investment rate} = \underset{(0.018)}{0.035} + \underset{(0.074)}{0.887} \times \text{Savings rate}$$

(The numerical values in parentheses are standard errors and $R^2 = 0.91$.) They argue that the estimate of the coefficient of the savings rate, 0.887, is way too high to support the view that international capital markets are highly integrated across countries.

Feldstein and Bacchetta (1989) named the coefficient of the savings rate as the savings retention coefficient.

4 The provincial GDP statistics are known to be very inaccurate. For example, the sum of provincial GDP is much larger than the value of GDP for the nation as a whole. Mr Ichiro Otani, a former representative of the IMF in China, pointed out the importance of this fact.

5 Conceptually, a fundamental difference exists between the state that finances its activities by tax and the state that earns its income by using enterprises it owns.

6 Except for Xizang, Ningxia, and Chongqing. The data are available for the first two autonomous regions from 1992 to 2002. The data for Chongqing is available from 1996 when it was separated from Sichuan and became the fourth municipality under the central government.

7 This does not mean that the allocation of capital is efficient. It is well known that the capital allocation mechanism suffers badly from both adverse selection and moral hazard problems because of the soft budget constraints.

8 The first period (1952–54) is three years.

9 We can perform the F-test to judge which estimate is more reliable. The value of F statistic is 5.314 under the null hypothesis that the province specific constants are all zero. The F statistic is computed by $\{(0.071 - 0.504)/(28 - 1)\}/\{0.504/(28 \times 7 - (28 + 1))\} = 5.314$. The null hypothesis is rejected at the 1 per cent significance level.

10 Constant terms in Equation (4.2) reflect the national policies how to allocate the funds for investment. For example, the estimate of constant for Shanghai is –0.028, while its value for Gansu is 0.454.

11 The final period in our analysis (2000–2002) is only three years.

12 The value of the F statistic is $-2.661 = \{(0.102 - 0.772)/30\}/(0.772/(31 \times 4 - (31 + 1)))$. Again the null hypothesis is rejected at the 1 per cent significance level.

13 A similar observation is reported in Boyreau-Dbray and Wei (2004). Their work was brought to the attention of the author after the present chapter was written in Japanese in March 2004.

14 The value of the savings retention coefficient of Japan takes on statistically significant negative values because of the importance of public investment. See Dekle (1996) and Yamori (1995). This is not the case for Canada, the US and the UK.

References

Bayoumi, Tamin and Andrew Rose (1993) "Domestic Savings and Intra-national Capital Flows," *European Economic Review* 37, 1197–1202.

Boyreau-Debray, Genevieve and Shang-Jin Wei (2004) "Can China Grow Faster? A Diagnosis of the Fragmentation of its Domestic Capital Market," *IMF Working Paper*, WP/04/76.

Dekle, Robert (1996) "Saving–investment Associations and Capital Mobility: on the Evidence from Japanese Regional Data," *Journal of International Economics* 41, 53–72.

Feldstein, Martin and Phillips Bacchetta (1989) "National Saving and International Investment," *Working Paper 3164*, NBER.

Feldstein, Martin and Charles Horioka (1980) "Domestic Saving and International Capital Flows," *The Economic Journal* 90, 314–29.

Helliwell, John and Ross McKitrick (1998) "Comparing Capital Mobility across Provincial and National Borders," *Working Paper 6624*, NBER.

Ishikawa, Shigeru (1990) *Kaihatsu Keizaigaku no Kihon Mondai*. Tokyo: Iwanami Shoten (in Japanese).

Kojima, Reitsu (1997) *Gendai Chugoku no Keizai*. Tokyo: Iwanami Shoten (in Japanese).

Obstfeld, Maurice and Kenneth Rogoff (2000) "The Six Major Puzzles in International Macroeconomics: Is there a Common Cause?" *Working Paper 7777*, NBER.

Sinn, Stefan (1992) "Saving–investment Correlations and Capital Mobility: on the Evidence from Annual Data," *The Economic Journal* 102, 1162–1170.

Yamori, Nobuyoshi (1995) "The Relationship between Domestic Savings and Investment: the Feldstein–Horioka Test Using Japanese Regional Data," *Economic Letters* 48, 361–6.

Part II

Micro-Agents: Transformation of the Behavioral Principle

Trade Credit, Financing, and Enforcement Institutions

5

Trade Credit and Imperfect Enforcement

Noriyuki Yanagawa

5.1 Introduction

Trade credit is an important financial mechanism and has recently received a considerable degree of attention in the academic literature (see, for example, McMillan and Woodruff, 1999). It is difficult to supply trade credit, however, if payment cannot be enforced effectively. Thus, the importance of informal enforcement mechanisms or relational contracting has been stressed (McMillan and Woodruff, 1999). It is crucially important to determine whether or not informal enforcement mechanisms are working well in sustaining trade credit in each developing and transition economy.

Allen *et al.* (2003) have shown that in China, the informal sector is very active, and that this is a central reason for this country's rapid rate of economic growth. In China, the present-day legal enforcement mechanism is relatively weak. Instead, informal enforcement and corporate governance mechanisms play important roles in the Chinese economy. These authors, however, have not explained what kind of informal mechanisms actually work in China. This chapter introduces the hypothesis that state-owned firms or quasi-state-owned firms play important roles as trade credit mechanisms in the Chinese economy. State-owned firms have a "relationship" with the enforcement sector, and this "relationship" may help to enhance informal mechanisms for enforcement.

This chapter is structured as follows: In section 5.2 a simple model of trade credit is presented, and this is followed in section 5.3 by a more general model for endogenously determining trade volumes. Section 5.4 includes the analysis of a survey regarding the financing behaviors of firms in China. Conclusions are discussed in section 5.5.

5.2 A simple model of trade credit

For the purposes of explanation we consider the case where a buyer and seller trade just one unit of a given product. The value of the product for the buyer is V, and the cost of the product is C. By assuming $V > C$, this trade is considered to be efficient. Usually, the trading price P is determined to be between V and C in order to realize a trade transaction. Even if it is impossible for the buyer to pay the price immediately, the seller can provide trade credit, and an efficient transaction can be realized. It is assumed in this instance, however, that enforcement for the payment contract is imperfect. Even if buyers promise to pay the contracted price, they may not pay the total promised payment by the promised date. In such a situation, desirable trade may not be realized.

A simple Three Period Model is considered. At Period 1, the buyer and seller agree to trade a product; they make a contract specifying the payment schedule. In order to deliver the product at Period 1, the seller incurs the cost for production C and plans to receive payment sufficient for the cost. Conversely, the buyer receives the product at Period 1, but will get profit from the product, V, only at Period 2. The buyer may thus have to receive trade credit from the buyer. It is assumed here that the buyer has cash a at Period 1, and the buyer has to borrow $(P - a)$ from the seller. Also, for the sake of simplicity, no time discount is assumed between Period 1 and Period 2. As long as the buyer pays $(P - a)$ at Period 2 according to the contract, the seller can in the final analysis receive P.

If enforcement for the contract is imperfect, however, the situation above may change drastically. The seller has an incentive not to pay $(P - a)$ at Period 2. To formulate the default incentive for the buyer, the gross interest rate between Period 2 and Period 3 is assumed to be R. By delaying payment, the buyer receives $(R - 1)(P - a)$. Hence, the buyer has an incentive to postpone payment until Period 3.

The delay of payment mentioned above may have a negative impact on the profit of the seller because the payment comes so late. To highlight this point, it can be assumed that the seller discounts the gain at Period 3. In other words, the discounted present value of payment P at Period 3 is δP $(\delta < 1)$. For simplicity, it is also assumed that the buyer has to pay the contracted payment at Period 3. This assumption seems too simple, but general situations can be characterized by using this simple formulation. By assuming very low δ, for example, cases can be examined where the buyer does not pay the contracted payment for some considerable time. Thus, the assumption is not restricted to describing the situations under consideration.

5.2.1 The case of no enforcement

In the case of there being no enforcement mechanism at all, the seller cannot expect a return at Period 2. The expected gain of the seller is

$$R = a + \delta(P - a) \tag{5.1}$$

Even if the seller can set the price as high as possible, and $P = V$, R is

$$R^{MAX} = a + \delta(V - a). \tag{5.1'}$$

Hence, if δ is sufficiently low, the following condition is satisfied:

$$R^{MAX} = a + \delta(V - a) < C \tag{5.2}$$

That is,

$$\delta < (C - a)/(V - a). \tag{5.3}$$

No transaction is realized since the seller cannot expect a sufficient return.

5.2.2 The case of imperfect enforcement

In the case of imperfect enforcement, suppose that there is a probability s that contract enforcement works. This probability may depend upon the legal structure of the country and the character of the trade. The ownership structure of the buyer and seller may also affect the probability of enforcement, a point explained below. Here it can be assumed that contract enforcement works to enforce promised payment at Period 2. In other words, the enforcement mechanism cannot impose a penalty for default. In this situation, the expected gain of the seller may be expressed as follows:

$$R = a + s(P - a) + (1 - s)\ \delta(P - a) \tag{5.4}$$

By defining $m = s + (1 - s)\delta$, (5.4) can be written as

$$R = a + m(P - a). \tag{5.5}$$

Even if the seller can set $P = V$, the maximum profit of the seller is

$$R^* = a + m(V - a). \tag{5.6}$$

The following propositions may be derived from this profit function:

Proposition 1
The profit function of the seller is an increasing function of a, s, and δ.

This proposition means that the enforcement mechanism is important for the profit of the seller. If the enforcement technology is too low (that is, s is very low), the buyer will tend to postpone payment until Period 3. Even if s is low, however, when a is sufficiently high or δ is close to 1, the seller's profit can still be high.

If the above R^* is sufficiently low (and lower than C), this seller may abandon attempts to sell the product to this buyer, even though $V > C$. If the legal enforcement mechanism works well, and R^* is lower than C, then efficient transactions cannot be realized. Hence, more implicit enforcements such as relational contracting may become necessary to improve the enforcement mechanism s.

Before examining this implicit mechanism, a more general model may be considered. In this general model, the optimal level of trade volume in this imperfect enforcement situation can be derived.

5.3 General model

It is assumed in the general model that the value function of the buyer is vX, and the cost function of the seller is cX, where X is the trade volume that is endogenously determined in the negotiation process of the buyer and the seller. It can be assumed here that the value function of the buyer is a constant return to scale, and the first best trade volume is infinite as long as $v > c$. If there is an imperfect enforcement problem, however, it is not optimal for the seller to provide an infinite supply to the buyer.

Suppose the buyer is a monopoly buyer of the product, and that the bargaining power of the buyer is 100 per cent. The equilibrium price is set to maximize the profit of the buyer under constraints that will be explained below. This supposition can simplify the explanation. Qualitative results are not affected, though the bargaining power is less than 100 per cent. The total amount of cash that the buyer has is assumed to be A.

In order to reduce the profit loss coming from the imperfect enforcement problem, the seller may use a nonlinear pricing contract. That is, the payment contract from the buyer to seller takes the form $T + PX$, where T is the fixed payment paid at Period 1, and P is the unit price that will be paid at the Period 2. Since the buyer has to pay T before the trade or simultaneously with the trade, there is no enforcement problem regarding T. By using these types of contracts, the seller can reduce the uncertainty of gain at Period 2.

As explained in the previous section, it is assumed that at Period 2, the contracted payment PX is enforced to be paid only with probability s and with probability $1 - s$ that the buyer can postpone payment until Period 3. From this delay in payment, the buyer may achieve some gain in interest, for example rPX. This gain generates an incentive for the buyer to postpone payment. Here this gain in interest is not considered explicitly, but rather just to simplify the argument. This assumption can be justified as long as r is small. Even if the gain in interest is considered explicitly, no qualitative results are affected. For the seller, the payment PX at Period 3 produces only the discounted present value δPX, where $\delta < 1$. In other words, delays in payment cause heavy damage to the seller.

In this situation, the buyer maximizes the following net profit function:

$$\text{Max}_{P,X,T}\ (v - P)\,X - T$$

If enforcement of the contract is perfect, the optimal solution is $P = c$, $T = 0$, and X is infinite. If the enforcement is imperfect, however, the monopoly buyer must consider the following constraints:

$$\begin{aligned} &\text{Max}_{P,X,T} && vX - T - sPX - (1 - s)PX \\ &\text{s.t.} && 0 \le T + sPX + (1 - s)\delta PX - cX \\ & && T \le A \\ & && c \le P \le v. \end{aligned}$$

If the seller sells X at price P, the total sale is PX. By the sales contract, the buyer pays T at Period 1 and promises to pay PX at tPeriod 2. The actual payment at Period 2, however, occurs with probability s and at Period 3 with probability $(1 - s)$. Thus, the objective function for the buyer is

$$vX - T - sPX - (1 - s)PX.$$

The first constraint is the individual rationality condition for the seller. Since the payment PX at Period 3 gives only δPX to the seller, the profit function of the seller becomes $T + sPX + (1 - s)\delta PX - cX$, and it must be equal to or higher than zero (outside option). The second condition is the liquidity constraint. Since it is assumed here that the seller only has cash A, and vX will only be realized at Period 2, the feasible T is A at maximum. It is also natural to set the third constraint that the promised price P must be lower than v and higher than the unit cost c. This constraint comes from the possibility of an "outside opportunity" for the seller in which he or she has a chance to sell the product to a third party at the price of c.

By defining $m = s + (1 - s)\delta$, the function can be rewritten as

$$\begin{aligned} &\text{Max}_{P,X,T} && (v - P)X - T \\ &\text{s.t.} && 0 \leq T + (mP - c)X \\ & && T \leq A \\ & && c \leq P. \end{aligned}$$

From the first constraint, if $c \leq mv$, the optimal trade amount becomes infinite, and the first best allocation can be realized. By setting $T = 0$ and $P = c/m$, the seller can realize nonnegative profits, and the buyer can realize infinite profits. If $c > mv$, however, the effective sales margin for the seller $(mP - c)$ cannot be positive, even if the price is set as high as possible. In this situation, therefore, $mP - c < 0$ and $X = T/(c - mP)$ (from the first constraint).

Using this result, the objective function can be rewritten as

$$\text{Max } (v - P)T/(c - mP).$$

Since this is a decreasing function of P under the situation of $c > mv$, optimal prices become $P^* = c$ and $T^* = A$. This means $X^* = A/c(1 - m)$, and the total trade credit becomes $P^*X^* = A/(1 - m)$.

From the relation $m = s + (1 - s)\delta$, $c > mv \leftrightarrow s < \dfrac{(c/v) - \delta}{1 - \delta}$. This leads to the following proposition:

Proposition 2

(1) If $s \geq s^* = \dfrac{(c/v) - \delta}{1 - \delta}$, the first best trade transaction can be realized, and the borrowing amount is infinite.

(2) If $s \leq s^* = \frac{(c/v) - \delta}{1 - \delta}$, the buyer borrows $\frac{A}{(1-\delta)(1-s)}$, and the trade amount is $\frac{A}{(1-\delta)(1-s)c}$.

This proposition means that the enforcement technology is an important factor for the determination of the trade credit level. If s is lower than s^*, the trade credit level is an increasing function of enforcement technology. Further in this model, enforcement technology becomes sufficiently high, and trade credits can be infinite. The initial cash holding level A is also an important factor in determining the trade credit level. The total level of borrowing is an increasing function of A. If A becomes higher, then the level of trade credit rises.

From this analysis, it seems evident that increases in enforcement technology are important factors for extending trade volume and trade credits. Improving legal mechanisms or government regulations would be one natural way to increase enforcement technology s. If legal mechanisms do not work well, however, more implicit mechanisms become necessary. In some cases, the long-term relationship between buyer and seller would be important to realize high s.

5.4 Who is responsible for enforcement in China?

5.4.1 Descriptive data

Who exactly provides enforcement in China? Two small-sample surveys on the financing behavior of firms (including trade credit) were conducted in Yichang City, Hubei Province (2001 IDE-DRC survey) and in Yibin City, Sichuan Province (2003 IDE-DRC survey). The survey conducted in Yibin City, Sichuan was also used for the econometric analysis presented in Chapter 9.

The 2003 IDE-DRC survey included 113 effective respondents; the average employment, sales, and net profits were 290.8, 17.682 million RMB and 0.595 million RMB, respectively. The surveyed companies are classified into small and medium-sized enterprises, and enjoyed reasonable levels of profits. Here, several questions about the role of the government in "enforcement technology" were asked (see Tables 5.1 to 5.3).

Table 5.1 shows the probability that respondents failed to collect their sales payments. 70 per cent (33 + 47/113) of respondents failed to collect sales payment for three years between 1998 and 2001. Of these, 29 per cent (33/113) finally gave up collecting the payment, and

Table 5.1 Have you ever failed to collect sales payments?

	No	*Yes, but collected finally*	*Yes, and could not collect at all*	*Total*
	31	47	33	113
How did you cope with failure to collect?				
Change transacting condition	1	19	7	29
Stop transaction		22	15	39
Suit		22	19	43

Note: Multiple responses were given regarding questions about trouble (rows).
Source: Institute of Developing Economies, *Development Research Centre Survey*.

41.5 per cent did finally collect. It can be seen here that about 30 per cent of the total number of transactions encountered a failure, or enforcement probability. Once companies got into trouble because they were not being repaid, about half stopped their transactions (22 out of 47 for group who finally collected, and 15 out of 33 for the group that gave up collection efforts), and brought lawsuits against the non-payers (22 out of 47 and 15 out of 33 respectively).

Again, who is responsible for contract enforcement? Respondents were asked whether or not they agreed that the government (both local and national) would resolve inter-firm conflicts (Table 5.2). 45 per cent (50/110) of the total agreed. State-owned and collectively owned firms that basically have supervisory departments in the government responded with a higher than average percentage (60 and 100 per cent).

It is often suggested that enforcement by the government has a bias in that the government may be inclined to protect its own local companies. Table 5.3 shows responses regarding whether or not the local courts give preference to local companies with regard to "execution of judgment." When suits were brought forth in the unpaid customer's hometown, no accused customer executed judgment by themselves; the courts only execute around half of the cases (4 out of 9), and 5 out of 9 cases remained unexecuted. When suits were filed in the accuser's hometown, the accused voluntarily executed judgment in 6 cases, and the courts forced execution in 15 out of 22. Only one case remained unexecuted. There seems to be a clear bias in enforcement of contracts and execution relative to whether parties are inside or outside the local administrative border.

Table 5.2 Do you agree that government will resolve inter-firm conflicts?

		State owned	*Collectively owned*	*Privately owned*	*Limited owned*	*Corporate share*	*Others*	*Total*
With admin.	Agree	6	2	5	22	3		38
Supervisory	Total	10	2	11	49	6	1	79
Without admin.	Agree			4	6	2		12
Supervisory	Total		1	9	18	3		31
Total	Total who agrees	6	2	9	28	5		50
	Total respondents	10	3	20	67	9	1	110

Source: Institute of Developing Economies, *Development Research Centre Survey*.

Table 5.3 Local bias in execution of judgment

	Your own home town	*Unpaid customer's home town*	*You and the unpaid customer are located in the same town*	*Total*
	22	9	7	39
Who executed judgment?				
Unpaid customer voluntarily executed	6		2	9
Court forced to execute	15	4	4	23
Not yet executed	1	5	1	7

Source: Institute of Developing Economies, *Development Research Centre Survey*.

According to the descriptive data, "enforcement technology" in China seems to have the following characteristics: First, the enforcement probability of the payment contract is well below 100 per cent; enforcement here appears to be imperfect, as assumed in the model. Secondly, enforcement appears to be carried out by local governments. Thirdly, court enforcement is biased toward protecting local firms.

In this environment, the model explicated in the previous section would predict that the ratio of cash on delivery and prepayment required is as much as the liquidity of the buyer.

Table 5.4a Ratio of payment timings: 2003 – Yibin, Sichuan

	Average share to total sales	*S.e.*	*Min.*	*Max.*	*Frequency*
Sales					
Post payment	62.27	34.48	0	0	98
Cash on delivery	46.39	28.51	1	100	79
Pre payment	25.17	25.86	0	100	63
Procurement					
Post payment	60.52	34.25	10	100	83
Cash on delivery	63.91	33.07	2	100	85
Pre payment	15.63	13.47	0	65	40

Note: These data show the average share of payment timing in total transactions. This is different from that of Chapter 9 where shares with particular transaction partners are shown.

Source: Institute of Developing Economies, *Development Research Centre Survey*.

Table 5.4b Ratio of payment timings: 2001 – Yichang, Hubei

	Average share to total sales	*S.e.*	*Min.*	*Max.*	*Frequency*
Sales					
Post payment	48.59	33.10	0	100	132
Cash on delivery	52.76	29.77	0	100	125
Pre payment	18.43	21.49	0	100	79
Procurement					
Post payment	41.88	28.89	0	100	94
Cash on delivery	67.38	30.36	0	100	127
Pre payment	17.59	22.40	0	100	49

Source: Institute of Developing Economies, *Development Research Centre Survey*.

Tables 5.4(a)–(b) shed light on this ratio both 2001 and 2003 IDE-DRC surveys. A higher trade credit level may be observed in the Yibin survey in 2003 (62 per cent) than in the Yichang survey in 2001 (49 per cent).

To determine how this difference evolved, an econometric test should be implemented. However, based on the descriptive data, the following situation may be presumed: The IDE-DRC 2001 survey in Yichang was conducted with firms in poor economic condition. Average sales in 2001 were 17.444 million RMB, roughly the same as those of the sample in the 2003 Yibin city survey. However, average profits were –3.56 million RMB. At that time, non-performing loans outstanding for all banks in the city reached an average of about 70 per cent. There was an intense effort by the banking sector to dispose of NPLs. In this emergent environment, trade credit claims were less protected, and the "enforcement technology" can be presumed to have been lower than in Yibin (2003 IDE-DRC surveys) where the economic situation is comparatively normal and stable. Further precise econometric tests are needed to determine why these differences in trade credit levels exist.

5.4.2 The perception of policy makers in China

Policy makers in China have been giving some consideration to the role of government in conflict resolution and the imperfect enforcement of the law. Zhou (2004) points out that deficiencies in the legal system have led to instabilities in the financial system. This author refers to deficiencies in the "insolvency law" and accounting standards as well as bank loan fraud. In the current legal environment, a debtor can default on debts but can avoid "bankruptcy" by legally manipulating the level of assets. The creditor is, in reality, less well protected. Thus, the total recovery rate for non-performing loans across China from 1999 to 2004 is as low as 20 per cent. However, in cases where non-performing loans were sold to local governments and these local entities executed disposal by themselves, the recovery ratio reached above 30 per cent. This is far beyond the level expected (Zhou, 2004, 9).

5.5 Conclusion

The survey data discussed in this chapter support the idea that the role of local government is crucial in the provision of trade credit in China, although the mechanism is biased. Enforcement technology is an important factor in expanding trade volume and trade credit. When the enforcement mechanism does not work well, many sellers may be unprepared to trade. If state-owned firms have special relationships with the government that are related to enforcement, there is a possibility that state-owned sellers will have high *s* for any customers or state-owned buyers that can show high *s* for their trade. Therefore, state-owned firms or quasi-state-owned firms that have special relations with the local government might play an active role in relational contracting or trade credit in the Chinese economy.

As Allen *et al.* (2003) have pointed out, the informal sector of the Chinese economy has played an important role in promoting the high growth rates of the economy. However, their research has not explained that the mechanisms of the informal sector, or reasons why the informal sector is working well. The evidence presented in this chapter indicates that the local government–state-owned firms nexus may play a positive role in trade credit. Of course, this mechanism is probably not the best for improving the environment of trade credit since it is a "biased" mechanism. Private firms cannot access the special technology of enforcement, and the power of local governments may be effective only within local areas. In order to reduce the bias of the system, the Chinese government may have to devote efforts to establishing more formal enforcement mechanisms.

References

Allen, Franklin, Jun Quan, and Meijun Quan (2003) "Law, Finance, and Economic Growth in China," ILE, University of Pennsylvania Law School, Research Paper 3–21.

McMillan, John and Christopher Woodruff (1999) "Interfirm Relationships and Informal credit in Vietnam," *Quarterly Journal of Economics* 114(4), 1285–1320.

Roland, Gerald and Thierry Verdier (2003) "Law Enforcement and Transition," *European Economic Review* 47, 669–85.

Zhou, Xiaochuan (2004) "Improving Legal System and Financial Ecology," Speech at the "Forum of 50 Chinese Economists," December 2, Beijing, China.

6

Trade Credits and Chinese Law

Osamu Takamizawa

6.1 Background

6.1.1 How can we measure the "usefulness of law"?

It is often stated that although laws exist on paper in China, they do not work in practice. Generally speaking, legal studies do not make use of quantitative tools to measure the degree of "usefulness". When our project is complete, a hint may be given. Until then, we had better to keep in our mind that all arguments related this question are only qualitative studies – a patchwork of conclusions based on individual experiences.

6.1.2 When does the "usefulness of law" become important?

In what kind of circumstances do people become aware of the "usefulness of law"? When the economy is booming, or active fiscal expenditure is progressing, people do not recognize the effectiveness of law as a significant factor. On the other hand, when the economy is sluggish or in depression, or there is no room for further fiscal expenditure, law could do little to improve matters. However, when legal institution building is conditioned on international investment, finance and trade, or the legal justification of fiscal expenditure is questioned, the usefulness of having an established legal framework is clear. Generally in the intermediate situation, the importance of law is recognized in terms of the resolution and prevention of conflicts, especially in respect of trade credit.

6.1.3 What is the definition of a "firm" in relation to trade credit?

When we consider "trade credit," if bank and non-bank financial institutions are included, we must refer to financial laws and regulations.

When we consider those workers who have an independent second business besides their main employment, they are also entrepreneurs in this context. If we do not take these into account, we will refer to substantive law including security or insurance or procedural laws, including bankruptcy, regarding the problem of account receivables, leasing fee, or bills and notes, and the lending and borrowing of money through methods other than financial institutions.[1] "*Zhaizhuangu* (Debt equity swap)" should also be considered.

6.1.4 Critiques of the idea of "Chinese law as a mere model" and "civil cases were always dealt without the involvement of the government"

In traditional Chinese law, which was in place until modern westernized reforms started at the end of the Qing dynasty, it used to be a dominant and common perception both inside and outside China that "Chinese law" was only an idealized model which was not implemented in the real world. Furthermore, it was believed that civil disputes were usually resolved informally. A similar perception also existed with regard to the laws and regulations of the People's Republic of China. However, recent studies on China's legal history refute these theories.[2]

If we see the regulations under the basic code , "*lü*" ,we can say Chinese law was rigidly adhered to at least in criminal and administrative cases (the notions of "civil," "criminal," and "administrative" law are not traditional Chinese terms, but reflect the concepts from the modern point of view). Litigation documents dating from the Qing dynasty show that a huge number of civil disputes were resolved by judges or local magistrates. Here, it should be stressed that even civil disputes were resolved by formal courts. Judges acted in a paternalistic fashion and the incidents were settled after all the parties concerned submitted pledges to accept the judge's decision.[3] Therefore, it is more realistic to perceive historical China as a society where law is implemented and conflicts are resolved by formal judgments.

In the case of modern China, it is often questioned whether the law really functions as it is intended to do, answer might be given from the axes of time, geographical space and power space.

The *time* axis means policy implementation stages by the Chinese Communist Party: the first stage, reports of practices and experiences from various fields; the second stage, formulation of policy; the third stage, implementation of policy at the experimental sites; the fourth is legislation at the State Council as an administrative regulation; the fifth is the introduction of formal legislation at the National People's Congress as a law; the sixth is legislation of related regulations; the seventh is acceptance by the state organization and society. Depending upon the timing of the problem we face, the "usefulness of law" changes; the earlier stages we face, the worse law functions we feel. On the other hand, at more mature stages in the process, the smoother is the operation.

The *geographical space* axis implies levels of economic developments, or where the problem takes place; the budget of courts is affected by the local government. More prosperous governments can afford to hire excellent staff and facilities, which affects the quality of legal service available.

The *power space* axis indicates the levels of the legal system hierarchy: central governments = Supreme Court; province = higher court; region = middle court; county = county court; and finally, town and township village = local society. Higher levels of courts can provide a satisfactory level of legal service with excellent staffs. However, at the town or village level, law becomes only one method out of many to resolve disputes. The county level is intermediate.

Depending upon the position of these three axes, the image of Chinese law is different. Justice, or the nature of law, is "probabilistic," unlike the law that is taught in the classrooms of law faculties or law schools. The place where the probability of legal enforcement is high is a legal society. Otherwise the "trial and error" of the people themselves shapes the development of society.

6.2 Legal system

6.2.1 Procedural law

There is no legal system specially prepared for trade credit or other inter-firm relations, so in this section we survey the general legal system in China.

1. Discussions between *the parties concerned.*
Not only in China; this is a universal method to resolve disputes.

2. *People's Conciliation Committee*
This committee is often introduced as one of the representations of Chinese Law especially for dispute resolution. It is an autonomous system within local society or working units, but it does not resolve disputes amongst firms.

3. *Arbitration (based on Arbitration Law)*

Arbitration is the institution employed to resolve inter-firm disputes: *Minshisusonga* (Civil Procedure Law), Articles 257 to 261 provides related rules. When the contract has an arbitration clause or the parties sign a written agreement on arbitration after the dispute occurs, the court will not accept suit, and the arbitration will be implemented. Arbitration based on *Zhongcaifa* (Arbitration Law) (promulgated on 31 August 1994, enforced on 1 September 1995) is applied to disputes about contract or properties involving citizens, corporations and other forms of organization. It is not used in cases involving marriage, adoption, custody, maintenance, inheritance, administrative disputes, labor disputes, or contracts within agricultural or rural organization.

The arbitration committees are located at municipalities directly under the Central Government, the capital cities of provinces and autonomous regions, and other major cities. In cases where a party does not implement a decision of the arbitration committee, the aggrieved party can apply court to for execution.

When settlement comes out, adjudication documents based on the settlement will be formulated or a cancellation of the arbitration will be applied (Arbitration Law, articles 49 and 50). It is possible that the arbitrator may recommend conciliation (Arbitration Law, articles 51 and 52)

4. *Conciliation via law firm, notary public, legal service station*

Lawyers or notary public solicitors may help to achieve resolution by conciliation. In the rural areas, there are legal service stations, which are publicly established. These are staffed by public servants with legal knowledge, and they will provide a service at a fee.

5. *Conciliation by an administrative organization*

Administrative organizations service disputes resolution. In the planned economy period, this was the most widely accepted method.

6. *Resolution by court*

Courts will resolve disputes based on Civil Procedure Law (promulgated and enforced on April 9, 1991).

Courts in China consist of four levels: country-level courts, middle courts, higher courts and Supreme Court. The principle for judging cases is based on them being heard at two separate levels of court. Country courts may be the first instance, and the middle court the second; for more important cases, middle courts become the first instance, and higher courts the second. For the most important provincial cases, the higher court become the first instance and Supreme Court is the second. Only in the most important national cases will the Supreme Court become the only legal institution involved. In total, four levels and two instances is the system.

Termination of suits takes place in the following circumstances:

(a) Cancellation of suit; in a case settlement is formalized amongst the parties concerned, or the plaintiff abandons the suit. Even in this case, the permission of the court is necessary (Civil Procedure Law, article 131)

(b) Conciliation of the court (articles 9, 85 to 91); this is a conciliation by judges. Currently, the judge will ask whether the parties concerned wish to seek conciliation and if all the parties agree, conciliation will take place. In one party refuses conciliation, the judge will pass sentence. Formerly, conciliation was preferred. It is possible to introduce conciliation at any time between the beginning and the end of the suit; however, the agreement of all the parties concerned is necessary. This conciliation has an equivalent effect to adjudication.

(c) Adjudication by special procedure.

(c-1) Summary procedure (Civil Procedure Law, articles 142–6)

This procedure is used in a case where facts, right and duties are not contested. Small claims courts often use this procedure.

(c-2) *Mahnverfaren* (in German "summary procedure only for payment")(Civil Procedure Law, articles 189–92)

The creditor gets the title of an order for payment of certain amount of money or substitutes, or securities (*Zahlungsbefehl* in German) through the summary procedure.

(c-3) Publicizing the invalidation of endorsable bills, notes and cheques (Civil Procedure Law, articles 193–8)

This is the procedure to invalidate endorsable bills, notes and cheques when they were stolen, lost or perished.

(c-4) Bankruptcy procedure (Civil Procedure Law, articles 199–206)

This is the procedure required when a corporate body lacks the ability to make its repayment. The creditor requests bankruptcy and debt repayments through the court. Article 206 provides this procedure not applicable to non-corporate firm, individual firms, contracting firm in the rural, individual partnership.

(d) Ordinary procedure for sentence

If the case is not in those categorized above (c-1 to c-4), an ordinary adjudication will be undertaken.

(e) Execution

If, even after procedures of (b) to (d), the party concerned still does not implement the judgment, legal execution will be carried out. The procedure of property preservation will be undertaken (Articles 251–6).

6.2.2 Substantive law

In order to cope with default or limited capability of the party concerned, security or assignment of choice in action is institutionalized in basic laws. Basic law of security is *Minfatongze* (the General Principles of Civil Law) and *Danbaofa* (Guarantee Law). *Wuquanfa* (Property Law) and *Minfa* (Civil Code) are now being drafted. The registration of the main property of company (such as building or land-use right) is considered to be the necessary condition of validity of conveyance. This can be contrasted with the case of France and Japan, where registration is only the countering legitimacy against the third party. Whether this originated from the planned system or the German-type property action is a matter of some controversy. In our opinion, it is likely to be the legacy of the planned system, where the disposal of property required the permission of related departments of government. On the other hand, the safety of the transaction is also an important factor; in this context, if the permission of departments is the condition of validity, the party (e.g. the buyer) might feel somewhat more secure. On the other hand, this presents problems in terms of speed of conveyance process.

Assignment of choice in action is also a counteraction against default or limited capability.

6.3 Problems

6.3.1 Difficulties in execution

Even today, execution procedure does not progress smoothly. The main reason for this is limited legal capability – that is, the human or physical capability of legal institutions is limited, or the personnel or finance of a legal institution is not independent of local government or the Communist Party.

1 *Current situation and legislative development*

Against the difficulty of execution, legal organization has already taken some action. Here we will give some examples of institution building related to the implementation of debt disputes.[4]

(a) "Some problem related to real estate" (*People's Court Daily*, February 28, 2004, p. 3) Here the "Notice of Supreme Court, State Resource Department, Construction Department regarding problem of court execution" is introduced. This article attributed reason of issuance of this publicity to a lack of legal support and cooperation, and difficulty in resale due to the existence of immature markets.
(b) "Regulation by Supreme Court regarding real estate's evaluation, transaction (draft for inviting social comments)" proposed procedures on evaluation, auction, and fees on this service.
(c) "Supreme Court regulation regarding judges on credit dispute" (draft for inviting social comments: *People's Court Daily*, April 7, 2004, p. 2) proposed a guideline on the titled problem.
(d) "Supreme People's court regulation on some problems of seizing, distressing, freezing property" (draft for public opinion: *People's Court Daily*, May 27, 2004, p. 3).
(e) "Supreme People's Court's guideline regarding participation reallocation procedure of multi creditors" (draft for inviting public comments; *People's Court Daily*, July 15 , 2004, p. 3) proposed guideline of priority amongst creditors: the first priority is execution cost, the second is attachment cost, the third is secured creditor and the other creditors provided by law. The right of legal creditor whose claim is before due date are reserved. The fourth is any others.

2 *Trade associations, professional ethics, commercial morality, administrative permission, and administrative budget support*

Regarding payment, or credit, it is desirable that there exists a professional or commercial norm of morality for an individual region or industry. In order to facilitate this norm, establishing trade associations, which is independent from administrative organization, and can play an intermediate function between governments and business? However, these kind of associations are still under formation, and have not fully developed this role to date.

3 *Illegal debt collection with violence*

If none of the organizations of justice, administration nor trade associations are fully reliable, it is a universal phenomenon that people will attempt to collect debt illegally. China is no exception to this. Some examples are given below:
(a) Li Ruyin, Hou Qingxue, "You zhaiwu yinqide feifa jujinxingwei de rending" (Identifying illegal custody due to debt disputes) (*People's Courts Daily*, November 20, 2003, p. 3) argues that to restrain people

so as to force debt repayment can be applied by Article 238 of the Criminal Law. If the debt itself is suspected to be illegal, it can be attributable to kidnapping crime, or illegal custody crime. Some scholars argue that they are distinguished by the amount of debt.

(b) "Zhaiquanren feifataozhai buying yi qinfancaichanzui dingzui" (Illegal debt recollection should not be identified as a crime of violation of property right) (*People's Court Daily*, February 1, 2004, p. b4) argues that custody for forcing debt repayment is a crime that violates the personal liberty of the body. However, if it is simply offensive, and does not reach the degree of crime, it should be regarded as innocent. This argument comes from a theory that crime should be defined by its degree of harmfulness against society, which originated from Criminal Law theory of the former Soviet Union.

(c) "Ba maodunjiufen jiejue zai jiceng – laizi Guangzhoukaifaqu yufang yu chuzhi qunzhongxing tufashijian de baodao" (Disputes are resolved by the grass roots level – a report on prevention and resolution of mass violence at Guangzhou Industrial Districts (*Legal Daily*, May 8, 2004, p. 3) introduces disturbances which originated from wage arrears at Guangzhou. In order to resolve this, the local government provided a budget of 0.3 million RMB, then the courts pay the worker first on behalf of the firms , and then start legal resolution. In other words, if the local budget cannot afford to meet the potential costs, it is difficult even to start resolution.

6.4 Evaluation and interpretation of the current legal environment of trade credits

All these problems come, at least partly, from the fact that China is still in a process of transition from a planned economy to a market-based economy. The substantial implementation of the market mechanism started only 10 years ago. As we can see from the experiences of legal modernization and westernization of Japan, China, or Thailand in the nineteenth and twentieth centuries, it took 30 to 50 years for the development of a modern legal system.

Hypotheses to understand the current legal framework related to trade credit can be given as follows:

Hypothesis 1: Confusing payment is due to customs of the planned economy period, during which time the payment date was not controled rigorously, and this custom still affects the current situation. If management becomes rigorous, chaotic trade credit is perceived as a problem...

Hypothesis 2: Due to lax credit provision by banks, non-banks or government postponed the solution of problems. Once this credit provision is strictly managed, confused trade credit custom will also be perceived as a problem.

Hypothesis 3: The bankruptcy system has been so generous that it brought no actual pressure to bear on managers, employees, families or local society. Once the bankruptcy system began to reflect market principles, chaotic trade credit is also perceived as a problem.

Hypothesis 4: Taking the development and transition stages into consideration, legal implementation such as a civil suit for responsibility of debt repayment or bankruptcy should be carried out in a limited form. However, in the years to come, taking international pressures into consideration, strict implementation might be launched.

Hypothesis 5: The culture of bargaining and late repayments, such as parties wishing to renegotiate even after making the contract, might be a key feature of present-day Chinese society. This custom may not change until following deepened international interdependence, when inter-cultural friction might lower China's reputation.

Testing the hypotheses above, the most important issues concern bankruptcy, including the reconstruction of the corporate sector. The institution and implementation of a credit system might be transformed to address the defects of the bankruptcy system. More detailed examination of these hypotheses may be made in future work.[5]

Notes

1 Christian Wollschlaeger, "Historical Trends of Civil Litigation in Japan, Arizona, Sweden, and Germany: Japanese Legal Culture in the Light of Judicial Statistics," in Harald Baum (ed.), *Japan: Economic Success and Legal System* (Berlin: Walter de Gruyter, 1997), pp. 89–142, which analyzes resolution of civil disputes in modern Japan, is a good reference on this problem. The author defines that the basic nature of civil disputes is the debt problem, and implements analysis from two points of view: a summary of the instruments of collection of debt, and how the economic development affects this. The author also documents that any summary of instruments either in the formal or private situation, if available, is preferred to conventional suits, forms of this instruments are different from regions and period, this defines the characteristics of the dispute resolution procedure.

2 See Shigeo Nakamura (2004) "Was traditional Chinese Law a Mere Model?," *International Journal of Asian Studies* 1(1), 139–57; 1(2) 297–322. This is the translation of his 1979 work.

3 Regarding developments of theories, see Osamu Takamizawa (1990) "Kyuju nendai ni okeru Chugokuho image – Kamakura kaigi wo chushin ni,"

(Images of Chinese Law in the 1990's: Focusing of the Kamakura meeting), *Toyobunka* 84, 57–73. Also see the works of Shuzo Shiga's and Shigeo Nakamura's works that were referred to in the essay above.

Also see Osamu Takamizawa (1998) *Gendai Chugoku no Hunso to Ho, (Disputes and Law in Modern China)* Tokyo: The University of Tokyo Press,1998).

4 Except for (a) to (e), we also should consider the public system of supporting small firms activity and the honesty of corporations (including shareholders and management, it can be called corporate governance in broader meaning). Shen Kai (2004), "Zhongxiaoqiye xinyongdanbao jidai zhuanmen lifa" (Credit Guarantee System for Small and Medium Enterprise needs special legislation) (Fuyinbaokanziliao D413 Jingjifaxue/Laodongfaxue, vol. 1, 23) pointed out obstacles to small and medium-sized firm finance. The Small and Medium Sized Enterprises Promotion law promulgated in 2002 is too simple to promote financing to SMEs (small and medium-sized enterprises). Only policy guideline documents exist. Security system, particularly for SMEs, is hard to be established based on the market system, thus the public guarantee system is desirable. Currently, governments have established the credit guarantee organization. However, it is not efficient for them to bear 70 to 80 per cent of credit risk, and allows bank to take on more risks than they do at present. "Supreme People's Court regulation regarding trial on corporation disputes" (*People's Court Daily*,November 5 , 2004, p. 4). Article 49 of this regulation provides that the court will accept suit cases of controling shareholders' abuses of the rights of the corporation. Article 51 provides that the corporation and controling shareholder will bear joint liability in case these two parties cannot be clearly distinguished.

The sources of (a) to (d) in Chinese:

(a) "Sheji fangdichan zhixing de ruogan wenti," *People's Court Daily* February 28 2004, p. 3.

(b) "Zuigao renmin fayuan guanyu zhixingzhong pinggu, paimai, bianmai ruoganwentideguiding" *People's Court Daily*, January 15 2004, p. 3.

(c) "Zuigao renmin fayuan guanyu shenli xinyongzheng jiufen anjian ruogan wenti de guiding" *People's Court Daily*, April 7 2004, p. 2.

(d) "Zuigao renmin fayuan guanyu renminfayuan chafeng, kouya, dongjie caichan ruogan wenti de guiding (zhengqiuyijianbao)," *People's Court Daily*, May 27 2004, p. 3. Supreme People's Court Regulation on Seizing, Distressing, Freezing Property in Civil Execution of the People's Courts was promulgated on October 26 2004 and brought into force on the January 1 2005.

(e) "Zuigao renmin fayuan guanyu zhixingchengxuzhong duoge zhaiwuren canyufenpeiwentideruoganwenti (zhengqiuyijiangao)," *People's Court Daily*, July 16 2004, p. 3.

5 Here are some examples which should be considered:

(a) Wang Dongming, "Pochanshijian huhuan tongyi pochan lifa" (Practical world of bankruptcy calls for unified bankruptcy legislation) (*People's Courts Daily*, October 22 2003, p. 3) classifies development history of bankruptcy into three periods;

(i) Promulgation of bankruptcy law in 1986 to early 1990s: few cases were applied to bankruptcy law.

(ii) Middle of 1990s to early 2000s: policy-based selective implementation of bankruptcy law.

1994: Guowuyuan guanyu zai ruogan chengshi shixing guoyouqiye pochan youguan wenti de tongzhi (State Council's publicity regarding implementation of SOE (state-owned enterprise) bankruptcy at pilot site cities).

1996: Guojiajinjimaoyiweiyuanhui/Renminyinhang guanyu shixing guoyouqiye jianbingpochanzhong ruogan wenti de tongzhi (State Economic and Trade Committee and People's Bank of China's publicity regarding problems in implementing SOE merge and acquisition and bankruptcy. Guowuyuan guanyu ruoganchengshi shixing guoyouqiye jianbingpochan he zhigong zaijiuye youguan wenti de buchongtongzhi(State Council's publicity regarding on employment problem in implementing merge and acquisition and bankruptcy).

(iii) 2000s: market-based implementation; however, lack of unified rule. Policy-based implementation in (ii) is as follows; first, a working group on this issue is established at individual levels of government. Then, special rules regarding SOE bankruptcy, such as regarding land use right or security are provided. During this procedure of bankruptcy, the first priority was put on wage claim or re-employment arrangement. This procedure may neglect protection of non-labor-related claim. Or even if the dispute goes to suit, the judge would be more concerned by the laborer and re-employment problem. However, currently most of the SOEs have complete corporatization, the method above has already become out of date. Thus, the Supreme Court published a guideline on the acceptance of suit regarding bankruptcy. In June 2004, by the view of Liu Xiaomin, the first review of draft of the revised bankruptcy law could have been undertaken by the Executive Committee of the National People's Congress. Main points of the review were trustiness of the auditing report, the qualification of the auditor, the supervision of property of the bankrupt, agency who organizes bankruptcy procedure (mainly by court) (see Liu Xiaomin, "Wanshan pochanlifa rang pochanqiye nantao zhaiwu' (By completing bankruptcy legislation, stop false bankruptcy to pass through debt) (*Legal Daily*, May 13 2004, p. 12).

(b) Zhang Lu, "Yi guoyouhuobotudishiyongquan chuzi chengli gongsi, gongsi pochan shi gaitudishiyongquan kefou lieru pochan caichan" (Whether land use right offered by state for establishing the corporate can be counted as bankrupted asset?) By referring to "Zuigaorenminfayuan guanyu pochanqiye huobotudishiyongquan yingfou lieru pochancaichan deng wenti de pifu" (Approval in Reply of the Supreme People's Court on the issues of whether state offered land must be counted into property of bankrupt, April 16 2003), some argue that mortgaged land should be counted as the property of the bankrupt. Article 50 of Chengzhenfaongdichangunlifa (the Adminstrative Law of the People's Republic of China on concerning Urban Real Estate) and Article 56 of the Guarantee Law also support this positive opinion. Others argue, referring to Article 58 of Tudiguanlifa (Land Administration Law) and Article 47 of Chengzhen guoyoutudishiyongquan churang he zhuanran Zanxing Tiaoli (Tentative Regulations on conveyance of use right of urban land owned by state), value of land use right should be evaluated as the monetary base, and counted as claim to the investor of bankrupted firm.

(c) Regarding trade credit practice, Hiroyuki Takahashi introduced payment instruments taking the example of the Japanese beer brewers operating in China. There are several kinds of practices.

(i) prepayment by bank credit card – that is, the brewer will send products after confirming the account;

(ii) settlement at the end of the month and payment is made on the 10th of next month by cash;

(iii) cash transactions;

(iv) mixture of ii and iii.

"Nippon no beer maker no shinshutu to Chugoku niokeru ryutu system no henka" (Transition in the Chinese Distribution System: Focusing on Entry into the Market by Japanese Breweries, *Gendai Chugoku* (*Modern China*), 78 (2004), 99–106).

References

Kaneko Yuka (2004) *Asia kiki to kin'yu housei kaikaku-houseibishien no jissenteki houhouron wo sagutte* (*The Asian Crisis and Financial Law Reform: In Search of Practical Aid for Legal Institution Building*. Tokyo: Shinzan-sha.

Xie Sichuan *et al.* (2003) Zhuanxingqi Zhongguo caichan zhidu bianqian yanjiu (*Study on the Development of Property Institutions During the Transition Period in China*), Economic Science Publisher.

7

Determinants of Trade Credits in China: An Empirical Investigation

Seiro Ito

7.1 Introduction

In their daily operations firms frequently make use of trade credits. Through the use of trade credits, firms can respond to short-term transaction needs: for buyers (customers), short-term financing allows them to choose the optimal inputs for their production which can contribute to subsequent product sales, and for sellers (suppliers), allowing for late payments provides a way of selling products to temporarily cash-constrained buyers. Given the short-term nature of such credits and the existence of collateral in the form of stocked products, sellers frequently offer trade credits. These allow for a richer combination of trade patterns, thereby enhancing efficiency in trade. If such credits are in the form of sellers accepting IOUs (or bills) from buyers, then such bills are typically underwritten by banks who supply transaction services to firms with deposit accounts. Sellers do not have to assume default risks, and such a transfer of risk makes sound economic sense because banks have more information on buyers through the transaction records on their accounts. Banks also have the advantage that they can thereafter withhold the long-term financing needed for undertaking fixed investment if firms fail to repay their trade credits.

In a developed market economy, trade credits are almost always guaranteed to be repaid because failing to do so typically means that banks will step in as the bill collectors. However, in an economy with an insufficient repayment enforcement mechanism and an underdeveloped banking system, the firms by themselves have to evaluate their trade partners' liquidity positions, solvency, and their own ability to enforce repayment. This limits the combination of trade patterns that can be chosen. Thus, the lack of the rule of law and underdeveloped nature of the banking system, which some have argued is a primary feature of corporate China, may result in real efficiency losses.

It is also arguable, however, that if the banking system is underdeveloped and it is permitted to renege on trade credits, those firms with greater enforcement power and higher levels of liquidity can act as agents to banks in that they can extend more credits to cash-constrained firms, and if a debtor tries to default opportunistically, these agent-acting firms can invoke their powerful enforcement mechanism to secure repayment. If these firms act as the enforcers of contracts and pre-empt any opportunistic behavior on the part of debtor firms, this can partially offset inefficiencies caused by insufficient trade credits. However, if these powerful firms misdirect trade credits to less profitable transactions or become sloppy about invoking their enforcement mechanism, they may simply act like bad bankers and become liabilities on the economy.[1]

Within the Chinese context, it may be that the state-owned enterprises have become liability firms. They are anecdotally believed to be inefficient, mostly because of their close ties to national and local authorities. However, one could argue that such ties endow them with more leverage in enforcing contracts. Such ties also allow them easier access to cash in the form of subsidies. During the transition period, when a well-developed banking system may take many years to emerge, conscientious state-owned firms have the potential to substitute, at least in part, for banks in providing short-term credits. This potential has never been explored, and the purpose of the present study is to undertake a preliminary investigation using data collected from firm transactions.

In an economy lacking an effective repayment enforcement mechanism, firms will try to borrow as much as possible while delaying repayments for as long as possible. When selling their own products, firms will try to reduce the use of postponed payments (their own credit), but when purchasing goods they will try to increase the use of postponed payments (trading partner's credit). If the use of trade credits is frequent and the amounts are large relative to total assets, they constitute an important source of financing for the firm.

This chapter will summarize the characteristics of "lending" and "borrowing" through trade credits. The focus will be on describing the nature of corporate finance during the transition from state planning to market-oriented resource allocation. With its immature private banking system, partially privatized firm ownership, and growing competition in output markets, it is of considerable interest to know if the sequence of steps toward privatization that China has chosen is consistent with a smooth transition. This naturally leads us to focus on the types of ownership, the presence of administrative boundaries and proximity to government in the determination of trade credits.

As Macmillan and Woodruff (1999) have illustrated, conventional theories of trade credit determination offer some predictions. The greater the relative bargaining power, *ceteris paribus*, the greater the level of trade credits obtained. The source of such bargaining power stems from market power, such as the presence of competitors or the presence of an industry group whose member firms as a whole jointly deter opportunistic actions by blacklisting. Another determinant is a firm's relative liquidity position. If a firm has better access to credits than its partner, and the firm has a comparative cost advantage in securing repayments than other credit suppliers, then the firm may be able to earn profits through financing its trading partner's repayment by using its own funds. Industry characteristics can also have an impact on a firm's relative liquidity position. For instance, the retail industry has a constant flow of cash income, and is in a better position to finance a partner's liquidity needs. Since our primary focus is on the financial transition from state planning to market forces, we will use these determinants as controls. The other variables we will consider are types of firm ownership, the presence of administrative boundaries, and the proximity to local authority.

7.2 Data

In January 2003 data were collected from firms in Yibin City, Szechuwan Province. The sample size was 120, with 112 effective responses, collected through interviews. Eighty five small and 18 medium-sized firms from all industries were sampled without a randomization (Table 7.1). These were the most geographically approachable firms, thus there may be a bias because the most marginally located firms are not included. However, at the time of sampling, there were 176 small and 25 medium-sized firms in the area (*National Industrial Statistics*, 2002), so the sample covered a considerable number of the firms located in and around the city center. There was an oversampling of medium-sized firms to ensure sufficient coverage of the larger state-owned firms. Although the selection bias cannot be considered to be serious, it may be that the sample overestimated the use of trade credits because

Table 7.1 Distribution of total assets, 2001

Size range	*Mean*	*Std*	*Obs.*
16–500	250.42	146.10	22
500–2,000	1,232.89	430.91	45
2,000–4,000	2,867.85	639.82	18
4,000+	8,939.63	7,610.78	18

Note: 103 firms gave total asset information. According to asset size, *Industrial Statistic* classifies small firms as below 4,000 yuan, medium-sized firms as between 4,000 and 40,000 yuan, and large firms as above 40,000 yuan.

geographically clustered firms may find it easier to extend and receive credits with nearby clusters than with remote firms.

Classified by ownership type, the sample contains 10 state-owned firms, 9 quasi-state-owned firms, 61 state-supervised firms, 29 independent, privately-owned firms, and 3 NAs. State-owned firms are firms classified according to the *State Owned Enterprises Law*. Quasi-state-owned firms include collective firms and limited or incorporated companies whose majority shareholders are government-owned holding companies. State-supervised firms consist of privately-owned firms which have supervisory authority in local government. This supervisory authority consists of an office that oversees firms and provides various kinds of assistances when needed. All other firms are classified as privately-owned. Allen *et al.* (2004) classified state-owned firms as the "formal" sector, and all other types as the "informal" sector. In this

Table 7.2 Definition of ownership types of sampled firms

State-owned	Firms classified as state-owned according to the *State-Owned Enterprises Law*.
Quasi-state-owned	Collective firms as classified by *Town and Village Enterprise Law*, and limited or incorporated companies whose majority shareholders are government-owned holding companies.
State-supervised	Privately-owned firms which have supervisory authority in local government.
Privately-owned	All other firms.

study the state-owned and quasi-state-owned firms are classified jointly as *government-owned*, while the latter two categories are regarded jointly as *nongovernment-owned* (Table 7.2).

When a firm sells a product with payment postponed (postpayment), the firms is offering trade credit. Conversely, when a firm buys a product postpayment, it is receiving credit. The two indices of trade credit used in this study are: (i) the amount of late payments in procurement (borrowing); and (ii) late payments in sales transactions (lending). Firms are asked to provide information on their largest trading partners in sales and procurements inside and outside the city boundaries. The city boundary distinction is used to see if administrative boundaries are significant in the provision of trade credits. We thus have four observations for the largest trading partners of each firms. Firms are also asked about the type of ownership of their trading partners. (Another measure of trade credits is days after delivery required to settle accounts, but this measure turned out not to produce uniform results across ownership types in our estimation.)

It is not always true that a trading partner with a large share in a firm's transactions exerts greater bargaining power, since it is the relative market power between the firm and its partner that determines the distribution of bargaining power.[2] Although sampling only the largest trading partners does not necessarily bias the estimates, there is a concern that the bargaining power of trading partners may be overestimated because of the collection of information on the largest trading partners in each category. Ideally, trading partners should be sampled from a pool of potential partners by noting that actual trading partners have been chosen from this pool. However, there exists no official list of firms for each product, nor is it possible to list all the firms able to supply products of characteristics demanded by buyers. Relying on the method of randomly selecting trading partners from actual trading partners would have led to a measurement error problem because firms may not record all transactions made in small amounts. Not only survey nonresponses reduce number of observations; nonrandomly placed nonresponses and measurement errors would also have cancelled out a significant portion of the benefits from randomization. These considerations led to the selection of the largest trading partners, but with some cautionary measures. Firms are asked about their market power in trading with partners, about the length of trading, and the uniqueness of their products, which are thought to affect distribution of bargaining powers. All of these factors are included in the estimations.

Table 7.3 Definition of variables used in regression

sales	sales in 100 yuan to main customer
manufact	a dummy variable for a partner firm in the manufacturing industry
distretail	a dummy variable for a partner firm in the distribution or retail industries
national	a dummy variable for a partner firm being government-owned
unq	a dummy variable for a good being designed specifically for sampled firm
rival	presence of competitors in sales, and presence of alternative suppliers in procurements
length	years of transaction with a partner firm
state	a dummy variable for a sampled firm being state-owned
qstate	a dummy variable for a sampled firm being either a collective firm or a firm whose majority shareholder is a public holding company
spoffice	a dummy variable for sampled firm having supervisory authority in local government
pvt	a dummy variable for sampled firm being privately-owned
tsales	total sales in 10,000 yuan of sampled firm in 2000
manufact	a dummy variable for the presence of a rival to the sampled firms
out	a dummy variable for a partner firm located outside the city boundary
proc	procurement in 100 yuan from a partner firm
tprofitA	ratio of total profits to total assets
cashA	ratio of cash holdings to total assets
liqLA	ratio of liquid liabilities to total assets
totA	total assets in 10,000 yuan
amount	amount borrowed from banks in 10,000 yuan
maturity	maturity of bank loans in days
irate	interest charged by banks
*lgv**	a set of dummy variables for what the firm expects from local government when in trouble. *lgvbk* indicates exerting an influence on banks' loan decisions, *lgvdspt* indicates intervening in disputes, *lgvsbsdy* indicates providing subsidies, *lgvprsnel* indicates sending personnel to firms, *lgvinfo* indicates sharing information.
$after_{s,c}$	the overall percentage that a sampled firm uses late payments
$bkchk_{s,c}$	the overall percentage that a sampled firm uses bank checks for payments
$bkplastic_{s,c}$	the overall percentage that a sampled firm uses credit cards for payments

7.3 Descriptive statistics

Tables 7.4 and 7.5 show descriptive statistics for trade credits in sales and procurement transactions, respectively. Table 7.3 gives description of each variable. Tables 7.6 and 7.7 consider lending and borrowing among various ownership types. Trading partners are classified into government-owned and non-government-owned firms. The classification is less fine than with the sampled firms because it is difficult to get detailed information on the exact type of ownership for trading partners, especially for those located outside the city.

In the sales transactions of Table 7.6 we see that lending is predominant in all types of ownership. This is especially the case for state-owned firms and quasi-state-owned firms. These firms provide more net trade credits than other ownership types, mostly through postpayments to trading partners. While state-owned firms offer more credits to buyers, they also receive more credits from sellers. This can be seen by comparing whether or not the trading partner is a government-owned firm. Both Table 7.6 and Table 7.7 suggest that sampled firms tend to offer more net trade credits to government-owned firms.

In procurements of Table 7.7, borrowing is predominant. State-owned firms in particular make no use of prepayments. At the same time they receive more net trade credits than any other ownership type. The peculiarity of government-owned firms is also confirmed in procurement transactions in that other ownership types provide more gross trade credits through prepayments to government-owned firms than to privately-owned firms, while using more or less the same proportions of postpayments as government- and non-government-owned firms.

These suggest that among the sampled firms state-owned firms make more use of trade credits than other ownership types, both in sales and in procurements. Since sales involve positive net lending and procurement positive net borrowing, state-owned firms offer more credits when selling while receiving more credits when procuring. There is a higher flow of trade credits through state-owned firms than through other ownership types.

We can statistically test the preceding analysis based on descriptive statistics by examining whether two different ownership types have equal means in lending and borrowing. To do this we will use Welch's *t* tests of unequal variances. The null is both have equal means, given unequal variances. The results are shown in Table 7.8 separately for lending (in sales) and borrowing (in procurements). In the left table,

Table 7.4 Descriptive statistics of sales transactions

	Min.	*10%*	*25%*	*Median*	*75%*	*90%*	*Max.*	*Mean*	*Std*	*0s*	*NAs*	*n*
days	0.00	3.00	10.00	30.00	35.00	66.00	180.00	32.23	34.46	1	0	81
cod	0.00	0.00	0.00	20.00	60.00	90.00	100.00	32.57	36.69	33	0	81
bef	0.00	0.00	0.00	0.00	10.00	20.00	100.00	6.79	15.09	57	0	81
after	0.00	0.00	20.00	70.00	100.00	100.00	180.00	61.63	42.23	13	0	81
manufact	0.00	0.00	0.00	0.00	1.00	1.00	1.00	0.47	0.50	43	0	81
distretail	0.00	0.00	0.00	0.00	1.00	1.00	1.00	0.30	0.46	57	0	81
national	0.00	0.00	0.00	0.00	1.00	1.00	1.00	0.38	0.49	50	0	81
sales	1.61	3.47	4.25	5.52	6.26	7.38	9.11	5.33	1.60	0	0	81
unq	0.00	0.00	0.00	0.00	1.00	1.00	1.00	0.33	0.47	54	0	81
rival	0.00	0.00	1.00	1.00	1.00	1.00	1.00	0.85	0.36	12	0	81
length	1.00	3.00	4.00	7.00	12.00	17.00	37.00	8.61	6.81	0	0	81
state	0.00	0.00	0.00	0.00	0.00	0.00	1.00	0.10	0.30	73	0	81
qstate	0.00	0.00	0.00	0.00	0.00	0.00	1.00	0.09	0.28	74	0	81
spoffice	0.00	0.00	0.00	1.00	1.00	1.00	1.00	0.59	0.49	33	0	81
pvt	0.00	0.00	0.00	0.00	0.00	1.00	1.00	0.22	0.42	63	0	81
tsales	0.00	0.02	0.05	0.09	0.17	0.31	0.95	0.15	0.17	0	0	81
manuf	0.00	0.00	0.00	1.00	1.00	1.00	1.00	0.74	0.44	21	0	81
tprofitA	–1.24	–0.02	0.00	0.01	0.03	0.07	0.27	0.01	0.15	0	0	81
cashA	0.00	0.01	0.02	0.04	0.07	0.14	0.54	0.06	0.08	0	0	81
liqLA	0.01	0.22	0.39	0.51	0.69	0.88	4.86	0.60	0.58	0	0	81
totA	0.00	0.02	0.08	0.16	0.30	0.64	3.64	0.29	0.48	0	0	81
lgvbk	0.00	0.00	0.00	0.00	1.00	1.00	1.00	0.43	0.50	46	0	81
lgvdspt	0.00	0.00	0.00	0.00	1.00	1.00	1.00	0.46	0.50	44	0	81
lgvsbsdy	0.00	0.00	0.00	0.00	0.00	0.00	1.00	0.05	0.22	77	0	81
lgvprsnel	0.00	0.00	0.00	0.00	0.00	1.00	1.00	0.12	0.33	71	0	81
lgvinfo	0.00	0.00	0.00	0.00	1.00	1.00	1.00	0.43	0.50	46	0	81
amount	0.00	0.01	0.01	0.03	0.06	0.13	1.00	0.07	0.14	0	19	81
irate	2.00	5.21	5.75	6.35	7.02	7.60	9.20	6.32	1.25	0	20	81
maturity	6.00	7.20	12.00	12.00	21.00	36.00	96.00	18.05	14.97	0	19	81

Note: Multiple answers are allowed for *lgvbk, lgvdspt, lgvsbsdy, lgvprsnel, lgvinfo*. See footnotes of Table A7.2 for a description of other variables.

Table 7.3 Descriptive statistics of procurement transactions

	Min.	*10%*	*25%*	*Median*	*75%*	*90%*	*Max.*	*Mean*	*Std*	*0s*	*NAs*	*n*
days	0.00	1.00	7.00	20.00	30.00	31.00	90.00	21.20	17.85	1	0	70
cod	0.00	0.00	0.00	20.00	90.00	100.00	100.00	38.29	42.49	30	0	70
bef	0.00	0.00	0.00	0.00	0.75	20.00	100.00	9.44	24.36	52	0	70
after	0.00	0.00	0.00	60.00	100.00	100.00	100.00	52.14	43.57	22	0	70
manufact	0.00	0.00	0.00	0.00	1.00	1.00	1.00	0.36	0.48	45	0	70
distretail	0.00	0.00	0.00	0.00	1.00	1.00	1.00	0.30	0.46	49	0	70
national	0.00	0.00	0.00	0.00	1.00	1.00	1.00	0.31	0.47	48	0	70
proc	0.59	2.97	3.81	4.94	5.79	6.69	8.75	4.78	1.59	0	0	70
rival	0.00	0.00	1.00	1.00	1.00	1.00	1.00	0.76	0.43	17	0	70
length	0.00	3.00	5.00	7.00	11.00	16.10	53.00	9.07	8.60	1	0	70
state	0.00	0.00	0.00	0.00	0.00	0.10	1.00	0.10	0.30	63	0	70
qstate	0.00	0.00	0.00	0.00	0.00	0.00	1.00	0.07	0.26	65	0	70
spoffice	0.00	0.00	0.00	1.00	1.00	1.00	1.00	0.59	0.50	29	0	70
pvt	0.00	0.00	0.00	0.00	0.00	1.00	1.00	0.24	0.43	53	0	70
tsales	0.00	0.02	0.05	0.09	0.16	0.30	0.95	0.15	0.18	0	0	70
manuf	0.00	0.00	0.00	1.00	1.00	1.00	1.00	0.69	0.47	22	0	70
tprofitA	–1.24	–0.01	0.00	0.01	0.04	0.08	0.27	0.01	0.16	0	0	70
cashA	0.00	0.01	0.02	0.04	0.07	0.15	0.30	0.06	0.06	0	0	70
liqLA	0.01	0.19	0.33	0.47	0.69	0.84	2.35	0.53	0.36	0	0	70
totA	0.00	0.03	0.08	0.15	0.29	0.64	3.64	0.29	0.51	0	0	70
lgvbk	0.00	0.00	0.00	0.00	1.00	1.00	1.00	0.44	0.50	39	0	70
lgvdspt	0.00	0.00	0.00	0.00	1.00	1.00	1.00	0.44	0.50	39	0	70
lgvsbsdy	0.00	0.00	0.00	0.00	0.00	0.00	1.00	0.03	0.17	68	0	70
lgvprsnel	0.00	0.00	0.00	0.00	0.00	0.10	1.00	0.10	0.30	63	0	70
lgvinfo	0.00	0.00	0.00	0.00	1.00	1.00	1.00	0.41	0.50	41	0	70
amount	0.00	0.01	0.01	0.02	0.05	0.13	1.00	0.07	0.15	0	17	70
irate	2.40	5.30	5.79	6.54	7.20	7.78	15.00	6.60	1.67	0	18	70
maturity	6.00	6.20	12.00	12.00	24.00	36.00	96.00	18.23	15.65	0	17	70

Note: See footnotes of Table A7.2 for a description of other variables.

Table 7.6 Prepayments/sales, postpayments/sales, and net borrowing between various ownership types

	Min.	*10%*	*25%*	*Median*	*75%*	*90%*	*Max.*	*Mean*	*Std*	*0s*	*NAs*	*n*
preSG.in	0.00	0.00	0.00	0.00	0.00	0.00	0.00	0.00	0.00	3	0	3
preSG.out	0.00	0.00	0.00	0.00	0.00	0.00	0.00	0.00	0.00	2	2	4
preSP.in	0.00	0.00	0.00	0.00	0.00	24.00	60.00	8.57	22.68	6	0	7
preSP.out	0.00	0.00	0.00	0.00	0.00	30.00	60.00	10.00	24.50	5	2	8
preQG.in	0.00	0.00	0.00	0.00	0.00	0.00	0.00	0.00	0.00	3	0	3
preQG.out	0.00	0.00	0.00	0.00	0.00	0.00	0.00	0.00	0.00	2	0	2
preQP.in	0.00	0.00	0.00	0.00	1.50	26.00	50.00	8.67	20.27	4	0	6
preQP.out	0.00	0.00	0.00	0.00	10.00	29.00	50.00	10.00	18.48	4	0	7
preVG.in	0.00	0.00	0.00	0.00	10.00	28.00	100.00	9.78	21.98	15	1	24
preVG.out	0.00	0.00	0.00	0.00	10.00	20.00	100.00	9.00	22.69	14	4	24
preVP.in	0.00	0.00	0.00	0.00	10.00	24.00	30.00	7.28	10.65	22	1	38
preVP.out	0.00	0.00	0.00	0.00	20.00	30.00	50.00	11.22	15.07	21	2	39
prePG.in	0.00	0.00	0.00	0.00	0.00	36.00	100.00	13.33	33.17	7	2	11
prePG.out	0.00	0.00	0.00	0.00	0.00	34.40	92.00	12.44	30.56	7	0	9
prePP.in	0.00	0.00	0.00	0.00	10.00	17.00	20.00	5.59	7.47	10	3	20
prePP.out	0.00	0.00	0.00	10.00	16.50	56.00	100.00	17.79	28.66	8	1	20
postSG.in	0.00	20.00	50.00	100.00	100.00	100.00	100.00	66.67	57.73	1	0	3
postSG.out	60.00	63.00	67.50	75.00	82.50	87.00	90.00	75.00	21.21	0	2	4
postSP.in	30.00	36.00	50.00	100.00	100.00	100.00	100.00	75.71	31.55	0	0	7
postSP.out	30.00	65.00	100.00	100.00	100.00	100.00	100.00	88.33	28.58	0	2	8
postQG.in	0.00	20.00	50.00	100.00	100.00	100.00	100.00	66.67	57.73	1	0	3
postQG.out	70.00	73.00	77.50	85.00	92.50	97.00	100.00	85.00	21.21	0	0	2
postQP.in	0.00	15.00	30.00	45.00	90.00	100.00	100.00	53.33	40.83	1	0	6
postQP.out	0.00	18.00	32.50	60.00	100.00	100.00	100.00	60.71	40.66	1	0	7
postVG.in	0.00	0.00	20.00	80.00	100.00	100.00	100.00	65.22	41.87	5	1	24
postVG.out	0.00	0.00	0.00	85.00	100.00	100.00	100.00	60.50	45.59	6	4	24
postVP.in	0.00	0.00	10.00	30.00	80.00	100.00	100.00	44.68	39.69	8	1	38
postVP.out	0.00	0.00	0.00	20.00	80.00	100.00	100.00	38.11	40.90	12	2	39

Table 7.6 Prepayments/sales, postpayments/sales, and net borrowing between various ownership types – *continued*

	Min.	*10%*	*25%*	*Median*	*75%*	*90%*	*Max.*	*Mean*	*Std*	*0s*	*NAs*	*n*
postPG.in	0.00	0.00	80.00	100.00	100.00	100.00	100.00	75.56	43.33	2	2	11
postPG.out	0.00	6.40	30.00	80.00	100.00	100.00	100.00	59.78	42.14	1	0	9
postPP.in	0.00	0.00	2.00	50.00	80.00	94.00	100.00	47.47	38.34	4	3	20
postPP.out	0.00	0.00	3.50	60.00	95.00	100.00	100.00	53.53	41.54	5	1	20
netSG.in	−100.00	−100.00	−100.00	−100.00	−50.00	−20.00	0.00	−66.67	57.73	1	0	3
netSG.out	−90.00	−87.00	−82.50	−75.00	−67.50	−63.00	−60.00	−75.00	21.21	0	2	4
netSP.in	−100.00	−100.00	−100.00	−100.00	−50.00	−12.00	30.00	−67.14	49.23	0	0	7
netSP.out	−100.00	−100.00	−100.00	−100.00	−100.00	−35.00	30.00	−78.33	53.07	0	2	8
netQG.in	−100.00	−100.00	−100.00	−100.00	−50.00	−20.00	0.00	−66.67	57.73	1	0	3
netQG.out	−100.00	−97.00	−92.50	−85.00	−77.50	−73.00	−70.00	−85.00	21.21	0	0	2
netQP.in	−100.00	−100.00	−90.00	−45.00	−6.00	11.00	20.00	−44.67	50.86	0	0	6
netQP.out	−100.00	−100.00	−100.00	−60.00	−7.50	11.00	20.00	−50.71	52.31	0	0	7
netVG.in	−100.00	−100.00	−100.00	−75.00	0.00	10.00	100.00	−55.44	55.66	3	1	24
netVG.out	−100.00	−100.00	−100.00	−80.00	0.00	10.00	100.00	−51.50	57.70	4	4	24
netVP.in	−100.00	−100.00	−80.00	−30.00	0.00	14.00	30.00	−37.39	44.46	5	1	38
netVP.out	−100.00	−100.00	−70.00	0.00	0.00	30.00	50.00	−26.89	49.16	8	2	39
netPG.in	−100.00	−100.00	−100.00	−100.00	−80.00	36.00	100.00	−62.22	72.42	0	2	11
netPG.out	−100.00	−100.00	−100.00	−80.00	−10.00	16.80	84.00	−47.33	63.63	1	0	9
netPP.in	−100.00	−94.00	−70.00	−45.00	−2.00	0.00	10.00	−41.88	37.69	3	3	20
netPP.out	−100.00	−100.00	−90.00	−50.00	3.00	56.00	100.00	−35.74	62.76	1	1	20

Note: SG is state–government transactions, SP is state–private transactions, QG is quasi-state–government transactions, QP is quas-state–private transactions, VG is state-supervised–government transactions, VP is state-supervised–private transactions, PG is private–government transactions, PP is private–private transactions. Quasi-state-owned firms are collective firms and firms whose majority shareholder is a public holding company. State-supervised firms are under the supervision of a local government. Private firms are all other firms. Government firms are state-owned and quast-state-owned firms. Net borrowing in sales transactions is prepayments – postpayments.

Table 7.7 Prepayments/procurement, postpayments/procurement and net borrowing between various ownership types

	Min.	*10%*	*25%*	*Median*	*75%*	*90%*	*Max.*	*Mean*	*Std*	*0s*	*NAs*	*n*
preSG.in	0.00	0.00	0.00	0.00	0.00	0.00	0.00	0.00	0.00	3	1	4
preSG.out	0.00	0.00	0.00	0.00	0.00	0.00	0.00	0.00	0.00	4	2	6
preSP.in	0.00	0.00	0.00	0.00	0.00	0.00	0.00	0.00	0.00	6	1	7
preSP.out	0.00	0.00	0.00	0.00	0.00	0.00	0.00	0.00	0.00	4	2	6
preQG.in	0.00	0.00	0.00	0.00	25.00	70.00	100.00	25.00	50.00	3	2	6
preQG.out	0.00	10.00	25.00	50.00	75.00	90.00	100.00	50.00	70.71	1	0	2
preQP.in	0.00	0.00	0.00	0.00	5.00	8.00	10.00	3.33	5.77	2	2	5
preQP.out	0.00	0.00	0.00	5.00	10.00	20.00	30.00	8.33	11.69	3	1	7
preVG.in	0.00	0.00	0.00	0.00	0.00	13.00	100.00	7.22	23.72	15	2	20
preVG.out	0.00	0.00	0.00	0.00	15.00	26.00	100.00	12.47	26.07	9	7	22
preVP.in	0.00	0.00	0.00	0.00	0.00	20.00	90.00	5.70	16.58	29	6	43
preVP.out	0.00	0.00	0.00	0.00	0.00	15.00	100.00	8.89	24.82	28	10	46
prePG.in	0.00	0.00	0.00	0.00	100.00	100.00	100.00	40.00	54.77	3	3	8
prePG.out	0.00	0.00	0.00	0.00	5.00	46.00	100.00	15.71	37.35	5	1	8
prePP.in	0.00	0.00	0.00	0.00	10.00	20.00	70.00	7.14	15.86	14	3	24
prePP.out	0.00	0.00	0.00	0.00	10.00	20.00	50.00	8.33	14.26	13	1	22
postSG.in	100.00	100.00	100.00	100.00	100.00	100.00	100.00	100.00	0.00	0	1	4
postSG.out	20.00	44.00	80.00	100.00	100.00	100.00	100.00	80.00	40.00	0	2	6
postSP.in	0.00	0.00	20.00	90.00	100.00	100.00	100.00	63.33	49.67	2	1	7
postSP.out	0.00	0.00	0.00	40.00	85.00	94.00	100.00	45.00	52.60	2	2	6
postQG.in	0.00	0.00	0.00	50.00	100.00	100.00	100.00	50.00	57.73	2	2	6
postQG.out	0.00	10.00	25.00	50.00	75.00	90.00	100.00	50.00	70.71	1	0	2
postQP.in	0.00	18.00	45.00	90.00	95.00	98.00	100.00	63.33	55.08	1	2	5
postQP.out	0.00	0.00	7.50	45.00	63.75	82.50	100.00	42.50	39.72	2	1	7
postVG.in	0.00	0.00	0.00	50.00	100.00	100.00	100.00	49.44	43.72	6	2	20
postVG.out	0.00	0.00	0.00	60.00	95.00	100.00	100.00	49.33	45.43	6	7	22
postVP.in	0.00	0.00	0.00	40.00	100.00	100.00	100.00	45.38	44.66	15	6	43
postVP.out	0.00	0.00	0.00	60.00	100.00	100.00	100.00	[illegible]	44.63	13	10	46

Table 7.7 Prepayments/procurement, postpayments/procurement and net borrowing between various ownership types – *continued*

	Min.	*10%*	*25%*	*Median*	*75%*	*90%*	*Max.*	*Mean*	*Std*	*0s*	*NAs*	*n*
postPG.in	0.00	0.00	0.00	0.00	80.00	92.00	100.00	36.00	49.80	3	3	8
postPG.out	0.00	0.00	0.00	80.00	90.00	100.00	100.00	51.43	48.80	3	1	8
postPP.in	0.00	0.00	10.00	60.00	100.00	100.00	100.00	50.95	41.58	5	3	24
postPP.out	0.00	0.00	10.00	60.00	80.00	100.00	100.00	48.09	41.43	5	1	22
netSG.in	100.00	100.00	100.00	100.00	100.00	100.00	100.00	100.00	0.00	0	1	4
netSG.out	100.00	100.00	100.00	100.00	100.00	100.00	100.00	100.00	0.00	0	2	6
netSP.in	0.00	0.00	20.00	90.00	100.00	100.00	100.00	63.33	49.67	2	1	7
netSP.out	0.00	0.00	0.00	40.00	85.00	94.00	100.00	45.00	52.60	2	2	6
netQG.in	–100.00	–70.00	–25.00	50.00	100.00	100.00	100.00	25.00	95.74	1	2	6
netQG.out	–100.00	–80.00	–50.00	0.00	50.00	80.00	100.00	0.00	141.42	0	0	2
netQP.in	–10.00	10.00	40.00	90.00	95.00	98.00	100.00	60.00	60.83	0	2	5
netQP.out	–10.00	–4.00	0.00	90.00	100.00	100.00	100.00	54.29	54.12	2	0	7
netVG.in	–100.00	0.00	0.00	45.00	100.00	100.00	100.00	42.22	56.00	5	2	20
netVG.out	0.00	0.00	15.00	60.00	100.00	100.00	100.00	54.67	41.55	3	7	22
netVP.in	–90.00	0.00	0.00	30.00	100.00	100.00	100.00	39.68	50.39	12	6	43
netVP.out	–100.00	–5.00	0.00	20.00	100.00	100.00	100.00	35.22	55.86	12	10	46
netPG.in	–100.00	–100.00	–100.00	0.00	80.00	92.00	100.00	–4.00	95.29	1	3	8
netPG.out	–100.00	–100.00	–50.00	70.00	90.00	100.00	100.00	21.43	89.52	1	1	8
netPP.in	–40.00	0.00	0.00	50.00	100.00	100.00	100.00	43.81	46.31	4	3	24
netPP.out	–40.00	–2.00	0.00	35.00	100.00	100.00	100.00	42.50	47.11	4	2	22

Note: SG is state–government transactions, SP is state–private transactions, QG is quasi-state–government transactions, QP is quasi-state–private transactions, VG is state-supervised–government transactions, VP is state-supervised–private transactions, PG is private–government transactions, PP is private–private transactions. Quasi-state-owned firms are collective firms and firms whose majority shareholder is a public holding company. State-supervised firms are under the supervision of a local government. Private firms are all other firms. Government firms are state-owned and quasi-state-owned firms. Net borrowing in procurement transaction is prepayments – postpayments.

Table 7.8 P-values of T-tests on equality in group means of postpayments

	Lending in sales				*Borrowing in procurement*			
	State	*Qstate*	*Supervised*	*Private*	*State*	*Qstate*	*Supervised*	*Private*
State	0.77	0.43	0.19	0.20	0.81	0.56	0.21	0.26
Qstate	0.49	0.67	0.86	0.82	0.44	0.67	0.69	0.74
Supervised	0.03	0.18	0.30	0.91	0.42	0.85	0.94	0.92
Private	0.12	0.48	0.36	0.88	0.54	0.72	0.76	0.81

Note: State is state-owned firms, qstate is quasi-state-owned firms, supervised is state-supervised firms, private is private firms. The upper diagonal gives the test results between different ownership types for trades inside the city boundary, diagonal entries give the results between inside and outside the city boundary for the same ownership types, and lower diagonal gives the results of different ownership types for trade outside the city boundary. All test statistics are based on Welch's *t*-tests that assume unequal variances. *p* values give probabilities that the null of equal means is correct.

we test whether one ownership type, say *state*, has the same mean as another. The upper-right diagonal gives the results for inside-city comparisons, e.g., $state_{in}$ vs $qstate_{in}$. Diagonal entries give results between lending for inside-city and outside-city lending for the same ownership types, i.e, $state_{in}$ vs $state_{out}$. The lower-left diagonal gives the results for outside-city comparisons, e.g., $state_{out}$ vs $qstate_{out}$.

Our results reveal, first, an invariance to city boundary. The diagonal elements in both tables show relatively high values for the same ownership types. This implies that firms do not consider administrative boundaries at the municipal level to be a deterrent to trade. This is somewhat surprising given the anecdotal evidence that suggests local favoritism in court rulings and government protection. Secondly, we see that state-owned firms behave differently from the other types of firms in trade credit transactions. This is seen from the relatively small values in the rows and columns for *state* in both tables. The results of Tables 7.6 and 7.7 that state-owned firms borrow and lend more are also confirmed by group mean comparisons.

Regarding trade credit transactions with government-owned firms, in their lending behavior state-supervised firms behave differently from other firm types. Privately-owned firms differ from state- and quasi-state-owned firms in lending to those government-owned firms located outside the city. In borrowing, state-owned firms differ from the others. This is predictable as they only use postpayments in procurement transactions with government-owned firms (Table 7.9). This may be indicative of the leniency of state-owned and government-owned firms in their efforts to collect trade credits.

Table 7.9 P-values of T-tests on equality in group means of postpayments to government-owned firms

	Lending in sales				*Borrowing in procurement*			
	State	*Qstate*	*Supervised*	*Private*	*State*	*Qstate*	*Supervised*	*Private*
State	0.59	0.74	0.62	0.61	0.13	0.37	0.00	0.00
Qstate	0.55	0.88	0.62	0.61	0.19	0.83	0.88	0.99
Supervised	0.20	0.15	0.02	0.15	0.23	0.99	1.00	0.94
Private	0.35	0.22	0.57	0.22	0.28	0.96	0.81	0.51

Note: See footnote of Table 7.8.

If we consider the number of days required for payments to be collected, Table 7.10 indicates that in sales transactions there are similarities between state-owned and quasi-state-owned firms, and between state-supervised and private firms. In procurements, state-owned firms again behave differently from the others. For transactions with government-owned firms, Table 7.11 shows a similarity between state-supervised and private firms in outside-city sales, and between state and quasi-state-owned firms in inside-city procurements.

Table 7.10 P-values of T-tests on equality in group means of days

	Days in sales				*Days in procurement*			
	State	*Qstate*	*Supervised*	*Private*	*State*	*Qstate*	*Supervised*	*Private*
State	0.84	0.90	0.24	0.29	0.90	0.57	0.12	0.34
Qstate	0.92	0.72	0.53	0.45	0.19	0.50	0.69	0.92
Supervised	0.19	0.11	0.85	0.76	0.04	0.83	0.30	0.63
Private	0.15	0.10	0.60	0.80	0.14	0.96	0.75	0.42

Note: See footnote of Table 7.8.

Table 7.11 P-values of t-tests on equality in group means of days to government-owned firms

	Days in sales				*Days in procurement*			
	State	*Qstate*	*Supervised*	*Private*	*State*	*Qstate*	*Supervised*	*Private*
State	0.34	0.10	0.21	0.98	0.89	0.92	0.58	0.81
Qstate	0.26	0.38	0.45	0.73	0.73	0.69	0.68	0.50
Supervised	0.65	0.64	0.16	0.56	0.26	0.28	1.00	0.35
Private	0.25	0.16	0.94	0.94	0.33	0.27	0.77	0.97

Note: See footnote of Table 7.8.

7.4 Estimation

7.4.1 Econometric issues

The balance sheet data used here are for 2000, and the data for trade credit transactions are from 2001. However, noting the possible endogeneity of *cashA* if they are serially correlated (which they are), we also estimate allowing for endogeneity, using industry classifications (*distretail, manfact, manuf*), and a firm's overall lending and borrowing in trade credits ($after_s$, $after_c$, $bkchk_s$, $bkchk_c$, $plastic_s$, $plastic_c$) as instruments. These may influence the cash balance of firms, but are unlikely to influence lending to or borrowing from specific firms. Another issue concerns sampling. Since medium-sized firms have been oversampled, we will use a sampling weight of:

$$w = \left(\frac{85}{176}\right) \Big/ \left(\frac{18}{25}\right) = 0.67077,$$

on medium-sized firms. Weighting is unnecessary if asset size turns out not to affect trade credits, which is the case. Thus we will not use these weights, although we use firm size (*totA*) as a regressor.

7.4.2 FGLS-SUR

We will undertake a preliminary investigation of the determinants of trade credits using GLS. Firms are asked the percentages of transactions done with pre- and post-payments. This implies that in the case of gross borrowing, for example, one needs to estimate a system of the following:

$$y_{1i} \times \text{sales}_i = postpayments_{1i} = (\mathbf{X}_{1i}' \times sales_i)\beta_1 + u_{i1} \times sales_i,$$

$$y_{2i} \times proc_i = prepayments_{2i} = (\mathbf{X}_{2i}' \times proc_i)\beta_2 + u_{i2} \times proc_i,$$

where $y_{1i} = \dfrac{postpayments_{1i}}{sales_i}$ and $y_{2i} = \dfrac{prepayments_{2i}}{procurement_i}$ Note that there will be heteroskedastic disturbances because we are implicitly multiplying u_{1i}, u_{2i} with volumes $s_{1i} = sales_i$, $s_{2i} = proc_i$, respectively, in each equation. Denoting $\tilde{y}_{gi} = s_{gi}y_{gi}$, $\tilde{\mathbf{x}}_{gt} = s_{gi}\mathbf{x}_{gi}$, $\tilde{u}_{gt} = s_{gi}u_{gi}$ for $i = 1, 2$ and $g = 1, 2$, we have an FGLS-SUR form of:

$$\begin{pmatrix} \tilde{y}_{1i} \\ \tilde{y}_{2i} \end{pmatrix} = \begin{pmatrix} \tilde{\mathbf{x}}'_{1i} & 0' \\ 0' & \tilde{\mathbf{x}}'_{2i} \end{pmatrix} = \begin{pmatrix} \beta_1 \\ \beta_2 \end{pmatrix} = \begin{pmatrix} \tilde{u}_{i1} \\ \tilde{u}_{i2} \end{pmatrix},$$

or

$$y_i = X_i\beta + u_i, \tag{7.1}$$

where we have dropped the tildes for notational simplicity. To perform an FGLS, we first compute a consistent estimate of the heteroskedasticity robust covariance matrix Ω with plain SUR (which is identical to system OLS), then estimate an FGLS-SUR estimator. The heteroskedasticity consistent covariance matrix estimator is given as (see Wooldridge, 2002, 7.49):

$$\hat{V} = \left(\sum_{i=1}^{N} X_i \hat{\Omega}^{-1} X_i\right)^{-1} \left(\sum_{i=1}^{N} X_i' \hat{\Omega}^{-1} \hat{u}_i \hat{u}_i' \hat{\Omega}^{-1} X_i\right) \left(\sum_{i=1}^{N} X_i \hat{\Omega}^{-1} X_i\right)^{-1}. \tag{7.2}$$

A complication arises as we have different numbers of observations in each equation. We used **0** in $\mathbf{x}_{gi}$ if g is not observed when g' is. We have chosen a conservative, smaller degree of freedom of the two in computing p values.

7.5 Estimated results

In this section, we will use regression to examine if observations based on the descriptive statistics of the last section can be confirmed. We run regressions of trade credits on firm characteristics and trading partner characteristics. Table 7.12 is the base regression.[3] Table 7.13 estimates (7.1) with bank-related variables. Due to NAs in bank-related variables, Table 7.13 has a smaller number of observations.

In the W-FGLS-SUR of Table A7.1 in **A**, estimated parameters for state-owned firms become insignificant. This is because state-owned firms are larger in scale and are included in the medium-sized firm category where we have used weights of 0.67. However, there is no strong evidence, besides from $totA_c$ is significantly negative in Table 7.13, from our estimation results in Table A7.2, Table A7.1 and Table 7.12 that firm asset size matters for trade credits. Hence it is reasonable to assume that ignoring weights does not seriously affect estimates, and that one can stand by the results in Tables 7.12 and 7.13.

The general pattern emerging from Tables 7.12 and 7.13 is that:

- The amounts of lending by state-owned ($state_s$), quasi-state-owned ($qstate_s$), state-supervised ($spoffice_s$), and private (pvt_s) firms are not significantly different. This is consistent with state-owned firms *not* acting as financier-cum-enforcer in trade credit transactions.

Table 7.12 Estimation of trade credits

	Lending and borrowing				Days			
	FGLS-SUR			GMM	FGLS-SUR			GMM
	(1)	(2)	(3)	(4)	(5)	(6)	(7)	(8)
	LENDING				DAYS REQUIRED FOR COLLECTION			
$state_s$	0.871***	0.767**	0.72***	0.516	0.123***	0.116***	0.099***	–0.013
	(0.196)	(0.232)	(0.245)	(0.465)	(0.022)	(0.024)	(0.025)	(0.035)
$qstate_s$	0.882***	0.834***	0.92***	1.059***	0.121***	0.116***	0.13***	0.032
	(0.175)	(0.25)	(0.233)	(0.434)	(0.024)	(0.027)	(0.024)	(0.035)
$spoffice_s$	0.737***	0.714***	0.707***	0.565*	0.125***	0.123***	0.142***	0.032
	(0.18)	(0.235)	(0.222)	(0.378)	(0.024)	(0.027)	(0.026)	(0.032)
pvt_s	0.906***	0.914***	1.008***	1.029**	0.122***	0.122***	0.135***	0.038
	(0.209)	(0.242)	(0.233)	(0.443)	(0.027)	(0.029)	(0.026)	(0.04)
$manuf_s$	–0.099	–0.079			0.01	0.012		
	(0.132)	(0.127)			(0.013)	(0.014)		
$tsales_s$	–0.212*	–0.201	0.066	0.456*	0.016*	0.017**	–0.022	0.005
	(0.15)	(0.167)	(0.206)	(0.305)	(0.012)	(0.013)	(0.025)	(0.02)
$manufact_s$	0.096	0.082			0.004	0.004		
	(0.118)	(0.114)			(0.01)	(0.011)		
$distretail_s$	0.041	0.019			–0.001	–0.001		
	(0.115)	(0.114)			(0.011)	(0.011)		
$national_s$	0.142**	0.178***	0.154***	0.448***	0.006	0.008	0.005	0.006
	(0.073)	(0.065)	(0.058)	(0.14)	(0.009)	(0.011)	(0.011)	(0.01)
$sales_s$	–0.028*	–0.042**	–0.04**	–0.094**	–0.014***	–0.015***	–0.015***	–0.008*
	(0.021)	(0.021)	(0.024)	(0.042)	(0.003)	(0.003)	(0.003)	(0.005)

Table 7.12 Estimation of trade credits – *continued*

	Lending and borrowing				*Days*			
	FGLS-SUR			*GMM*	*FGLS-SUR*			*GMM*
	(1)	*(2)*	*(3)*	*(4)*	*(5)*	*(6)*	*(7)*	*(8)*
	LENDING				DAYS REQUIRED FOR COLLECTION			
$rival_s$		–0.017	0.022	0.381**		0.001	0.008	0.032**
		(0.14)	(0.159)	(0.226)		(0.007)	(0.008)	(0.015)
$length_s$		0.012***	0.01*	0.025**		0.001	0	0.001
		(0.005)	(0.006)	(0.013)		(0.001)	(0.001)	(0.001)
una_s		–0.012	–0.007	0.154		0.002	0.004	0.005
		(0.085)	(0.081)	(0.127)		(0.014)	(0.014)	(0.012)
$tprofitA_s$			–0.487**	–2.435**			–0.045	–0.05
			(0.212)	(1.757)			(0.056)	(0.123)
$cashA_s$			0.234	–5.677***			–0.028	0.293
			(0.427)	(2.311)			(0.065)	(0.27)
$totA_s$			0.074	0.049			0.019**	0.013
			(0.096)	(0.141)			(0.01)	(0.011)
$lgvbk_s$			–0.116	0.127			–0.002	–0.015*
			(0.103)	(0.128)			(0.011)	(0.01)
$lgvdspt_s$			–0.24***	–0.155			–0.004	0.011
			(0.086)	(0.146)			(0.015)	(0.011)
$lgvsbsdy_s$			–0.327*	–0.213			0.062**	0.041*
			(0.234)	(0.226)			(0.031)	(0.027)
$lgvprsnel_s$			0.242*	0.369*			0.015	0.029*
			(0.183)	(0.266)			(0.021)	(0.022)

Table 7.12 Estimation of trade credits – *continued*

	Lending and borrowing				*Days*			
	FGLS-SUR			*GMM*	*FGLS-SUR*			*GMM*
	(1)	*(2)*	*(3)*	*(4)*	*(5)*	*(6)*	*(7)*	*(8)*
	LENDING				DAYS REQUIRED FOR COLLECTION			
$lgvinfo_s$			0.048	–0.233**			–0.006	0.01
			(0.097)	(0.118)			(0.016)	(0.015)
out_s	–0.087**	–0.058	–0.068**	–0.015	0.002	0.003	0.002	0.002
	(0.053)	(0.051)	(0.04)	(0.055)	(0.004)	(0.004)	(0.004)	(0.005)
$state_c$	0.906***	0.942***	0.9***	2.855***	0.079***	0.084***	0.1***	0.196***
	(0.23)	(0.255)	(0.251)	(0.594)	(0.017)	(0.018)	(0.02)	(0.037)
$qstate_c$	0.99***	1.003***	0.955***	1.295***	0.083***	0.087***	0.092***	0.143***
	(0.19)	(0.209)	(0.213)	(0.436)	(0.018)	(0.018)	(0.019)	(0.026)
$spoffice_c$	0.566***	0.598***	0.561***	0.603***	0.086***	0.091***	0.093***	0.109***
	(0.185)	(0.215)	(0.196)	(0.305)	(0.02)	(0.02)	(0.017)	(0.022)
pvt_c	0.667**	0.703***	0.78***	0.827***	0.084***	0.09***	0.097***	0.124***
	(0.214)	(0.239)	(0.219)	(0.337)	(0.022)	(0.021)	(0.02)	(0.025)
$manuf_c$	0.067	0.07			0.005	0.005		
	(0.111)	(0.109)			(0.011)	(0.011)		
$tsales_c$	–0.079	–0.096	0.035	0.32	0.026*	0.024	0.034*	0.075**
	(0.323)	(0.309)	(0.395)	(0.425)	(0.02)	(0.019)	(0.025)	(0.033)
$manufact_c$	0.03	0.056			0	0.002		
	(0.087)	(0.089)			(0.007)	(0.007)		

Table 7.12 Estimation of trade credits – *continued*

	Lending and borrowing				*Days*			
	FGLS-SUR			*GMM*	*FGLS-SUR*			*GMM*
	(1)	*(2)*	*(3)*	*(4)*	*(5)*	*(6)*	*(7)*	*(8)*
	LENDING				DAYS REQUIRED FOR COLLECTION			
distretail$_c$	–0.059 (0.101)	–0.034 (0.103)			0.002 (0.009)	0.004 (0.009)		
national$_c$	–0.06 (0.076)	–0.083 (0.081)	–0.099 (0.08)	–0.091 (0.113)	0 (0.004)	–0.002 (0.005)	0.001 (0.005)	0.006 (0.007)
proc$_c$	–0.017 (0.024)	–0.02 (0.026)	–0.016 (0.026)	0.008 (0.036)	–0.01*** (0.003)	–0.01*** (0.003)	–0.009*** (0.003)	–0.009*** (0.003)
rival$_c$		–0.064 (0.09)	–0.033 (0.089)	0.228* (0.159)		–0.007 (0.006)	–0.004 (0.006)	0.004 (0.013)
length$_c$		0.003 (0.006)	0.004 (0.005)	0.02*** (0.007)		0 (0)	0 (0)	0.001 (0.001)
tprofitA$_c$			0.459** (0.243)	3.533* (2.425)			0.017 (0.016)	0.058 (0.131)
cashA$_c$			–0.526 (0.729)	-10.063*** (2.872)			–0.107** (0.059)	–0.694*** (0.228)
totA$_c$			–0.03 (0.11)	–0.4** (0.196)			–0.01** (0.006)	–0.033*** (0.014)
lgvbk$_c$			0.043 (0.107)	–0.166 (0.13)			–0.001 (0.007)	–0.015* (0.009)
Igvdspt$_c$			–0.031 (0.12)	–0.318*** (0.117)			–0.011* (0.008)	–0.024*** (0.007)

Table 7.12 Estimation of trade credits – *continued*

	Lending and borrowing				*Days*			
	FGLS-SUR			*GMM*	*FGLS-SUR*			*GMM*
	(1)	*(2)*	*(3)*	*(4)*	*(5)*	*(6)*	*(7)*	*(8)*
	LENDING				DAYS REQUIRED FOR COLLECTION			
$lgvsbsdy_c$			–0.418**	–0.418*			–0.025**	–0.019
			(0.181)	(0.269)			(0.013)	(0.017)
$lgvprsnel_c$			0.085	–0.704***			–0.019*	–0.045***
			(0.202)	(0.249)			(0.014)	(0.016)
$lgvinfo_c$			0.06	0.358***			0.017**	0.027***
			(0.125)	(0.135)			(0.009)	(0.01)
out_c	–0.008	0.007	0.017	0.021	0.002	0.004	0.003	0.007*
	(0.045)	(0.05)	(0.05)	(0.077)	(0.004)	(0.004)	(0.004)	(0.005)
$corr_u$	0.905	0.909	0.862		0.992	0.991	0.949	
obs_s	156	156	156	156	156	156	156	156
oby_c	136	136	136	136	136	136	136	136
overID				1				0.9991

Notes: (1)–(3) (5)–(7) columns are estimated with FGLS-SUR to allow for parameters on sales and procurements to differ. (4) and (8) are estimated with GMM to allow for the endogeneity of *tprofitA*, *cashA*, using *manuf*, $after_s$, $after_c$, $bkchk_s$, $bkchk_c$, $bkplastic_s$, $bkplastic_c$ as instruments. lending is payments after delivery in sales transactions, borrowing is Total sum of payments before delivery and cash-on-delivery in procurements. days are number of days of after delivery until payment is completed. All regressors are interacted with either sales or procurements, except for *sales* or *proc* itself and global intercept. The tests use robust standard errors of $(\sum_{i=1}^{N} \mathbf{X}_i \hat{\Omega}^{-1} \mathbf{X}_i)^{-1} (\sum_{i=1}^{N} \mathbf{X}_i' \hat{\Omega}^{-1} \hat{\mathbf{u}}_i \hat{\mathbf{u}}_i' \hat{\Omega}^{-1} \mathbf{X}_i) (\sum_{i=1}^{N} \mathbf{X}_i \hat{\Omega}^{-1} \mathbf{X}_i)^{-1}$ where $\hat{\Omega}$ is constructed from OLS residuals of the first stage. Suffix$_s$ indicates sales transactions, $\hat{c}$ indicates procurement transactions. The number of observations ***obs*** are reduced in the estimations that include bank-related variables because of nonresponses, and $qnat_c$ is dropped due to singularities. ***corr*** is the correlation between residuals u_s and u_c ***overID*** is an overidentification test for the instruments used.

Table 7.13 Estimation of trade credits with bank-related variables

	Lending and borrowing					*Days*				
	FGLS-SUR				*GMM*	*FGLS-SUR*				*GMM*
	(1)	*(2)*	*(3)*	*(4)*	*(5)*	*(6)*	*(7)*	*(8)*		
	LENDING					DAYS REQUIRED FOR COLLECTION				
$state_s$	0.829***	0.718***	0.499**	0.617**	0.344	0.12***	0.112***	0.102***	0.093*	0.127***
	(0.194)	(0.234)	(0.261)	(0.322)	(0.342)	(0.022)	(0.024)	(0.024)	(0.047)	(0.039)
$qstate_s$	0.784***	0.731***	0.673***	0.59**	–0.102	0.11***	0.104***	0.108***	0.126***	0.126***
	(0.177)	(0.25)	(0.25)	(0.29)	(0.391)	(0.023)	(0.027)	(0.028)	(0.045)	(0.048)
$spoffice_s$	0.687***	0.654***	0.586***	0.269	–0.473	0.121***	0.117***	0.118***	0.161***	0.161***
	(0.177)	(0.234)	(0.238)	(0.294)	(0.365)	(0.024)	(0.027)	(0.028)	(0.038)	(0.041)
pvt_s	0.857***	0.857***	0.804***	0.608**	–0.244	0.118***	0.117***	0.121***	0.187***	0.185***
	(0.207)	(0.242)	(0.25)	(0.341)	(0.414)	(0.027)	(0.03)	(0.031)	(0.045)	(0.046)
$manuf_s$	–0.086	–0.063	–0.05			0.012	0.014	0.016		
	(0.131)	(0.128)	(0.119)			(0.013)	(0.014)	(0.014)		
$tsales_s$	–0.225*	–0.208	–0.218*	0.612*	–0.773	0.014	0.016	0.007	0.127***	0.148**
	(0.15)	(0.164)	(0.153)	(0.45)	(0.641)	(0.012)	(0.013)	(0.013)	(0.051)	(0.071)
$manufact_s$	0.097	0.085	0.064			0.003	0.003	0.002		
	(0.119)	(0.114)	(0.112)			(0.01)	(0.011)	(0.011)		
$distretail_s$	0.041	0.024	0.016			–0.002	–0.002	–0.002		
	(0.116)	(0.114)	(0.114)			(0.011)	(0.012)	(0.012)		
$national_s$	0.147**	0.181***	0.173***	0.11*	0.043	0.007	0.008	0.009	–0.006	0.016*
	(0.074)	(0.066)	(0.061)	(0.067)	(0.104)	(0.009)	(0.011)	(0.011)	(0.011)	(0.01)
$sales_s$	–0.023	–0.038**	–0.041**	–0.025*	0.005	–0.013***	–0.014***	–0.015***	–0.017**	–0.021***
	(0.021)	(0.021)	(0.021)	(0.017)	(0.032)	(0.003)	(0.003)	(0.003)	(0.004)	(0.004)

Table 7.13 Estimation of trade credits with bank-related variables – *continued*

	Lending and borrowing				*Days*			
	FGLS-SUR			*GMM*	*FGLS-SUR*			*GMM*
	(1)	*(2)*	*(3)*	*(4)*	*(5)*	*(6)*	*(7)*	*(8)*
	LENDING				DAYS REQUIRED FOR COLLECTION			
$rival_s$	–0.008	0.038	–0.119	0.235	0.002	0.003	0.014*	0.022*
	(0.138)	(0.14)	(0.174)	(0.185)	(0.008)	(0.008)	(0.01)	(0.014)
$length_s$	0.013***	0.012**	0.016**	0.005	0.001	0	0	0
	(0.005)	(0.006)	(0.007)	(0.01)	(0.001)	(0.001)	(0.001)	(0.001)
unq_s	–0.012	0.011			0.003	0.005		
	(0.085)	(0.083)			(0.014)	(0.014)		
$tprofitA_s$		–0.599***	–2.394***	–6.41***		–0.032	–0.619***	–0.741***
		(0.172)	(0.804)	(1.769)		(0.052)	(0.219)	(0.251)
$cashA_s$		0.452	2.624***	13.018***		–0.023	0.015	0.151
		(0.447)	(1.076)	(4.374)		(0.069)	(0.174)	(0.426)
$totA_s$		0.107	–0.379*	0.28		0.012**	–0.029	–0.056**
		(0.091)	(0.246)	(0.297)		(0.007)	(0.03)	(0.032)
$amount_s$			0.255	–0.647			–0.01	0.039
			(0.532)	(0.639)			(0.076)	(0.061)
$maturity_s$			0.007**	–0.005			0.002***	0.002***
			(0.004)	(0.005)			(0.001)	(0.001)
$irate_s$			0.039	0.083**			–0.008*	–0.011**
			(0.031)	(0.04)			(0.005)	(0.006)
$lgvbk_s$			–0.307***	–0.256**			–0.013	–0.034***
			(0.126)	(0.121)			(0.015)	(0.014)

Table 7.13 Estimation of trade credits with bank-related variables – *continued*

	Lending and borrowing					*Days*				
	FGLS-SUR				*GMM*	*FGLS-SUR*				*GMM*
	(1)	*(2)*	*(3)*	*(4)*	*(5)*	*(6)*	*(7)*	*(8)*		
	LENDING					DAYS REQUIRED FOR COLLECTION				
$lgvdspt_s$				–0.212**	–0.203**				–0.004	0.02*
				(0.092)	(0.106)				(0.014)	(0.012)
$lgvsbsdy_s$				–0.947***	–1.068***				0.091**	0.079**
				(0.159)	(0.344)				(0.04)	(0.035)
$lgvprsnel_s$				0.265*	0.318**				0.018	0.004
				(0.194)	(0.168)				(0.029)	(0.02)
$lgvinfo_s$				0.153*	0.18*				0.014	0.035**
				(0.102)	(0.124)				(0.015)	(0.013)
out_s	–0.078*	–0.052	–0.056	–0.042*	–0.073**	0.003	0.004	0.003	0.003	0.004
	(0.052)	(0.051)	(0.051)	(0.03)	(0.04)	(0.004)	(0.004)	(0.004)	(0.006)	(0.006)
$state_c$	0.364*	0.328*	0.353*	1.193***	0.817*	0.039**	0.035**	0.038**	0.103**	0.065**
	(0.23)	(0.245)	(0.245)	(0.359)	(0.531)	(0.017)	(0.017)	(0.019)	(0.031)	(0.029)
$spoffice_c$	–0.015	–0.049	–0.064	0.762***	0.769**	0.041**	0.038**	0.037**	0.094**	0.06**
	(0.166)	(0.178)	(0.179)	(0.29)	(0.451)	(0.019)	(0.018)	(0.019)	(0.029)	(0.027)
pvt_c	0.079	0.045	0.047	1.032***	0.81**	0.038**	0.035**	0.034**	0.103***	0.04**
	(0.185)	(0.194)	(0.195)	(0.322)	(0.476)	(0.02)	(0.019)	(0.02)	(0.035)	(0.029)
$manuf_c$	0.137	0.139	0.143			0.013	0.012	0.012		
	(0.11)	(0.115)	(0.117)			(0.012)	(0.012)	(0.013)		
$tsales_c$	–0.279	–0.269	–0.368	0.515	0.915*	0.008	0.008	0.019	0.046	0.08**
	(0.38)	(0.348)	(0.425)	(0.59)	(0.583)	(0.022)	(0.022)	(0.029)	(0.046)	(0.04)

Table 7.13 Estimation of trade credits with bank-related variables – *continued*

	Lending and borrowing					*Days*				
	FGLS-SUR				*GMM*	*FGLS-SUR*				*GMM*
	(1)	*(2)*	*(3)*	*(4)*	*(5)*	*(6)*	*(7)*	*(8)*		
	LENDING					DAYS REQUIRED FOR COLLECTION				
$manufact_c$	0.084	0.088	0.06			0.005	0.006	0.005		
	(0.084)	(0.091)	(0.095)			(0.007)	(0.007)	(0.008)		
$distretail_c$	–0.04	–0.043	–0.075			0.004	0.003	0.002		
	(0.113)	(0.113)	(0.114)			(0.01)	(0.01)	(0.01)		
$national_c$	–0.039	–0.04	–0.049	–0.132*	–0.344**	0.003	0.003	0.003	0.007	0.006
	(0.087)	(0.088)	(0.087)	(0.092)	(0.151)	(0.005)	(0.005)	(0.005)	(0.006)	(0.008)
$proc_c$	0.068***	0.058**	0.058**	–0.021	–0.005	–0.003	–0.004*	–0.003*	–0.007*	–0.005
	(0.028)	(0.028)	(0.027)	(0.03)	(0.056)	(0.003)	(0.003)	(0.003)	(0.004)	(0.004)
$rival_c$		0.061	0.089	–0.163*	–0.285		0.004	0.006	–0.007	0.003
		(0.093)	(0.095)	(0.107)	(0.239)		(0.006)	(0.006)	(0.01)	(0.014)
$length_c$		0.005	0.007	0.007*	0.006		0	0	0	0
		(0.006)	(0.006)	(0.005)	(0.005)		(0)	(0)	(0)	(0)
$tprofitA_c$			0.51***	–0.912	-2.209			0.011	0	–0.054
			(0.203)	(1.074)	(2.765)			(0.013)	(0.114)	(0.183)
$cashA_c$			–0.409	-1.132	-9.101***			–0.029	–0.042	–0.57***
			(0.774)	(1.37)	(3.268)			(0.055)	(0.124)	(0.23)
$totA_c$			0.063	–0.386*	–0.756**			–0.005	–0.019	–0.051***
			(0.101)	(0.278)	(0.318)			(0.007)	(0.02)	(0.02)
$amount_c$				0.365	2.047**				–0.054	0.041
				(0.622)	(0.996)				(0.045)	(0.058)

Table 7.13 Estimation of trade credits with bank-related variables – *continued*

	Lending and borrowing					*Days*				
	FGLS-SUR				*GMM*	*FGLS-SUR*				*GMM*
	(1)	*(2)*	*(3)*	*(4)*	*(5)*	*(6)*	*(7)*	*(8)*		
	LENDING					DAYS REQUIRED FOR COLLECTION				
$maturity_c$				0.009**	0.012*				0.001**	0.001**
				(0.005)	(0.008)				(0.001)	(0.001)
$irate_c$				–0.026	0.051				–0.003	0.004
				(0.033)	(0.048)				(0.003)	(0.003)
$lgvbk_c$				–0.036	0.008				–0.009	–0.023***
				(0.129)	(0.174)				(0.009)	(0.009)
$lgvdspt_c$				0.068	–0.059				–0.011	–0.022***
				(0.124)	(0.159)				(0.009)	(0.009)
$lgvsbsdy_c$				–0.502***	0.215				–0.039***	–0.011
				(0.158)	(0.356)				(0.015)	(0.021)
$lgvprsnel_c$				0.028	–0.135				–0.019	–0.027*
				(0.26)	(0.25)				(0.016)	(0.016)
$lgyinfo_c$				0.032	–0.011				0.017*	0.034***
				(0.126)	(0.162)				(0.01)	(0.009)
out_c	0.033	0.021	0.02	0.086*	0.125	0.005	0.004	0.004	0.004	0.002
	(0.048)	(0.051)	(0.052)	(0.057)	(0.105)	(0.004)	(0.004)	(0.004)	(0.005)	(0.006)
cor_u	0.901	0.904	0.884	0.742		0.991	0.989	0.986	0.741	
obs_s	156	156	156	113	113	156	156	156	113	113
obs_c	136	136	136	97	97	136	136	136	97	97
overID					1					1

Notes: Columns (1)–(4) (6)–(9) are FGLS-SUR, columns (5) and (10) are GMM. For details, see footnotes of Table 7.12.

- Lending is greater to government-owned (*national*$_s$) firms. This coincides with another finding – that state-owned and quasi-state-owned firms borrow more.
- Lending is greater when amounts (*sales*$_s$) are small.
- The higher the profit rate (*tprofitA*$_s$, *tprofitA*$_c$), the smaller the lending, and the greater the borrowing. If we assume weak exogeneity, this has a causal interpretation that profitable (and hence well-managed) firms lend less while being able to borrow more. If the exogeneity assumption is violated, this may entail a reverse causation that firms that lend more are making less profit due to lending, and firms who can get more loans can earn more profits because of borrowing. Although balance sheet variables are all predetermined, autocorrelation provides a way for the endogenous determination of profits. The correlation coefficient is .72 for $^{(\text{profits})}/_{(\text{total asset})}$ ratios between 2000 and 2001, hence it is not possible to know the direction in which causality runs. The problem of possible endogeneity can be resolved if one uses instruments. In the GMM estimation, we instrumented profits with own and partner's industry dummies and the overall use of late payments, bank checks, and credit cards which are all considered to be correlated with unobservable productivity, but not necessarily with the use of late payments in a *particular* transaction. Overidentification tests show the significance of using instruments. Profits remain significant in all but a borrowing regression with bank-related variables. Thus, we conclude that profits have a causal interpretation in most cases.
- Larger lending is offered:
  - to firms inside the city boundary relative to outside (*out*$_s$). This has a natural interpretation in line with local favoritism which was not detected when we tested equal means in Table 7.8.
  - by firms that do not expect local authority to intervene in the case of repayment disputes (*lgvdspt*$_s$), by firms that do not expect subsidies in the case of business difficulties (*lgvsbsdy*$_s$), by firms that expect personnel to be dispatched from local authority in the case of business difficulties (*lgvprsnel*$_s$). Estimates on disputes can be understood as firms that are not expecting government intervention have alternative ways to secure payments, such as those suggested in standard theories of trade credits, or they may have backed up all together not to offer trade credits. Estimates on subsidies have a similar interpretation.
  - by firms with higher cash holdings to total assets (*cashA*$_s$). This indicates more liquid firms are extending trade credits and receiving bank loans.

- Larger lending is offered, after adding bank-related variables (Table 7.13):
  - coefficients for quasi-state-owned and state-supervised firms become smaller. This indicates that firms receiving bank loans are more liquid.[4]
  - by firms that are charged higher interest rates by banks. This may indicate that banks see larger trade credit provision in sales as a sign of potential default.
- Larger borrowing is obtained:
  - by state-owned ($state_c$) and quasi-state-owned ($qstate_c$) firms in the sample (Table 7.12).
  - by firms with smaller cash holdings to total asset ratios ($cashA_c$ in Table 7.12, Table 7.13).
- Longer years of trading:
  - increases lending provided by sampled firms, but not after the inclusion of bank-related variables using IVs. This may indicate that firms with longer trading relationships are more profitable than others whose profitability is captured in bank lending patterns and instruments, and that longevity of relationship by itself does not have independent effects on credit provision.
- Firm size (proxied by total asset size $totA_s$, $totA_c$) does not affect trade credits.
- In Tables 7.12 and 7.13, the coefficients for each ownership type do not change significantly after the addition of local government variables. This indicates that their ability to extend trade credits is uncorrelated with ties to local government.

7.6 Concluding remarks

The financial transition from planned to market-oriented allocation is not well documented. As a first step to understand the process, this chapter has undertaken an examination of corporate financial characteristics using a unique dataset from a survey that focused on the determination of trade credits to small and medium-sized firms in China.

This chapter used descriptive statistics and GLS/GMM and shed light on the general trends of trade credits among firms of different ownership type. It found: First, an indication that trade credits are consistent with funding capacity and needs, as liquid firms extend more credits, and more cash-constrained firms receive larger credits.

Secondly, state-owned firms do not seem to act as a catalyst of trade credit flows in offering credits. State-owned and quasi-state-owned firms do not differ significantly from other ownership types in their credit provision to trading partners. They do obtain more trade credits than others which can suggest reneging on loan repayments. However, this is not necessarily the case. The theoretical model developed in Chapter 5 predicts a firm with a stronger enforcement technology to offer more credits to buyers. If this is true, the result we have that state-owned firms *receive* more credits can be interpreted as all other firms having stronger enforcement techniques toward state-owned firms, *not* vice versa. That is, state-owned firms have less bargaining power over gains from each bilateral trade. There is a body of evidence that state-owned firms are more tightly controled by local authority, hence better-behaved, and that, therefore, reneging on debts is less frequent than other ownership types. Of course, one needs to be careful when pushing this interpretation further because, although being controled in estimation, state-owned firms are generally larger in size and have more market power. Obviously, a more thorough investigation is warranted.

Another thing to note about the role of state-owned firms is that they may be just slacking on their financial management. They may simply be sloppy and miss their repayments, which can be interpreted as receiving larger sums in loans. One evidence from our data that counters to this possibility is the maturity of loans. In estimation of days to repay, we found no significant difference among ownership types. We may need to estimate loan and days as a system because they are simultaneously determined. To test a view that state-owned firms are less well behaved against otherwise require more detailed data on trades, and possibly more observation. This is left for future research.

Thirdly, profitability is associated with lower levels of lending and higher levels of borrowing. Given that all balance sheet variables are dated prior to trade credit transactions and they are instrumented, this indicates causality that better managed, profitable firms lend less while being able to borrow more.

Fourthly, ties to local government, which are proxied by what assistance firms expect when they are in trouble, does not seem to affect trade credit provisions and receipts in all ownership types. However, such a tendency does not extend beyond the city boundaries, because firms generally offer smaller loans to partners outside of the city boundary.

Fifthly, bank-related variables indicate that banks penalizes suppliers of trade credits in sales transactions by putting premiums on interest rates.

Some other issues remain to be explained. First, lending and borrowing can be considered as censored variables. One can use tobit models with endogenous variables as suggested, for example, by Smith and Blundell (1986), Newey (1987), and Wooldridge (2002). Secondly, one may wish to develop an explicit theoretical model that describes this chapter's conjecture that state-owned firms function as financier-cum-enforcers, to come up with more specific identification restrictions for testing. These and other issues remain for future study.

Notes

1 Allen *et al.* (2004) argues from the latter perspective, noting faster growth in the "private sector" (all firms with various types of private and local government ownership other than state-owned and publicly listed firms) despite its poorer legal and financial mechanisms, that there should "exist effective alternative financing channels and governance mechanisms, such as those based on reputation and relationships."

2 For example, consider the number of alternative trading partners as a "fall back" option in bargaining models.

3 Using additional instruments such as a dummy variable for owner-manager firm (*inscontrol*) and majority share in stock holdings (*maipercent*) does not affect results.

4 Whether sources of such liquidity are bank loans or inherent liquidity positions of firms, are not identified, however.

References

Allen, Franklin, Jun Qian and Maijun Qian (2004) "Law, Finance, and Economic Growth in China," *Center for Financial Institutions Working Papers*, Wharton School Center for Financial Institutions, University of Pennsylvania.

McMillan, John and Christopher Woodruff (1999) "Interfirm Relationships and Informal Credit in Vietnam," *Quarterly Journal of Economics* 114(4), 1285–1320.

Newey, Whitney K. (1987) "Efficient Estimation of Limited Dependent Variable Models with Endogenous Explanatory Variables," *Journal of Econometrics* 36(3), 231–50.

Smith, Richard J. and Blundell, Richard W. (1986) "An Exogeneity Test for a Simultaneous Equation Tobit Model with an Application to Labor Supply," *Econometrica* 54(3), 679–85.

Wooldridge, Jeffrey (2002) *Econometric Analysis of Cross Section and Panel Data*. Cambridge, MA: MIT Press.

Appendix: W-FGLS-SUR estimation of trade credits

Table A7.1 W-FGLS-SUR estimation of trade credits (with a global intercept)

	Gross borrowing			*Gross lending*			*Net borrowing*			*Days*		
	(1)	*(2)*	*(3)*	*(4)*	*(5)*	*(6)*	*(7)*	*(8)*	*(9)*	*(10)*	*(11)*	*(12)*
int	–0.005**	–0.004*	–0.003	0.001	0	–0.001	–0.002	0	0	0.13***	0.132***	0.131***
	(0.003)	(0.003)	(0.003)	(0.003)	(0.003)	(0.003)	(0.005)	(0.004)	(0.005)	(0.046)	(0.047)	(0.049)
int_s	0.004*	0.003	0.001	–0.001	0	0.002	0.001	–0.001	–0.004	0.258**	0.271**	0.284**
	(0.003)	(0.003)	(0.003)	(0.005)	(0.005)	(0.005)	(0.007)	(0.007)	(0.007)	(0.118)	(0.121)	(0.126)
$sales_s$	0.095**	–0.034	0.024	0.592***	0.656***	0.533**	–0.395*	–0.597**	–0.422*	2.425	–0.472	–1.815
	(0.054)	(0.093)	(0.088)	(0.203)	(0.228)	(0.234)	(0.242)	(0.308)	(0.315)	(2.509)	(2.618)	(3.009)
$manufact_s$	0.041	0.062**	0.061**	0.036	–0.008	–0.016	–0.003	0.061	0.056	–1.857**	–1.578*	–1.488*
	(0.035)	(0.033)	(0.033)	(0.11)	(0.112)	(0.11)	(0.128)	(0.127)	(0.13)	(1.016)	(1.103)	(1.139)
$distretail_s$	0.037	0.053**	0.062**	0.034	0.002	–0.022	–0.027	0.025	0.058	–2.512**	–2.053**	–2.222**
	(0.032)	(0.031)	(0.031)	(0.105)	(0.105)	(0.107)	(0.115)	(0.113)	(0.119)	(1.257)	(1.241)	(1.246)
$national_s$	–0.055**	–0.062**	–0.06**	0.137**	0.147***	0.149***	–0.205***	–0.228***	–0.222***	1.073	1	0.831
	(0.027)	(0.027)	(0.026)	(0.062)	(0.057)	(0.059)	(0.08)	(0.073)	(0.073)	(1.163)	(1.29)	(1.23)
uno_s		–0.015	–0.021		0.045	0.048		–0.032	–0.052		0.137	0.162
		(0.028)	(0.027)		(0.091)	(0.09)		(0.11)	(0.108)		(1.89)	(1.833)
$rivals_s$		0.145***	0.138***		–0.153	–0.127		0.327*	0.287*		1.695	1.894
		(0.057)	(0.054)		(0.141)	(0.139)		(0.218)	(0.213)		(1.496)	(1.493)
$length_s$		0	–0.001		0.008	0.011*		–0.012*	–0.015**		0.101	0.133*
		(0.002)	(0.002)		(0.007)	(0.007)		(0.008)	(0.009)		(0.096)	(0.102)
nat_s	0.11	0.148	0.175*	0.192	0.161	0.024	–0.135	–0.032	0.097	–3.986**	–3.812**	–5.191**
	(0.143)	(0.123)	(0.117)	(0.197)	(0.199)	(0.196)	(0.332)	(0.31)	(0.293)	(2.195)	(1.894)	(2.603)
$qnat_s$	–0.063**	–0.071**	–0.066**	0.021	0.039	0.009	–0.186	–0.214	–0.175	–1.125	–1.473	–2.046
	(0.029)	(0.043)	(0.04)	(0.182)	(0.196)	(0.168)	(0.202)	(0.233)	(0.195)	(2.238)	(2.229)	(2.117)
$spoffice_s$	0.035*	0.019	0.012	–0.189**	–0.172*	–0.168*	0.173*	0.151	0.13	–1.03	–1.271	–1.315
	(0.026)	(0.033)	(0.034)	(0.102)	(0.107)	(0.107)	(0.127)	(0.138)	(0.14)	(1.581)	(1.725)	(1.715)
$tsales_s$	0.06	0.118*	0.118*	–0.461***	–0.528***	–0.505**	0.301	0.437*	0.369	–1.369	–0.764	–5.301
	(0.074)	(0.079)	(0.09)	(0.168)	(0.187)	(0.251)	(0.243)	(0.277)	(0.327)	(1.711)	(1.865)	(4.384)

Table A7.1 W-FGLS-SUR estimation of trade credits (with a global intercept) – *cosntinued*

	Gross borrowing			*Gross lending*			*Net borrowing*			*Days*		
	(1)	*(2)*	*(3)*	*(4)*	*(5)*	*(6)*	*(7)*	*(8)*	*(9)*	*(10)*	*(11)*	*(12)*
$manuf_s$	–0.055*	–0.058*	–0.055*	0.118	0.127	0.121	–0.181	–0.188	–0.181	–1.401	–1.254	–1.217
	(0.038)	(0.037)	(0.038)	(0.134)	(0.136)	(0.133)	(0.162)	(0.161)	(0.162)	(1.601)	(1.592)	(1.586)
$tprofitA_s$			0.167**			–0.428**			0.589***			–4.263
			(0.083)			(0.185)			(0.23)			(4.66)
$cashA_s$			0.341			–0.066			0.821			–7.813
			(0.268)			(0.697)			(0.862)			(8.046)
$liqLA_s$			–0.053**			0.091			–0.17**			1.591*
			(0.026)			(0.074)			(0.09)			(0.989)
$totA_s$			–0.042			0.091			–0.032			5.527*
			(0.068)			(0.275)			(0.326)			(4.151)
out_s	0.053**	0.051**	0.048**	–0.082**	–0.061*	–0.058*	0.138**	0.108**	0.099**	0.312	0.4	0.456
	(0.03)	(0.026)	(0.026)	(0.045)	(0.037)	(0.038)	(0.07)	(0.053)	(0.055)	(0.385)	(0.445)	(0.446)
$proc_c$	0.489***	0.589***	0.495***	0.202*	0.176*	0.208*	0.184	0.3	0.211	1.08	0.654	0.076
	(0.154)	(0.172)	(0.182)	(0.133)	(0.129)	(0.133)	(0.261)	(0.262)	(0.258)	(1.378)	(1.616)	(2.094)
$manufact_c$	0.007	0.027	0.036	0.047	0.014	–0.008	–0.031	0.024	0.051	–0.51	–0.388	–0.352
	(0.087)	(0.084)	(0.087)	(0.042)	(0.047)	(0.048)	(0.116)	(0.117)	(0.125)	(0.803)	(0.8)	(0.839)
$distretail_c$	–0.041	–0.034	–0.023	0.128*	0.109*	0.098*	–0.17	–0.133	–0.12	–0.361	–0.258	–0.313
	(0.098)	(0.1)	(0.101)	(0.082)	(0.077)	(0.075)	(0.146)	(0.134)	(0.134)	(0.912)	(0.953)	(0.978)
$national_c$	–0.038	–0.066	–0.074	0.085*	0.126**	0.145**	–0.131	–0.194*	–0.211**	0.098	0.031	0.183
	(0.071)	(0.067)	(0.07)	(0.057)	(0.066)	(0.067)	(0.118)	(0.125)	(0.125)	(0.503)	(0.566)	(0.631)
$rival_c$		–0.121*	–0.102		0.084	0.053		–0.195**	–0.148*		0.158	0.344
		(0.078)	(0.081)		(0.068)	(0.062)		(0.106)	(0.099)		(0.643)	(0.679)
$length_c$		0	0.003		–0.007***	–0.008***		0.007	0.011**		0.057	0.067
		(0.004)	(0.004)		(0.003)	(0.003)		(0.006)	(0.006)		(0.08)	(0.084)

Table A7.1 W-FGLS-SUR estimation of trade credits (with a global intercept) – *cosntinued*

	Gross borrowing			*Gross lending*			*Net borrowing*			*Days*		
	(1)	*(2)*	*(3)*	*(4)*	*(5)*	*(6)*	*(7)*	*(8)*	*(9)*	*(10)*	*(11)*	*(12)*
nat_c	0.095	0.068	0.304*	–0.175**	–0.145*	–0.11	0.181	0.151	0.359	–0.798	–1.132	–0.504
	(0.257)	(0.241)	(0.212)	(0.101)	(0.1)	(0.151)	(0.272)	(0.269)	(0.325)	(1.342)	(1.626)	(1.539)
$qnat_c$	0.309**	0.266**	0.242*	–0.164*	–0.133*	–0.204**	0.532**	0.474**	0.506**	–0.427	–0.503	–0.686
	(0.157)	(0.158)	(0.177)	(0.1)	(0.093)	(0.122)	(0.236)	(0.229)	(0.274)	(1.382)	(1.382)	(1.463)
$spoffice_c$	–0.157*	–0.182*	–0.193**	–0.048	–0.024	–0.022	–0.076	–0.119	–0.129	–0.33	–0.391	–0.426
	(0.122)	(0.119)	(0.114)	(0.082)	(0.076)	(0.074)	(0.188)	(0.177)	(0.165)	(1.009)	(0.998)	(0.983)
$tsales_c$	0.432	0.406	0.175	–0.316**	–0.186	–0.108	0.833**	0.628*	0.399	–1.773	–3.028	–2.552
	(0.372)	(0.385)	(0.46)	(0.17)	(0.17)	(0.254)	(0.445)	(0.425)	(0.59)	(3.207)	(3.831)	(4.134)
$manuf_c$	0.203**	0.202**	0.211**	–0.097	–0.092	–0.108*	0.299**	0.295**	0.319**	1.219	1.11	1.068
	(0.117)	(0.109)	(0.105)	(0.084)	(0.085)	(0.079)	(0.169)	(0.161)	(0.149)	(1.01)	(1.052)	(1.029)
$tprofitA_c$			0.421**			0.243*			0.136			0.662
			(0.206)			(0.164)			(0.321)			(1.835)
$cashA_c$			–1.506***			1.502**			–3.023***			–7.717
			(0.627)			(0.701)			(1.182)			(9.214)
$liqLA_c$			0.203**			–0.074			0.265**			1.456*
			(0.098)			(0.087)			(0.15)			(1.11)
$totA_c$			0.12			–0.075			0.139			–0.279
			(0.128)			(0.12)			(0.233)			(1.198)
out_c	0.034	0.048*	0.045*	–0.013	–0.028	–0.026	0.049	0.076*	0.069*	0.572**	0.586**	0.519*
	(0.034)	(0.035)	(0.032)	(0.027)	(0.029)	(0.029)	(0.047)	(0.05)	(0.047)	(0.338)	(0.342)	(0.357)
$corr_u$	0.399	0.61	0.91	0.877	0.428	0.572	0.895	0.877	0.41	0.522	0.854	0.861
obs_s	154	154	154	154	154	154	154	154	154	154	154	154
obs_c	130	130	130	130	130	130	130	130	130	130	130	130

Notes: Weighted FGLS-SUR estimation. See footnotes of **Table 7–12** for a description of the variables.

Table A7.2 FGLS-SUR estimation of trade credits (with a global intercept)

	Gross borrowing			*Gross lending*			*Net borrowing*			*Days*		
	(1)	*(2)*	*(3)*	*(4)*	*(5)*	*(6)*	*(7)*	*(8)*	*(9)*	*(10)*	*(11)*	*(12)*
int	–0.001	–0.002	–0.001	0.001	0.001	0.001	0.001	0.001	0.001	0.19***	0.192***	0.196***
	(0.004)	(0.004)	(0.004)	(0.003)	(0.003)	(0.003)	(0.006)	(0.005)	(0.005)	(0.053)	(0.054)	(0.055)
int_s	0	0	–0.002	–0.001	0.001	0.002	–0.002	–0.004	–0.007	0.165	0.169	0.18*
	(0.004)	(0.004)	(0.004)	(0.005)	(0.005)	(0.005)	(0.007)	(0.007)	(0.008)	(0.13)	(0.133)	(0.137)
$sales_s$	0.104**	0.012	0.051	0.622***	0.561***	0.463**	–0.443**	–0.473*	–0.335	2.031	0.824	–0.248
	(0.051)	(0.089)	(0.082)	(0.201)	(0.218)	(0.225)	(0.235)	(0.289)	(0.29)	(2.905)	(3.358)	(3.611)
$manufact_s$	0.052*	0.067**	0.066**	–0.031	–0.044	–0.05	0.077	0.101	0.096	–1.128	–0.927	–0.827
	(0.034)	(0.032)	(0.031)	(0.121)	(0.116)	(0.115)	(0.129)	(0.125)	(0.125)	(1.086)	(1.154)	(1.19)
$distretail_s$	0.047*	0.062**	0.066***	0.027	0.018	–0.002	0	0.026	0.051	–1.392	–1.168	–1.183
	(0.029)	(0.029)	(0.028)	(0.115)	(0.112)	(0.113)	(0.121)	(0.118)	(0.121)	(1.384)	(1.309)	(1.326)
$national_s$	–0.058**	–0.068***	–0.072***	0.169***	0.177***	0.189***	–0.24***	–0.26***	–0.272***	0.852	0.78	0.61
	(0.025)	(0.027)	(0.027)	(0.064)	(0.061)	(0.061)	(0.076)	(0.075)	(0.074)	(1.094)	(1.143)	(1.176)
unq_s		–0.013	–0.013		0.043	0.041		–0.023	–0.032		–0.036	–0.091
		(0.03)	(0.028)		(0.089)	(0.088)		(0.106)	(0.103)		(1.45)	(1.406)
$rival_s$		0.127**	0.131***		–0.048	–0.034		0.172	0.164		0.837	1.107
		(0.058)	(0.054)		(0.131)	(0.125)		(0.203)	(0.188)		(1.328)	(1.272)
$length_s$		–0.002	–0.003**		0.009*	0.011**		–0.011**	–0.015**		0.027	0.047
		(0.001)	(0.001)		(0.006)	(0.006)		(0.007)	(0.007)		(0.082)	(0.09)
nat_s	0.039	0.099	0.101	0.203	0.173	0.092	–0.191	–0.091	–0.033	–3.295*	–3.123*	–4.055**
	(0.114)	(0.11)	(0.108)	(0.177)	(0.188)	(0.185)	(0.268)	(0.277)	(2.0267)	(2.057)	(1.913)	(2.406)
$qnat_s$	–0.077***	–0.081**	–0.064**	0.05	0.012	–0.011	–0.201	–0.171	–0.121	–1.612	–1.894	–2.623
	(0.028)	(0.038)	(0.037)	(0.169)	(0.177)	(0.161)	(0.191)	(0.21)	(0.186)	(2.056)	(2.136)	(2.081)
$spoffice_s$	0.031	0.018	0.012	–0.202**	–0.205**	–0.201**	0.183*	0.176	0.16	–1.272	–1.375	–1.559
	(0.025)	(0.031)	(0.034)	(0.1)	(0.107)	(0.106)	(0.124)	(0.138)	(0.138)	(1.521)	(1.547)	(1.601)
$tsales_s$	–0.049**	0.023	0.032	–0.309***	–0.32**	–0.211	0.101	0.195	0.057	–0.413	0.041	–2.862
	(0.027)	(0.049)	(0.06)	(0.129)	(0.138)	(0.178)	(0.167)	(0.2)	(0.224)	(1.351)	(1.504)	(2.626)

Table A7.2 FGLS-SUR estimation of trade credits (with a global intercept) – *continued*

	Gross borrowing			*Gross lending*			*Net borrowing*			*Days*		
	(1)	*(2)*	*(3)*	*(4)*	*(5)*	*(6)*	*(7)*	*(8)*	*(9)*	*(10)*	*(11)*	*(12)*
manuf_s	–0.045	–0.046*	–0.044	0.109	0.103	0.098	–0.149	–0.149	–0.143	–0.545	–0.479	–0.588
	(0.035)	(0.035)	(0.035)	(0.134)	(0.134)	(0.13)	(0.16)	(0.158)	(0.157)	(1.521)	(1.551)	(1.532)
$\mathit{tprofitA}_s$			0.132**			–0.443***			0.573***		-2.683	
			(0.072)			(0.174)			(0.197)			(4.769)
cashA_s			0.419*			–0.062			0.764			-5.281
			(0.271)		(0.641)		(0.803)		(9.422)			
liqLA_s		–0.06**		0.081		–0.167**		1.162				
		(0.028)			(0.073)			(0.088)			(1.176)	
totA_s			–0.026			–0.04			0.091			3.636*
			(0.049)		(0.245)		(0.279)		(2.49)			
out_s	0.042**	0.032*	0.031*	–0.093**	–0.072*	–0.067*	0.137**	0.105**	0.096*	–0.046	–0.047	–0.052
	(0.025)	(0.021)	(0.021)	(0.048)	(0.048)	(0.049)	(0.065)	(0.057)	(0.059)	(0.447)	(0.508)	(0.514)
proc_c	0.549***	0.685***	0.626***	0.165	0.169	0.185*	0.263	0.395*	0.34	–0.133	–0.068	–0.495
	(0.165)	(0.179)	(0.2)	(0.144)	(0.136)	(0.143)	(0.276)	(0.274)	(0.292)	(1.559)	(1.806)	(2.147)
$\mathit{manufact}_c$	0.005	0.03	0.031	0.059*	0.016	–0.008	–0.042	0.027	0.046	–0.167	0.015	0.062
	(0.083)	(0.084)	(0.09)	(0.037)	(0.043)	(0.044)	(0.102)	(0.109)	(0.119)	(0.658)	(0.674)	(0.714)
$\mathit{distretail}_c$	–0.128*	–0.102	–0.105	0.1*	0.057	0.043	–0.204*	–0.128	–0.121	–0.647	–0.432	–0.444
	(0.099)	(0.102)	(0.105)	(0.072)	(0.075)	(0.074)	(0.127)	(0.125)	(0.128)	(0.781)	(0.853)	(0.863)
$\mathit{national}_c$	–0.073	–0.113*	–0.129**	0.109**	0.147**	0.151**	–0.184**	–0.255**	–0.271**	–0.073	–0.256	–0.157
	(0.076)	(0.073)	(0.076)	(0.059)	(0.068)	(0.07)	(0.102)	(0.121)	(0.125)	(0.428)	(0.456)	(0.478)
rival_c		–0.144**	–0.118*		0.05	0.024		–0.187**	–0.142*		–0.449	–0.352
		(0.073)	(0.08)		(0.055)	(0.053)		(0.098)	(0.102)		(0.553)	(0.577)
length_c		0	0.003		–0.006**	–0.007**		0.006	0.009*		0.019	0.025
		(0.005)	(0.005)		(0.003)	(0.003)		(0.006)	(0.006)		(0.048)	(0.049)
nat_c	0.237	0.232	0.408***	–0.238**	–0.227**	–0.276**	0.45**	0.441**	0.674***	0.114	0.101	1.149
	(0.197)	(0.182)	(0.163)	(0.114)	(0.111)	(0.144)	(0.269)	(0.255)	(0.286)	(1.17)	(1.16)	(1.063)

Table A7.2 FGLS-SUR estimation of trade credits (with a global intercept) – *continued*

	Gross borrowing			*Gross lending*			*Net borrowing*			*Days*		
	(1)	*(2)*	*(3)*	*(4)*	*(5)*	*(6)*	*(7)*	*(8)*	*(9)*	*(10)*	*(11)*	*(12)*
nat_c	0.237	0.232	0.408***	–0.238**	–0.227**	–0.276**	0.45**	0.441**	0.674***	0.114	0.101	1.149
	(0.197)	(0.182)	(0.163)	(0.114)	(0.111)	(0.144)	(0.269)	(0.255)	(0.286)	(1.17)	(1.16)	(1.063)
$qnat_c$	0.285**	0.241*	0.252*	–0.17**	–0.155**	–0.206**	0.52**	0.464**	0.493**	–0.347	–0.459	–0.68
	(0.157)	(0.153)	(0.179)	(0.096)	(0.091)	(0.115)	(0.224)	(0.217)	(0.267)	(1.382)	(1.396)	(1.47)
$spoffice_c$	–0.215**	–0.235**	–0.245**	–0.041	–0.028	–0.027	–0.143	–0.177	–0.187	–0.792	–0.867	–0.928
	(0.115)	(0.112)	(0.109)	(0.076)	(0.07)	(0.069)	(0.173)	(0.163)	(0.157)	(0.897)	(0.906)	(0.911)
$tsales_c$	0.228	0.199	0.058	–0.199*	–0.071	–0.019	0.578*	0.397	0.179	1.128	0.643	1.652
	(0.339)	(0.352)	(0.387)	(0.137)	(0.127)	(0.171)	(0.38)	(0.395)	(0.475)	(2.299)	(2.611)	(3.145)
$manuf_c$	0.179*	0.177*	0.187**	–0.089	–0.081	–0.089	0.273*	0.262*	0.275**	1.308*	1.294	1.275
	(0.116)	(0.107)	(0.108)	(0.085)	(0.083)	(0.078)	(0.172)	(0.163)	(0.159)	(1.015)	(1.041)	(1.035)
$tprofitA_c$			0.567***			0.125			0.447*			1.451
			(0.164)			(0.17)			(0.293)			(1.45)
$cashA_c$			–1.286**			1.144**			–2.385**			–6.492
			(0.625)			(0.684)			(1.206)			(7.74)
$liqLA_c$			0.129			–0.055			0.192			1.213
			(0.104)			(0.089)			(0.158)			(0.99)
$totA_c$			0.067			–0.028			0.087			–0.598
			(0.072)			(0.066)			(0.126)			(0.657)
out_c	–0.011	0.018	0.011	–0.002	–0.02	–0.015	–0.01	0.034	0.023	0.388	0.494*	0.457
	(0.044)	(0.05)	(0.049)	(0.03)	(0.032)	(0.032)	(0.055)	(0.061)	(0.059)	(0.338)	(0.363)	(0.372)
$corr_u$	0.538	0.624	0.9	0.943	0.504	0.611	0.895	0.944	0.484	0.587	0.864	0.938
obs_s	154	154	154	154	154	154	154	154	154	154	154	154
obs_c	130	130	130	130	130	130	130	130	130	130	130	130

Notes: FGLS-SUR estimation with a global intercept. See footnotes of Table 7.12 for a description of the variables.

8

Determinants of Debt, Bank Loans, and Trade Credit of Private Firms in the Transition Period: The Case of Myanmar

Fumiharu Mieno

8.1 Introduction

This chapter examines the fund-raising behaviors of firms under a primitive financial system during the initial stages of a transition economy. Specific attention is given to the case of the Myanmar economy in the late 1990s.

In a transition economy, financial development processes generally coincide with the growth of real sectors. In the macroeconomic dimension, the separation of fiscal and financial sectors is a key policy issue. At the center of policy disputes are issues involving imputation of the government and state-owned enterprise debt. The role of the new state banks in financing the government sector is also a major concern. In the microeconomic dimension, the financial sector expands rapidly in term of deposits and financial assets with the new entry of private banks and this is reflected in the growth of real sectors. However, the function of the financial system on the supply side develops more slowly than the growth of deposits. It takes some time for newly emerged financial institutions to accumulate the information and know-how to develop credit successfully. Immature legal systems also cause malfunctions in loan transactions. Consequently, in the early stages of a transition economy, the gap between the growth of the financial assets in banks and intermediation with the real sector persists and expands.

Under such financial situations, entrepreneurs seek to raise funds in the most advantageous fashion using choices such as the following: (i) self-financing; (ii) bank borrowing; and (iii) informal borrowing. Previous studies show that under such primitive financial systems, trade credit may play a significant role. McMillan and Woodruff (1999) recently observed the state of trade credit transactions in Vietnam. They concluded that trade credit played a significant role in firms' fund raising and was determined by various factors, including the social and business network among entrepreneurs. In this volume, Ito (Chapter 7) examines the determinants of trade credit in mainland China, focusing primarily on the role of state-owned enterprises. In contrast to these studies, the focus of this chapter is on characteristics of behaviors in more backward transition economies where firms are in their infancy, and the function of banks is marginal. The relationship between trade credit and other fund sources, such as debt in general and bank borrowing, is also of concern.

The structure of this chapter is as follows. Section 8.2 includes a brief overview of the development of Myanmar's financial system in the 1990s. An explanation of data is provided in section 8.3. Section 8.4 includes descriptive statistics regarding the fund raising of firms. An empirical analysis of the determinants of debt financing, bank borrowing, and trade credit is presented in section 8.5. Concluding observations and remarks are to be found in section 8.6.

8.2 Development of the economy and the financial system in Myanmar

Since economic reforms were first implemented under the military regime (see Table 8.1), the Myanmar economy has experienced an average annual growth rate of real GDP of around 6.5 per cent (1994 to 1998).[1] In the early 1990s the military authority implemented wholesale economic reforms based on the liberalization of foreign trade and an increase in the inflow of capital. Fiscal reforms as well as the privatization of state-owned enterprises and financial institutions were also instituted.

Since these reforms, the private sector has seen an accelerated growth in the level of capital inflows and the growth of the domestic sector.[2] In the banking sector, government banks have been reorganized from a mono-bank system to several independent policy-based banks. Private banks were also admitted. From 1992 to 1997, twenty private banks were established and started taking on business. As Table 8.2 indicates, private banks have been growing rapidly. The annual growth rates of total assets and deposits are on average 155.1 per cent and 195.5 per cent respectively during the period 1993–1999. Although loans on the asset side have also grown, the rate is much lower than

Table 8.1 Major macroeconomic indicators

	1994/95	*1995/96*	*1996/97*	*1997/98*	*1998/99*	*1999/00*
Real GDP growth (%)	7.5	6.9	6.4	5.7	5.8	10.9
Fiscal deficit (million Kyat)	–30,807.2	–40,082.6	–52,398.2	–58,524.9	–94,162.4	–110,700.7
Fiscal deficit (rate of GDP) (%)	–6.5	–6.6	–6.6	–5.2	–5.8	–5.1
Issues of Treasury Bonds (million Kyat)	54.7	872.4	2,390.5	4,213.5	25,653.1	42,195.5
CPI growth rate (annual average) (%)	24.1	25.2	16.3	33.1	30.1	15.6

Source: Calculated by author from *Statistical Yearbook (2002)* (Central Statistical Organization, 2002) and other sources.

Note: CPI growth rate is compared with previous years, others are of fiscal year (April to March).

Table 8.2 Main items of private bank balance sheets

	1994/95	*1995/96*	*1996/97*	*1997/98*	*1998/99*	*1999/00*	*2000/01*	*2001/02*
Total assets (Million Kyat)	6,676	20,231	48,966	85,062	139,849	230,588	384,101	597,174
Assets								
Loan and advances (%)	52.7	48.0	53.6	59.4	43.5	42.1	41.6	51.8
Security investment (%)	0.5	1.1	3.7	2.3	14.2	0.4	0.4	0.3
Treasury bonds (%)	0.6	2.4	2.3	5.2	6.6	25.6	26.3	17.9
Liabilities								
Deposits (%)	72.5	77.6	75.6	68.4	79.2	80.7	84.5	81.6
Capital Account (%)	12.6	7.6	9.7	8.7	6.4	5.8	5.0	4.6
Growth rate of total Assets (%)	178.2	203.0	142.0	73.7	64.4	64.9	66.6	55.5
Growth of deposits (%)	206.8	224.5	135.7	57.1	90.5	68.0	74.3	50.1
Growth of loans (%)	171.7	176.4	169.8	92.5	20.6	59.5	64.6	93.7
Growth of Treasury bonds (%)	2.6	1137.5	129.4	292.3	107.2	540.4	71.0	5.9

Source: *Statistical Yearbook 2000, 2002* (Central Statistical Organization), p. 315.

that of deposits. This is reflected in two factors: First, the high inflation rate (an average of 24.1 per cent in the period 1994–1999) and interest rate ceilings made real interest rates negative; hence, the loan business was not very profitable, and this probably discouraged private banks from expanding their loan activities. Secondly, it was not easy for newly emerging banks to find new and eligible customers as fast as they could gain depositors; it took considerable time to acquire the information necessary for credit transactions.

It is worth noting that the growth gap between the increase of deposits and credits have been balanced by holding treasury bonds, particularly after 1999. The fiscal deficit seemed to worsen, and the balance of treasury bonds increased after 1998. A substantial part of the resources mobilized from households by banks was directed to financing the fiscal deficit.[3]

Another characteristic of the private banking sector is the fact that most major banks are established and formed by major business groups engaging in the "real" sectors of the economy, particularly in the export of primary sector products and in non-manufacturing sectors such as construction or real estate. For example, Yoma Bank (established in 1993) is a 100 per cent subsidiary of First Myanmar Investment (FMI), one of the largest holding companies in Myanmar. It is dominated by one Myanmar Chinese family, and business has been developed primarily in the non-manufacturing sector, with over 40 subsidiaries and affiliates. Similarly, Asia Wealth Bank, the largest bank in Myanmar in 1999, was established in 1994 under the initiative of the Olympic group, one of the largest construction conglomerate groups (it controls 15 firms engaged in export and construction; see Wang, 2004). These facts suggest that the financial function of private banks on the credit side may be biased toward these banks' group firms or internal markets.[4]

8.3 Data

In any consideration of the financial system in Myanmar, the corporate financial structure of private firms may be examined using micro data. Though Myanmar can be classified as a transition economy, the role of state-owned enterprises is becoming increasingly limited. This survey was thus designed to focus on privately owned firms. Data used in this study include firm profiles, balance sheets, various financial situations, and the characteristics of owners. The data cover 167 small and medium-sized firms in the manufacturing, trade, and service sectors.

Data were collected using a survey administered by a private information company at Yangon during a period from October to December 2003. Industries were classified into export, manufacturing and service sectors, and 10 sub-sectors. For each sub-sector, several firms were selected. Administrators visited the head offices of firms that accepted invitations to be included in the survey. Managers were then interviewed using the prepared survey instrument.

Only 89 of the 167 firms in the sample had data available for balance sheets, financing for investments, and sources of working capital. In addition, some large firms that hold private banks and belong to major business groups such as FMI or the Olympic group were excluded from the analysis. This was due primarily to the design and sample selection. Thus, analysis is restricted to those firms which do not have special relationships with private banks.

8.4 Descriptive observation

8.4.1 Debt ratio and bank borrowing

8.4.1.1 Balance sheet

The basic features of fund raising may be checked with three different types of indices. First, Table 8.3 shows the capital structure of all sampled firms classified by sector and size. Balance sheet data cover the years 1999 through 2001, and values in the table indicate an average for the three years. For all firms, the average debt ratio is 15.9 per cent. This ratio consists mainly of bank borrowing (6.0 per cent), accounts payable (4.1 per cent), and other liabilities (3.0 per cent). The debt ratio is surprisingly low; this implies that firms in the sample primarily depend upon self-financing. Only 33 of the 89 sampled firms (37 per cent) utilize bank loans as a tool for fund raising.

Comparing by sectors, debt financing is relatively higher in the exports sector (a debt ratio of 21.5 per cent and bank borrowing of 11.1 per cent), and lower in manufacturing (13.7 per cent, 4.7 per cent). On the sub-sector level, debt financing seems most active for agriculture (24.6 per cent in exports of agricultural products, 26.0 per cent in livestock, and 20 per cent in manufacturing of agricultural products).

There does not seem to be a linear relation between the size of a firm and its debt financing. Based on assets, firms were classified into three groups: large (over 10 million Kyat), medium-sized (1–10 million Kyat), and small (under 1 million Kyat). A comparison shows that medium-sized firms are most dependent on debt financing; large and small firms appear equally dependent on debt. Larger firms seem to be located quite distant from the bank loan market.

Table 8.3 Capital structure of sample firms

	All	*Size*				*Export*		
	Sample	*Large*	*Medium*	*Small*	*Total*	*Textile*	*Agric. Product*	*Livestock*
No. of Sample	89	11	48	30	12	5	5	2
Debt Ratio	15.9	10.3	18.6	13.8	21.5	16.7	24.6	26.0
L1 Deferred Payment, Note Payable	4.1	1.8	4.0	5.2	3.9	4.9	1.4	7.6
L2 Bank Borrowing	6.0	5.6	8.1	2.7	11.1	5.1	17.0	11.5
No. of Firms Borrowing	33	4	11	4	8	2	4	2
Rate of Firms Borrowing	37.1	36.4	22.9	13.3	66.7	40.0	80.0	100.0
L3 Borrowing from Affiliation	0.8	1.0	0.6	1.0	1.8	2.7	0.0	4.3
L4 Borrowing from Owners and Managers	0.9	0.0	1.2	0.6	2.3	1.3	4.3	0.0
L5 Borrowing from Others	1.2	0.2	1.2	1.5	0.3	0.0	0.3	1.1
L6 Other Liabilities	3.0	1.7	3.4	2.8	2.1	2.7	1.7	1.5
Capital Account	83.1	87.5	80.1	86.2	78.5	83.3	75.4	74.0
C1 Paid up Capital	37.2	46.7	35.5	36.5	42.2	52.1	32.3	42.5
C2 Retained Earrings	27.8	31.3	24.3	32.0	25.6	20.6	28.1	31.5
C3 Capital Surplus and Others	18.1	9.4	20.3	17.7	10.7	10.6	15.0	0.0

Table 8.3 Capital structure of sample firms – *continued*

	Manufacturing				*Service*				
	Total	*Agric. products*	*Industries*	*Consumer products*	*Total*	*Service general*	*Construc-tion*	*Consumer service*	*Retail distributor*
No. of Sample	47	3	33	11	30	6	7	8	9
Debt Ratio	13.7	20.0	10.9	14.1	17.2	7.4	13.8	13.7	29.6
L1 Deferred Payment, Note Payable	3.2	0.0	4.0	3.2	5.7	4.3	5.0	1.6	10.9
L2 Bank Borrowing	4.7	16.7	3.0	4.2	6.0	0.0	2.5	8.6	10.4
No. of Firms Borrowing	16	1	13	2	9	0	3	3	3
Rate of Firms Borrowing	34.0	33.3	39.4	18.2	30.0	0.0	42.9	37.5	33.3
L3 Borrowing from Affiliation	0.6	0.0	0.0	0.8	0.7	0.0	0.8	1.2	0.7
L4 Borrowing from Owners and Managers	0.5	0.0	0.8	0.4	0.8	0.0	2.7	0.8	0.0
L5 Borrowing from Others	1.5	3.3	1.6	1.3	1.0	0.4	0.7	0.8	1.9
L6 Other Liabilities	3.3	0.0	1.5	4.2	2.9	2.7	2.1	0.8	5.7
Capital Account	85.8	79.9	86.8	86.0	80.7	92.6	86.2	86.3	63.4
C1 Paid up Capital	41.4	30.6	46.3	40.7	28.8	23.1	45.2	31.2	17.6
C2 Retained Earrings	26.4	19.3	25.7	27.3	30.8	49.1	22.5	25.0	30.3
C3 Capital Surplus and Others	18.0	30.1	14.8	18.0	21.1	20.4	18.6	30.1	15.5

The figures present the percentage. In case of "No. of Firms Borrowing," the figures are number of firms

Note: In some cases total sum is not 100 per cent due to the inconsistency of original data

Source: Author.

Table 8.4 Fund raising for capital

		By sector		
	All	*Export*	*Manufacturing*	*Service*
No. of firms	89	16	44	29
Borrowing from government bank (%)	1.9	0.0	2.1	2.2
Borrowing from private bank (%)	6.4	11.9	8.5	0.8
Borrowing from others (%)	2.2	0.0	3.0	1.7
Self-financing and support from family and relatives (%)	80.3	84.8	81.5	76.7
Others (%)	9.3	3.3	4.9	18.7

		By previous job		
	Government	*SOE*	*Trader*	*Family business*
No. of firms	7	6	26	37
Borrowing from government bank (%)	7.1	3.3	0.0	1.8
Borrowing from private bank (%)	5.5	0.0	11.0	6.5
Borrowing from others (%)	0.0	8.3	1.9	2.5
Self-financing and support from family and relatives (%)	87.4	53.9	78.3	80.5
Others (%)	0.0	34.5	8.8	8.7

Source: Author.

8.4.1.2 Financing initial capital

Table 8.4 indicates the methods used for financing initial capital at a given establishment. Somewhat similar to the observations regarding balance sheets, self-financing and financing from family and relatives appear to be the overwhelming factors, amounting to 80.3 per cent of the total. Sampled establishments appear to rely on bank borrowing only at a rate of 8.3 per cent on average. In the service sector, the level of bank borrowing is particularly low.

A possible relationship between financing and the founders' previous occupation can also be observed. Government servants appear to have greater access to loans from government banks, but the officers of state-owned enterprises seem to rely more heavily on equities. To a relatively high degree, traders and independent owners depend upon private bank loans.

8.4.1.3 Fund mobilization for investment and working capital

Table 8.5 shows the methods of fund raising for investment in equipment and working capital. For the five surveyed years, 28 out of 89 sampled firms have implemented investment in equipment, but bank loans have been used in only nine cases. In all cases, loan types have been those of transaction rather than syndicate. According to the table, the share of bank loans is substantially high, amounting to 22.8 per cent. Shares appear to be moderately higher in the export and service sectors while lower in manufacturing. However, this trend is ambiguous due to the small sample size. On working capital, only 32 of the 89 firms borrow from banks, and the share of bank loans used for fund raising is, on average, 13.5 per cent in total.[5] Similar to investment in equipment, the share appears to be higher in the export sector.

The financial intermediation of banks seems to function well in supplying working capital to the trade (export) sector, which is the most traditional form of banking activity. It also seems to offer partial support for investment in equipment. Bank loan transactions are more active in the export and service sectors, and less active in the manufacturing sector.

8.4.2 Trade credit

As was seen in the balance sheet data, firms in the sample rely primarily on self-financing. Bank loans and deferred payments (trade credit) comprise the largest components in small firm debt finance. Since its share is almost the same as that of bank loans, trade credit in a sense plays a substantial role in the fund mobilization of firms, particularly in sales and procurement transactions. This subsection focuses on the features and background of trade credit.

Table 8.5 Method of fund raising for equipment investment and working capital

(a) Equipment investment

	All	*Export*	*Manufacturing*	*Service*
	28	4	18	6
Self-financing: investment from affiliates	8.9	0.0	13.9	0.0
Self-financing: investment from owner	60.2	52.8	62.5	58.3
Bank borrowing	22.8	33.3	14.2	41.7
Family, relative and friend	0.0	0.0	0.0	0.0
Others	8.1	13.9	9.4	0.0

Note: Calculated from the 28 firms which implemented equipment investment at late five years. Bank borrowing is positive in 9 firms.

(b) Working capital

	All	*Export*	*Manufacturing*	*Service*
	89	12	47	30
Self-financing	78.1	63.6	82.8	76.7
Bank borrowing	13.5	29.2	12.3	9.2
Family, relative and friend	4.2	2.5	2.8	7.2
Foreign counterpart	0.0	0.0	0.0	0.0
Others	3.7	4.8	2.1	5.7

Note: Bank borrowing is positive in 32 firms.

Source: Author.

8.4.2.1 Market environment of sales and procurements

The available sample of firms for data regarding sales/procurements transactions was 133, which was larger than that used for the balance sheet or other financial data. We will first consider market environments, which are closely related to trade credit. Table 8.6 shows the share of the largest customer of each firm. About half of the total (61 firms) face a competitive environment where the top share is under 25 per cent, whereas 8 firms face an oligopsonistic situation. In the group of large firms, none faces oligopsony, and the manufacturing sector appears in the more competitive environment. According to answers given on questions related to the market environment, about one half of the firms surveyed face tough competitors, and they consider

Table 8.6 Distribution of samples on product transaction

(a) Share of the largest customer

	Under 25%	*25–50%*	*50–75%*	*Over 75%*
by size				
Large	10	3	2	0
Medium	32	19	17	4
Small	19	14	8	4
by sector				
Export	3	5	6	2
Manufacturing	41	17	15	1
Service	17	14	6	5
Total	61	36	27	8

(b) Market condition

No significant competitors	11
Several competitors	62
Many competitors	45
Foreign-invested competitors	6
Imported goods as main competitors	6
Total	130

(c) Price setting

Price is set by firms (seller)	65
Price is set by customers (buyer)	20
Price is set by competitive condition	23
Depend on situation	21
Depend on exchange rate	1
Depend on the price of input	2
Total	132

Source: Author.

themselves to be price takers. The other half consider themselves to be price setters. However, there does not seem to be a correlation between the situation of price setting and the share of the largest customer.

8.4.2.2 Transactions with deferred payments

Table 8.7 shows the situation of sampled firms relative to acceptation of deferred payments in sales. The total average rate of deferred payments in the available 106 firms is 56.8 per cent. About 20 per cent of the sampled firms settle transactions solely with deferred payments; four firms settle transactions using only cash. Bargaining power seems to be independent of the rate of deferred payments.

According to answers given in the survey, firms weigh various factors, such as the track record and reputation of owners/managers, in deciding whether or not to accept deferred payments (supplying the credit). Personal relationships and profitability have secondary propriety in this decision. The factor of location seems to be unimportant.

Substantial numbers of the sampled firms (16 out of 98) have defaulted in the collection process of deferred payments. The average frequency of default in 16 firms is 3.1 times, and the table indicates that there may be a positive correlation between the share of the largest customers and the default frequency. The most common reaction to a customer that defaults is to terminate sales; very few firms resort the legal action. What is strikingly different compared with the

Table 8.7(a) Share of deferred payments in total transactions

			No. of Firms		
	Average	*Standard Deviation*	*Only Deferred*	*Only Cash*	*Total*
By sector					
Export	69.5	38.3	5	1	10
Manufacturing	53.3	29.4	11	2	62
Service	59.4	25.8	7	1	34
By the sales share of the largest customer					
Under 25%	53.6	30.6	9	0	52
25–50%	62.6	28.4	9	0	27
50–75	56.5	27.6	4	0	20
Over 75%	58.4	31.6	1	4	7
Total	56.8	29.4	23	4	106

Table 8.7(b) Main concern on decision of acceptance of deferred payments

Experience of the transaction	50
Reputation and characteristics of the customers	44
Profitability	22
Personal relationship	34
Location	2
The way for payment	5
Others	3

Table 8.7(c) Frequency of default

	Average	*No. of firms*
By the share of deferred payments		
Under 25%	2.10	10
25–50%	2.17	6
50–75%	3.69	36
Over 75%	2.75	20
By sector		
Export	1.75	4
Manufacturing	3.86	37
Service	3.60	20
By the vintage of firms		
Over 10 years	3.94	35
Over 5 years	3.69	16
Over 2 years	2.56	9
Under 2 years	2.00	1
Total	3.08	72

Table 8.7(d) Reaction to default

Termination of transaction	54
Personal negotiation	16
Suit in the court	1
No way	13

Source: Author.

case of China presented by Yanagawa in Chapter 5 of this volume is that lawsuits are very rare. The function of law in Myanmar seems to be very limited, and many firms indicate that they have no way to cope with default.

8.4.2.3 Deferred payments against the largest trade counterpart

Table 8.8 includes aggregated figures for the situation of deferred payments for each of the largest customers. As with the data shown in Table 8.7, deferred payments represent around half of total transactions. About 20 per cent of sampled firms use only deferred payments as a method of settlement, and about 12 per cent of the sampled firms only use cash for settlements.

According to Table 8.9, 81 out of 98 firms set the same cost for deferred payments as for cash settlements. This means that in most

Table 8.8 Share of deferred payments in total transactions with the largest customer

			No. of firms		
	Average	*Standard deviation*	*Only deferred payments*	*Only cash*	*Total*
Export	51.0	46.1	4	3	10
Manufacturing	46.4	30.5	7	8	62
Service	62.1	29.8	9	1	31
Total	51.6	32.5	21	12	103

Source: Author.

Table 8.9 "Interest rate" in trade credits with the largest customer

	All firms		*Firms with a price difference*	
	Average (%)	*No. of Firms*	*Average (%)*	*No. of Firms*
Export	0.00	10		
Manufacturing	0.82	57	4.51	12
Service	0.67	31	4.12	5
Total	0.69	98	4.40	17
By frequency of default	*Average (%)*	*No. of Firms*		
None	0.7	82		
Once	0.0	2		
Twice	0.0	3		
Three times	1.2	6		
Over four times	2.0	5		

Source: Author.

cases, the "interest rate" for trade credit is zero. Observing the difference between the cost of cash settlements and deferred payments in the remaining 17 cases, the average annual "interest rate" is 4.4 per cent. It appears that there is no linear relationship between the "interest rate" and the frequency of default. However, the "interest rate" for customers that have defaulted more than three times in the past seems larger than the average.

Table 8.10 Share of deferred payments in total transaction with the largest traders procurement

(a) Share of deferred payments in total transactions

	Average	*Standard deviation*	*No. of firms* Only deferred payments	*Only cash*	*Total*
Export	28.6	39.3	1	4	7
Manufacturing	32.9	36.2	10	32	70
Service	22.4	31.5	3	21	38
Total	29.3	35.0	14	57	115

(b) "Interest rate" in trade credit

	All firms		*Firms with a price difference*	
	Average (%)	*No. of Firms*	*Average (%)*	*No. of Firms*
Export	0.00	7		
Manufacturing	0.32	70	5.58	4
Service	2.15	38	20.47	4
Total	0.91	115	13.03	8

By frequency of default	*Average (%)*	*No. of Firms*
Once	3.2	20
Twice	0.0	3
Three times	0.0	2
Over four times	5.3	1

Source: Author.

Another aspect of trade credit via deferred payments may be seen in the procurement process of the sampled firms. Table 8.10 summarizes the situation of payments in this process. The percentage of deferred payments is only 29.3 per cent, and 57 of the 115 available firms indicated that they pay only in cash. Firms appear to see themselves making primarily cash-based settlements in their own payments. For 51 of the 58 firms that accept deferred payments, there is no difference between the cost for cash and the cost for deferred payments. Using the same calculations as in case of sales, the average "interest rate" in seven firms is 13.0 per cent. The "interest rate" for procurements seems substantially higher than in the case of sales.

Although a clear conclusion cannot be made because of the small sample size, information was obtained on the function of trade credits in the severe environments of financial markets where bank loans rarely function. First, in contrast to bank borrowings which are biased toward only a small number of firms in the financial market, it can be seen that trade credits in the form of deferred payments are used widely as a method of fund raising. The trade credit appears to play a complementary role to the incomplete bank loan transaction.

Secondly, in most cases trade credits are supplied free of interest. Even in cases where the interest is not zero, levels are negligible. Third, defaults in transactions involving trade credits occur frequently. In an environment that lacks enforcement, firms deciding whether or not to supply the trade credits evaluate customers on the basis of their track record of transactions and personal relationships. They deal with defaults mainly through threatening termination.

8.5 Estimation of the determinants of debt, bank loans, and trade finance

This section examines the determinants of the methods used by firms for fund mobilization. First, we estimate the determinants of the capital structure of a firm's debt ratio and bank borrowing. The analysis then proceeds to consider the determinants of trade credit in the form of deferred payments both by indices of the capital structure and by share in transactions with the largest traders.

8.5.1 Determinants of the capital structure

8.5.1.1 Model and variables

A standardized estimation method is used for the determination of a debt ratio (total liabilities over total assets) and a bank borrowing ratio (bank borrowings over total assets, L2 in Table 8.3), considering the agency cost of external finance. Tittman and Wessels (1988 and subsequent years) reveal that the agency cost of each external financial method is the major cause for the differences found in capital structures. Many studies, such as those of Suto (2003) Lee *et al.* (1999) and Mieno (2006), indicate that such a view is also applicable to developing countries in East Asia such as Malaysia, Korea, and Thailand.

The estimation model is as follows:

$$y_i = c + \alpha_1 X_{1i} + \alpha_2 X_{2i} + \alpha_3 X_{3i} + \alpha_3 X_4 + u_k \; (i = 1,2,\ldots n)$$

where c is a constant, u is an error term, and n is the sample size.

Explanatory variables are as follows:

X_1: vector of control variables
ASSET: total assets
RETEAR: retained earnings
Risk: proxy of risk factor

X_2: vector of the variables related to characteristics of firms
INVE: the attitude for equipment investments
VINTAGE: vintage (age) of the firm

X_3: the vector of the variables related to characteristics of owner and manager
BR: the relationship with banks: (BR is 1 if some owners or managers participate in the management or equity holding of banks at the same time, zero otherwise.)
NOCM: Number of firms in the possession of the owner of the sampled firm (proxy of diversification and size of the owners' business).
OWNER1-4: dummy variables for the owners' previous job including (1) government servants (2) staff of state enterprises (3) traders, and (4) staff of private firms, respectively.

X_4: An industrial dummy variable for 10 sub-sectors

X_1 was adopted because previous studies indicate that there is a positive correlation between firm size and debt ratio. In these studies, total assets were employed as the index of firm size. The availability of self-finance or cash flow is a basic factor for the debt ratio. It is well known that using cash flow or profit ratio as a proxy is the most appropriate index of self-financing. However, neither index is available for analysis here, so retained earnings from the balance sheet was adopted for this study. For the risk factor (known to be a negative factor for debt rates), a modified score value was used based on the answers to a question relative to future prospects of the business: 0 for "getting worse," 1 for "no change," and 2 for "improving." Although the effect of taxes is an important factor for capital structure, relevant data were not available.

Variables on X_2 were selected as follows: One of the most basic factors for a firm's demand of funds is the source for investment in equipment. Investment behavior can influence capital structure. The index score for investment behavior was prepared in qualitative form. The score is based on answers to a question regarding future investment schedules as follows: 2 for "scheduling the new investment," 1 for "unfixed," and 0 for "no plan." Focus is placed on the age of firms. It appears that substantial time is required for firms and banks to establish a stable relationship on loan transactions. Mutual reliance and the accumulation of information seem to be formed through a trial and error process starting with the initial staged transaction.

On X_3, each variable is selected as follows: As mentioned earlier, most existing firms were founded after the economic reforms in the early 1990s. Survey data indicate that the ownership and managerial structures of firms remain underdeveloped. In expanding or diversifying the business, entrepreneurs often establish new firms. It is often the case that entrepreneurs run multiple firms that are related to the same business as a response to complicated and ambiguous government regulations. In addition, entrepreneurs often organize joint ventures and coordinate investments through business networks centered on business communities such as the federation of commerce.

In order to capture such factors, explanatory variables related to the qualitative characteristics of owners and managers are introduced as follows: (i) a dummy variable of owner and manager involvement in the banking business in form of equity holding or managing; (ii) the number of firms owned by the owners of the sampled firms (this can be understood as a proxy for the real size of business and/or the affluence of cash flow for owners); and (iii) dummy variables related to the previous jobs of owners before establishing the firms. This final variable is introduced because of a lack of financial skills in the business network due to their work experience in government and private sectors.

Industrial dummy variables for 10 sub-sectors are also introduced. It is well known that differences in industries can explain the difference in the degree of information asymmetry and other factors related to capital structure.

8.5.1.2 Estimation method

It has been noted that among the 89 sample firms, the debt ratio of 27 and the bank borrowing of 33 are non-positive. For such features of the dependent variables, three types of estimation methods are employed: Ordinal Least Squares, the Tobit model and the Probit model.

The Tobit model is an estimation method designed for observations where some aspects of dependent variables below a particular level are unobservable. Parameters are calculated using the Most Likelihood Estimation. The model is as follows:

$$y_i^* = x_i\beta + u_i$$

$$y_i = \begin{cases} y_i^* & if\, y_i^* > 0 \\ 0 & if\, y_i^* < 0 \end{cases}$$

where x_i is the vector of independent variables (including the constant), and β is a parameter of these variables.

Logarithmic likelihood functions are the sum of the probabilities of $y_i = 0$ and $y_i = y_i^*$ expressed as follows:

$$\ln L = \sum_{i\in(y_i=0)} \ln\Phi\left(\frac{-x_i\beta}{\sigma}\right) + \sum_{i\in(y=y^*)} \left\{\ln\Phi\left(y_i - \frac{-x_i\beta}{\sigma}\right) - \ln\sigma\right\}$$

On the other hand, the Probit model is a method for estimation where dependent variables are limited to a qualitative form – zero or one. The model is as follows:

$$y_i = x_i\beta + u_i$$

$$y_i = \begin{cases} 1 & if\, y_i^* > 0 \\ 0 & if\, y_i^* = 0 \end{cases}$$

The probability for $y_i = 1$ is $P_i = F\left(\sum_{k=1}^{K} x_i\beta\right)$, and the likelihood functions can be formulated as $L = \prod_{y_i=1} P_i \prod_{y_i=0} (1 - P_i)$. In the Probit model, F is assumed to be normally distribution for the estimation process.

The Tobit and Probit models can give better results in estimations where the dependent variable of a large part of the sample is zero. On the other hand, the difference between the Tobit and Probit estimations is noteworthy. Parameters from the Tobit estimation show the effect of independent variables of non-zero samples on the levels of the dependent variables. The Tobit model cannot adequately capture the difference if the independent variables are determinants of a state that is positive instead of zero. Conversely, the Probit model evaluates only the difference between zero and a positive state and ignores information on the degree of change within the positive zone. It is more suitable for capturing the initial and marginal insulation from zero to positive.

8.5.1.3 Estimation result

Results for estimations of the debt and bank borrowing ratios are summarized in Tables 8.11 and 8.12. In several of these estimations, some industrial dummy variables are omitted because of a lack of conver-

Table 8.11 Estimation results of the debt ratio

	Tobit model		*Probit model*		*OLS*	
Parameter	*Estimate*	*t-statistic*	*Estimate*	*t-statistic*	*Estimate*	*t-statistic*
C	56.380	4.871 [.000]	2.658	3.058 [.002]	43.200	4.641 [.000]
ASSET	–0.835	–0.203 [.839]	0.000	0.570 [.569]	0.000	–0.407 [.685]
RETEAR	–0.422	–3.374 [.001]	–0.013	–1.261 [.207]	–0.252	–2.618 [.011]
RISK	–0.397	–0.147 [.883]	–0.281	–1.200 [.230]	1.239	0.555 [.581]
Characteristics of firm						
INVSCHA	3.583	0.593 [.553]	1.102	2.376 [.017]	4.561	0.908 [.367]
VINTAGE	–0.472	–1.888 [.059]	–0.041	–1.649 [.099]	–0.269	–1.364 [.177]
Characteristics of Owner						
BR	12.184	1.883 [.060]	1.268	2.009 [.045]	8.815	1.683 [.097]
NOCOM	–9.185	–3.254 [.001]	–0.568	–2.346 [.019]	–5.736	–2.527 [.014]
OWNER 1	–15.542	–1.839 [.066]	–0.435	–0.681 [.496]	–11.031	–1.563 [.123]
OWNER 2	–42.087	–2.930 [.003]			–17.923	–2.271 [.026]
OWNER 3	–8.590	–1.544 [.123]	0.273	0.569 [.569]	–7.162	–1.520 [.133]
OWNER 4	–8.686	–1.427 [.153]	0.189	0.369 [.712]	–7.024	–1.360 [.178]
Adj–R				0.288		0.217

Note: The figures in parentheses present P-values of coefficients.
C: constant term, ASSET: total assets, RETEAR: retained earnings, RISK: index of risk, INVSCHA: attitude of equipment investment, VINTAGE: Vintage (Age) of the Firm, BR: index of participant of banking business, NOCOM: No. of firms owned by the sample firm's owner. OWNER: owner's previous job: (1) government servant, (2) staff of state owned enterprise, (3) trader, (4) staff of private company

Source: Author.

Table 8.12 Estimation results of bank borrowing

	Tobit model		*Probit model*		*OLS*	
Parameter	*Estimate*	*t-statistic*	*Estimate*	*t-statistic*	*Estimate*	*t-statistic*
C	–24.792	–1.068	–1.251	–1.422	10.293	2.004
		[.286]		[.155]		[.049]
ASSET	0.000	0.357	0.000	0.874	0.000	0.189
		[.721]		[.382]		[.851]
RETEAR	–0.588	–2.154	–0.021	–1.977	–0.148	–2.469
		[.031]		[.048]		[.016]
RISK	–2.403	–0.400	–0.134	–0.568	0.325	0.222
		[.089]		[.570]		[.825]
Characteristics of firm						
INVSCHA	31.600	2.014	1.110	1.810	5.083	1.639
		[.044]		[.070]		[.105]
VINTAGE	0.519	1.075	0.020	1.028	0.107	0.872
		[.282]		[.304]		[.386]
Characteristics of owner						
BR	0.545	0.043	0.018	0.037	–0.727	–0.225
		[.966]		[.970]		[.823]
NOCOM	6.100	1.080	0.386	1.710	–0.200	–0.141
		[.280]		[.087]		[.888]
OWNER 1	–7.748	–0.519	0.149	0.249	–7.141	–1.603
		[.604]		[.804]		[.113]
OWNER2					–5.355	–1.046
			[.299]			
OWNER3	–22.096	–1.843	–0.867	–1.867	–6.877	–2.283
		[.065]		[.062]		[.025]
OWNER4	–28.993	–1.884	–1.162	–1.909	–7.216	–2.204
		[.060]		[.056]		[.031]
Adj–R				0.337		0.189

Note: The figures in parentheses present P-values of coefficients.
C: constant term, ASSET: total assets, RETEAR: retained earnings, RISK: index of risk, INVSCHA: attitude of equipment investment, VINTAGE: Vintage (Age) of the Firm, BR: index of participant of banking business, NOCOM: No. of firms owned by the sample firm's owner. OWNER: owner's previous job: (1) government servant, (2) staff of state-owned enterprise, (3) trader, (4) staff of private company

Source: Author.

gence in the likelihood functions of both the Probit and Tobit models due to the small sample size and the large number of explanatory variables. All industrial dummy variables are omitted from the tables.

First, there are generally consistent results on the controling variables. RETEAR, a proxy of self-finance, is significantly positive in both the debt and the bank-borrowing ratios. This confirms the fact that self-financing occurs prior to debt in fund mobilization. The signs of the parameters of investment attitude, INVE, are positive in most cases, and are statistically significant for the Probit model in the case of debt and in both the Probit and Tobit models in the case of bank borrowing. On the risk factor, signs are negative, but these parameters are not statistically significant. Results of the estimation indicate that a firm's fund-raising behavior is basically caused by the fund demand for investments; external finance is subordinate to internal finance. These basic tendencies are common to most economies and are also observed in the sampled firms of Myanmar.

Secondly an unexpected trend was found in effects of the vintage of firms. Parameters for the debt ratio are negative and statistically significant. Results for bank borrowing are not statistically significant. These results suggest that firms are dependent on debt financing in their initial stages and tend to gradually change toward having an increased reliance on self-financing. Insignificant results for bank borrowing imply that debt financing in the early stages is in the nature of trade credit or other informal financial sources. It may be that entrepreneurs start their business depending on informal borrowing. Through the growing process, they move past the initial situation and toward more reliance on self-finance. Banks do not seem to play a significant role in this process.

Thirdly, results indicate that the owner relationship with private banks (variable BR) is positive relative to the debt ratio, but insignificant relative to bank borrowing. Owner involvement does not appear to be a factor that encourages transactions with bank loans. Results also indicate that firms whose owners are involved in the running of private banks are relatively highly dependent on other debt instruments, presumably informal credit. It would seem that the purpose for owners being involved in private banks is not for strengthening the credit relationship with the bank, but rather for the diversification of their businesses.

Fourthly, in NCM, the proxy of diversification and scale of owners' business parameters are negative and significant relative to debt ratio. They are positive and significant in case of the Probit model relative to bank borrowing. Firms owned by entrepreneurs whose businesses are relatively large seem to retain affluent cash flows and also appear to be independent of informal credit. They are comparatively active in transactions of bank loans.

Finally, with regard to the issue of an owner's previous job, results show that entrepreneurs rooted in the private sector (such as traders and staff of private firms) have less access to bank loans than entrepreneurs from public sectors like government or state-owned enterprises. These results may indicate the existence of a disparity between government and private sectors in relation to networks in the financial market.

8.5.1.4 Interpretation of results

The results of estimations may be summarized as follows: investment in equipment leads to large demand for funds. Firms appear to choose debt as a resource of fund raising if self-financing is not sufficient to meet the demand. In this, fund raising seems to be determined by a "pecking order." However, self-financing is virtually dominant, and debt is largely subordinate to this. Although entrepreneurs depend on debt in their initial stages, they change this situation as they grow. Considering the fact that there is very little bank borrowing, debt finance consists of trade finance and other informal financial methods. Some firms with affluent cash and diversification of their businesses are relatively active in bank borrowing. There is no evidence to support a specific relationship between bank loan transactions and owners' managerial or shareholding participation in private banks.

8.5.2 Determinants of trade credit

The determinants of trade credit were analyzed using two types of estimation. The first was one form of capital structure, the deferred payments ratio over total assets on the balance sheet (deferred payments, note payable over total assets, L1 in Table 8.3). In this case, the estimation model was the same as that used previously. The second estimate was the ratio of deferred payments to the total amount of transactions with the largest trader on procurement. In the latter case, information related to customers was also available for use as explanatory valuables in the estimation.

8.5.2.1 Data and model

In the first estimation, the treatment of data and explanatory variables are the same as those used previously. In the second estimation, information related to customers and the relationship with the largest trader in procurement is added in explanatory variables as follows:

RTRASUP: share of the largest trader out of total transactions (procurement)
EXPERIS: transaction experience (months)
RELATIONS: relationship with the trader (4 dummy variables): (1) "friend" (2) "relative" (3) "family", and (4) "others"
LOCATIONS: location of the head office (4 dummy variables): (1) "in the city" (2) "in the township" (3) "in Myanmar", and (4) "abroad"

In the case where the share of the largest trader for procurement is too large (monopsony in the extreme case), the trader can request firms to compress deferred payments by exerting a considerable amount of bargaining power. Long-term transaction experience can help accumulate information. With regard to information and enforcement problems, kinship and geography are perhaps the most basic factors to be considered.

8.5.2.2 Results of estimations

Results of the estimations are shown in Tables 8.13 and 8.14. For estimations of the deferred payments ratio over total assets, the results for the debt ratio and bank borrowings differ as follows:

First, the parameters for retained earnings are not statistically significant. As seen in the previous section, in most cases of trade credit there are no interest charges. This means that the capital cost for trade credit is no higher than the opportunity cost. These results indicate that preference order is indifferent to self-financing for firms with access to trade credit.

Secondly, parameters for attitude regarding equipment investment are significantly positive, as are the estimates of debt ratio and bank borrowing. This suggests that trade credit functions to match the demand in funds for investment.

Thirdly, firm vintage is not statistically significant in the case of bank borrowing. The significant negative sign in the case of the debt ratio means that the debt mobilized initially is not of the nature of trade credit or bank borrowing.

Fourthly, results on the dummy variables for an owner's previous job suggest entrepreneurs rooted in private business (traders or workers in private companies) have more access to trade credit.

The results of the second type of the estimation are as follows: First, parameters of retained earnings are positive and statistically significant. Although the reason is not clear, these results indicate that traders are

Table 8.13 Estimation results of trade credit (deferred payments/total assets)

	Tobit model		*Probit model*		*OLS*	
Parameter	*Estimate*	*t-statistic*	*Estimate*	*t-statistic*	*Estimate*	*t-statistic*
C	−17.475	−0.732	−0.824	−1.067	23.363	2.257
		[.464]		[.286]		[.027]
ASSET	−0.270	−1.442	−0.812	−1.431	0.000	−1.047
		[.149]		[.152]		[.299]
RETEAR	−0.369	−1.311	−0.011	−1.132	−0.130	−1.215
		[.190]		[.257]		[.229]
RISK	−0.080	−0.013	−0.222	−1.061	2.834	1.143
		[.989]		[.289]		[.257]
Characteristics of Firm						
INVSCHA	29.145	2.031	0.761	1.667	10.181	1.823
		[.042]		[.095]		[.073]
VINTAGE	−0.287	−0.547	0.003	0.175	−0.315	−1.439
		[.585]		[.861]		[.155]
Characteristics of Owner						
BR	−15.137	−1.035	−0.554	−1.138	2.106	0.362
		[.300]		[.255]		[.719]
NOCOM	−5.946	−0.916	−0.140	−0.633	−2.360	−0.935
		[.360]		[.527]		[.353]
OWNER1	11.180	0.619	0.964	1.473	−2.899	−0.369
		[.536]		[.141]		[.713]
OWNER2					−3.937	−0.449
			[.655]			
OWNER3	18.977	1.515	0.943	2.211	1.018	0.194
		[.130]		[.027]		[.846]
OWNER4	18.668	1.353	0.967	2.058	0.335	0.058
		[.176]		[.040]		[.954]
Adj–R				0.205		0.039

Note: The figures in parentheses present P-values of coefficients.
C: constant term, ASSET: total assets, RETEAR: retained earnings, RISK: index of risk, INVSCHA: attitude of equipment investment, VINTAGE: Vintage (Age) of the firm, BR: index of participant of banking business, NOCOM: No. of firms owned by the sample firm's owner. OWNER: owner's previous job: (1) government servant, (2) staff of state owned enterprise, (3) trader, (4) staff of private company.

Source: Author.

Table 8.14 Estimation results of trade credit ("deferred payments/total transaction" with the largest traders)

	Tobit model		*Probit model*		*OLS*	
Parameter	*Estimate*	*t-statistic*	*Estimate*	*t-statistic*	*Estimate*	*t-statistic*
C	–159.021	–2.976 [.003]	–3.239	–2.701 [.007]	–24.703	–0.910 [.367]
ASSET	–0.001	–0.857 [.391]	0.000	–1.199 [.231]	0.000	–0.414 [.681]
RETEAR	0.781	1.812 [.070]	0.020	1.922 [.055]	0.274	1.177 [.244]
BANKLOAN	–0.127	–0.136 [.892]	–0.012	–0.579 [.563]	–0.171	–0.387 [.700]
RISK	1.721	0.197 [.844]	0.003	0.014 [.989]	2.593	0.498 [.621]
Characteristics of firm						
INVSCHA	62.131	2.536 [.011]	1.435	2.640 [.008]	18.595	1.577 [.120]
VINTAGE	0.118	0.147 [.883]	–0.006	–0.305 [.761]	0.072	0.147 [.884]
Characteristics of owner						
BR	26.353	1.136 [.256]	0.184	0.353 [.724]	12.021	0.949 [.346]
NOCOM	–6.706	–0.685 [.493]	0.016	0.067 [.947]	–3.023	–0.583 [.562]
OWNER1	25.526	0.923 [.356]	1.052	1.475 [.140]	6.006	0.369 [.713]
OWNER2	24.948	0.675 [.500]	0.992	1.154 [.248]	–4.407	–0.246 [.807]
OWNER3	9.858	0.512 [.608]	0.590	1.264 [.206]	–4.525	–0.411 [.683]
OWNER4	25.611	1.058 [.290]	0.986	1.720 [.085]	5.874	0.455 [.651]
Relationship with the trader						
RTRASUP	–0.492	–0.225 [.822]	–0.005	–0.147 [.883]	–0.008	–0.707 [.482]
EXPERIS	–0.013	–0.626 [.531]	0.000	–0.816 [.414]	0.000	0.018 [.985]
RELATIONS1	53.482	1.657 [.098]	0.496	0.706 [.480]	21.074	1.276 [.207]
RELATIONS2	83.390	2.283 [.022]	1.198	1.446 [.148]	35.851	1.844 [.070]

Table 8.14 Estimation results of trade credit ("deferred payments/total transaction" with the largest traders) – *continued*

	Tobit model		*Probit model*		*OLS*	
Parameter	*Estimate*	*t-statistic*	*Estimate*	*t-statistic*	*Estimate*	*t-statistic*
RELATIONS3	139.783	2.183 [.029]			89.264	2.268 [.027]
LOCATIONCU (1)	32.572	0.562 [.574]			13.189	0.344 [.732]
LOCATIONCU (2)	8.869	0.180 [.857]	0.252	0.213 [.831]	−1.154	−0.040 [.969]
LOCATIONCU (3)	3.132	0.186 [.852]	0.192	0.285 [.775]	−1.419	−0.145 [.885]
LOCATIONCU (4)			0.195	0.304 [.761]		
Adj–R				0.277		−0.022

Note: The figures in parentheses present P-values of coefficients.
C: constant term, ASSET: total assets RETEAR: retained earnings, RISK: index of risk, INVSCHA: attitude of equipment investment, VINTAGE: Vintage (Age) of the firm, BR: index of participant of banking business, NOCOM: No. of firms owned by the sample firm's owner. OWNER: owner's previous job: (1) government servant, (2) staff of state-owned enterprise, (3) trader, (4) staff of private company, BANKLOAN: bank borrowing, RTRASUP: the share of the largest trader, EXPERIS: span of experience of transaction (years), RELATIONS: personal relationship (1) Friend, (2) Relatives, (3) Family, LOCATIONCU: location of the head office: (1) in the same city, (2) in the same township, (3) in Myanmar, (4) abroad

Source: Author.

willing to supply trade credit to firms that have affluent cash flow and a strong ability to repay. On attitude toward investment, the results are positive and statistically significant, as in all previous cases.

Results on the features of and the relationship with traders are as follows: First, the size of and experience with transactions are not statistically significant. No evidence was found that the share of deferred payments is determined by mutual bargaining power or track record. Secondly, in cases using the Tobit model, trade credit transactions are active within the family, relatives and friends. This implies that kinship is still an important factor in determining the availability of trade credit. No evidence was found relative to the location factor.

8.5.2.3 Interpretation of results on trade credit

Under a severe financial market where debt financing and bank loan transactions are very inactive, trade credit seems to play a modest role in fund raising. These methods are seen as similar to genuine self-financing. Trade credit is utilized more actively by entrepreneurs who were previously engaged in the private sector and do not retain an intimate relationship with banks. With the exception of the most primitive social relationship, kinship, determinants of trade credit remain ambiguous.

8.6 Concluding remarks

In this chapter features of the financial system in Myanmar were observed, and econometric tests were undertaken on determinants of decisions in fund raising. Several clear features were identified: In Myanmar, firms depend to a large extent on self-financing. Although banks have grown rapidly in financial assets, bank loans play only a marginal role as a source of funding for firms. No business network has been formed or is functional for promoting bank loan transactions. On the other hand, even those firms that started with debt financing tend to shift to self-financing in the growth process. In such environments, trade credit as debt financing in the form of deferred payments seems to be a major source of funds. However, such methods appear to be determined solely by kinship, the most primitive factor, and do not seem to be widespread.

In Myanmar, the private sector in the real economy has grown considerably, and this seems to be driving the growth of the financial sector. In spite of the rapid expansion of financial assets, the function of financial institutions for the private sector is very limited. This is due partly to that sector's limited ability to get information and macroeconomic instability. The financial sector functions to support the government sector in order to finance the fiscal deficit.

To a substantial degree, trade credit functions as a means of debt financing. However, compared with the cases of Vietnam and mainland China, transactions in Myanmar do not seem to expand through business and/or personal networks or other social factors. This means that even in the case of trade credit, transactions are not automatically formed in a transition economy. Rather, certain factors or conditions may play a significant role in forming social relationships that are the basis for trade credit transactions.

In Myanmar, firms have grown mostly through self-financing, rather than through borrowing from the bank or even trade credits. This suggests that in the early stages of a transition economy, the growth of the real sector may come first, regardless of the development of the financial system.

Notes

1 The criticism is often made that statistics on the GDP growth rate released by the Myanmar government after 1999/2000 are unrealistically high (in real terms, 10.9 per cent in 1999/2000, 13.7 per cent in 2000/2001 and 10.5 per cent in 2001/2002), and that they are not reliable. According to estimates of the Economic Intelligent Unit (which estimates and releases the growth rate after 2001/2002), the rates are 5.3 per cent in both 2001/2002 and 2002/2003.

2 Economic growth in Myanmar in the 1990s seems to have been biased toward the non-manufacturing sector. The share in real GDP of manufacturing remains at 6.8 to 7.1 per cent and has been almost constant through the 1990s. On the other hand, the trade and service sector has grown substantially in shares (21.5 to 24.0 per cent and 6.5 to 9.0 per cent from 1993 to 1999).

3 Calculating using data from the *Statistical Yearbook*, 27.2 to 38.1 per cent of the fiscal deficit can be presumed to be absorbed by the market in form of treasury bonds, most of which were held by private banks in 1998/1999 to 1999/2000. These are remarkable figures compared with those of 4.6 to 7.2 per cent in 1995/1996 to 1996/1997.

4 Wang (2004) reported similar characteristics in the Kanboza Bank. Shares for this bank grew rapidly after the bank run in 2003. On the other hand, many small private banks are owned by the government or military-related holding companies (such as Myawaddy bank which is owned by Myanmar Economic Holdings). Generally, such entities are said to be inactive in the banking business.

5 Questionnaires regarding fund raising for working capital (flow level) are limited to explicit methods such as bank borrowing, borrowing within kinship, and/or self-financing. In fact, trade credit in the form of expanding deferred payments must be materially functional as working capital. Care should be used in interpreting the different meanings of Table 8.5.1 and Table 8.3 (which shows the share of methods in stock level).

References

Lee, Jong-Wha and Young Soo Lee, Byung-Sun Lee (2000) "The Determination of Corporate Debt in Korea," *Asian Economic Journal* 14(4), 333–56.

McMillan, John and Christopher Woodruff (1999) "Interfirm Relationships and Informal Credit in Vietnam," *The Quarterly Journal of Economics* 114(4), 1285–1320.

Mieno, Fumiharu (2006) "Fund Mobilization and Investment Behavior in Thai Manufacturing Firms in the Early 1990s," *Asian Economic Journal*, 20(1), 95–122.

Petersen, Mitchell A. and Raghuram G Rajan (1997) "Trade Credit: Theories and Evidence," *The Review of Financial Studies*, 10(3), 661–91.

Suto, Megumi (2003) "Capital Structure and Investment Behaviour of Malaysian Firms in the 1990s – A Study of Corporate Governance before the Crisis," *Corporate Governance: an International Review*, 11(1), 25–39.

Titman, Sheridan and Roberto Wessels (1988) "The Determinants of Capital Structure Choice," *Journal of Finance*, 43(1), 1–19.
Mya Than and Myat Thein (2000) *Financial Resources for Development in Myanmar: Lessons from Asia*. Singapore: Institute of Southeast Asian Studies.
Myat Thein (2003) *Economic Development of Myanmar*. Singapore: Institute of Southeast Asian Studies.
Wang, Sandra (2004) "Private Banks in Myanmar (1990–2003)," Mimeograph.

Savings and Lending Decisions and the State

9

Household Savings Decisions and Institutional Development: The Case of Rural Households in China

Hisatoshi Hoken

9.1 Introduction

Household savings decisions are key factors in determining the stability and development of an economy. Higher household savings contribute to stable macroeconomic development, particularly in the transition process from a planned economy to a market economy. Institutional settings essentially determine whether or not stability can be accomplished. In China's planned economy, economic surplus was strictly controled by government planning and the living standard of households were kept artificially low. Households could only afford marginal expenses, and household savings decisions did not work. Those systems were maintained by state-owned enterprises (SOE) in urban areas and by peoples' communes in the rural regions.

At the start of the transition process, however, communes collapsed, and the agricultural production responsibility system gradually started to introduce commercial agriculture in rural areas. The SOEs assumed the right to decide operational matters, including wage levels for employees. In this transition process, financial flows in the economy changed substantially. Household decisions about savings became an important factor in the financial flows throughout China.

However, the financial system of China continues to be strictly regulated by the government, especially in rural areas. The Rural Credit Cooperative (RCC), under the control of the Agricultural Bank of China (ABC), has been playing an exclusive role in formal finance during the transitional period. While the monopolistic position of the RCC leads to a loss of efficiency and produces disciplinary problems in management, the restriction of competition among financial institutions also helps to curtail moral hazard behavior among financial intermediaries and promotes financial deepening in the economy as a whole.

Relative to the above discussion, a theory of "financial restraint" has recently attracted much attention. A financial restraint policy implies that the government can create rent opportunities for financial institutions through deposit rate controls and restrictions on competition. These rents create a "franchise value" which attracts further investment into the financial industry. In particular, Hellmann *et al.* (1997, 1998) evaluate the ways in which financial restraint creates incentives for financial institutions to develop a deposit-taking infrastructure in rural areas, thus contributing to the mobilization of household savings.

It is debatable whether or not a financial restraint policy has been properly practiced in China. This chapter focuses on the impact of financial infrastructures in rural areas on the saving decisions of rural households in China. Specifically, rural households will probably hold more financial assets offered by financial institutions as their access to the financial network improves, and the creditability of formal financial institutions increases. At the same time, these households will hold fewer assets in the form of cash, gold, and jewels. Whether or not establishments of rural financial stations have effects on portfolio selection in rural households during the period of economic transition can be tested by using household micro data. A primary contribution of this chapter is to introduce variables related to the foundation of rural financial stations into a portfolio selection model and to estimate effects qualitatively.

When we investigate the portfolio selection of rural households in less developed countries (LDCs), it is necessary to pay attention to the variability of household income. Rural households in LDCs are likely to face a substantial risk of income variability. Because of this risk and imperfect information, formal insurance arrangements are seldom available, and poor households must use self-insurance mechanisms to mitigate risk and cope with income shocks. Therefore, variability and level of income appear to influence the portfolio selections of rural households. Characteristics of portfolio selections of rural household in connection with the variation of income are also examined in this chapter.

The chapter is structured as follows: section 9.2 describes the structure of financial flows in China using a flow-of-funds table to clarify the importance of the household sector in terms of financial flows. Based on the aggregated data of rural household panel surveys, characteristics of financial behavior on rural households are examined. Section 9.3 considers the specific example of four villages from Shanxi Province and estimates portfolio selection on cash and savings deposit holdings using household panel data. A summary of major findings and concluding remarks is presented in section 9.4.

9.2 Characteristics of financial behavior in the household sector and in rural households

9.2.1 Change of I–S balance by sectors since 1978

First, we examine the structure of financial flows in China using the flow-of-funds table. Figure 9.1 presents the change in I–S (investment–savings) balances since 1978. In this figure, economic units are separated into four distinct sectors: household, enterprise (including the financial sector), government, and foreign sectors. The values presented in Figure 9.1 are the difference of savings minus investments divided by total GDP.[1]

Figure 9.1 shows that the level of household savings has been higher than that of household investment, and that the household sector has been characterized by a surplus of money flow. At the time of the introduction of the first economic reforms in 1978, the I–S level of the household sector was roughly in balance. Since 1978, the level of savings in the household sector has been increasing, and the I–S balance has been in consistent surplus. The level of surplus was below 10 per cent of the GDP during the 1980s. Since then, the surplus has grown still further, maintaining a value over 15 per cent. The large amount of funds has been provided by the household sector. Surplus for the household sector, however, decreased to about 10 per cent in 2000. This decline may be due to a stagnation in the growth of income and a real-estate boom in urban areas. In contrast to the household sector, the I–S balance on the enterprise sector has been in deficit. This means that the enterprise sector has been conducting investment activity aggressively. The large amount of investment funds used was raised by external financing. Since the mid-1980s, the deficit of the enterprise sector has grown rapidly, and the deficit soon rose to a level of 10 to 15 per cent. Due to the economic stagnation caused by the Tiananmen incident, the deficit decreased toward the end of the 1980s. However, the Chinese economy has experienced an economic boom, and enterprises have conducted aggressive investment activities since the Southern Tour Lecture by Deng Xiaoping in 1992. Consequently, the level of the deficit was about 15 per cent in the middle of the 1990s.

Figure 9.1 also shows that the government and foreign sectors have been keeping equilibrium in I–S balances and are not so influential relative to the financial flows in China. Although the government sector showed a surplus before the introduction of the economic reforms, this surplus decreased rapidly, and the I–S balance had reached a level of equilibrium by the end of the 1980s. This seems to indicate that the capital surplus of the government sector had been transferred to

Figure 9.1 Change of I–S balance since 1978

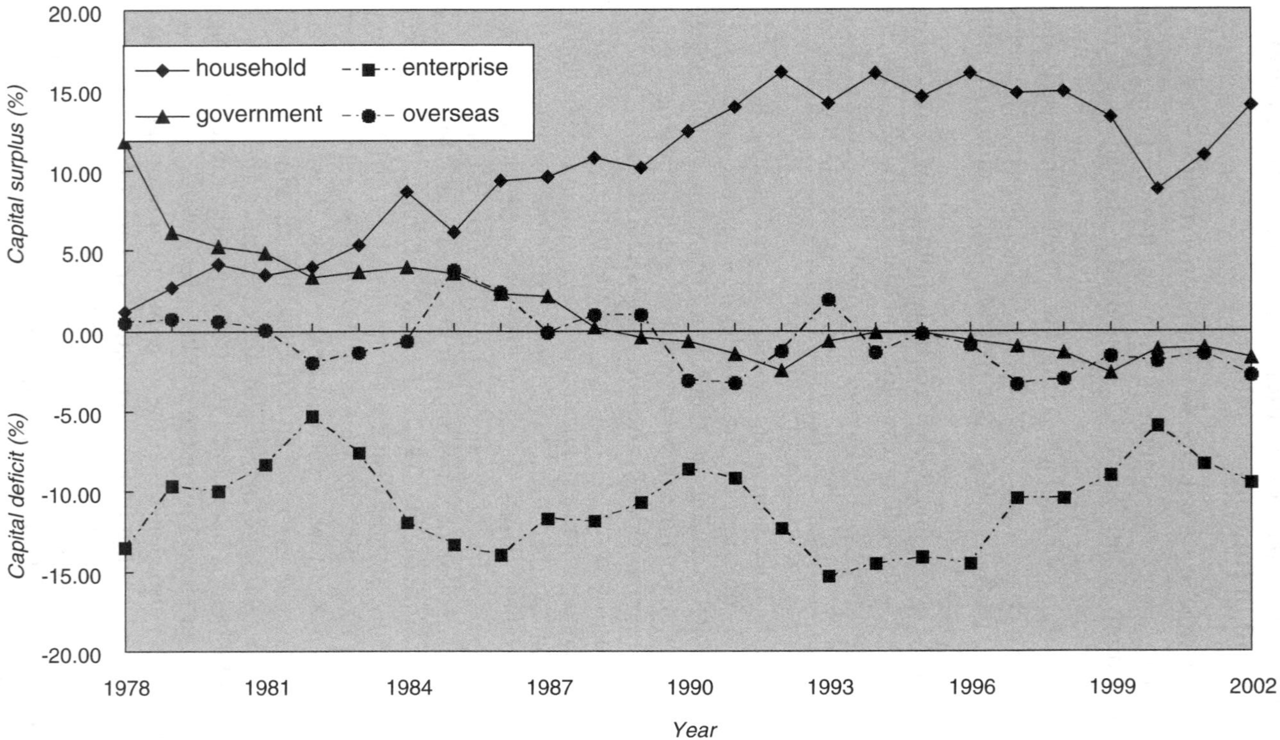

Source: Tang (2003); The People's Bank of China, *Quarterly Statistical Bulletin* (various issues).

the household sector. This was partially due to liberalization and reforms in the rural area; an agricultural production responsibility system was introduced, and free markets for agricultural products were restored. The implications of the above findings are: (i) that the surplus of savings in the household sector has been transferred to become investment funds in the enterprise sector; and (ii) that the structure of those financial flows has sustained rapid and continuous economic growth in China. Furthermore, the low level of dependence on government spending and foreign capital contributes to the stability of the Chinese economy. Because the surplus of the household sector has been used for investment funds in the form of lending, these funds for investment can be raised without the adoption of an inflationary money supply policy. In this sense, the financial structure of China can be contrasted with that of Eastern Europe and the CIS after economic transition.[2]

In order to make clear the importance of savings deposits in the household sector, a composite of household financial assets is presented in Figure 9.2. Considerable amounts of financial assets are in the form of savings deposits, and these account for about 60–70 per cent of total financial assets. The percentage share of currency holdings, in contrast, has been decreasing gradually from 20 per cent to 10 per cent. The percentage share of securities holdings and reserves for the insurance business has been rising since the mid-1990s. This is due to a boom in the stock market and reforms of the insurance system.

9.2.2 Characteristics of saving behavior in rural households

From the above, it may appear that the mobilization of savings from the household sector in China has been accomplished during the transition from a planned economy to a market economy. However, the mechanism of mobilization and the structure of household saving decisions have not been studied sufficiently from a microeconomic viewpoint, and it is necessary to analyze this mechanism using household micro data. The rural household becomes the focus for investigation of changes in financial behavior and characteristics of portfolio selection.

In order to examine the economic situation of the rural household, the "Rural Household Survey" (RHS) conducted by the National Statistics Bureau (NSB) provides the most comprehensive survey data. However, total average data and income class average data on the balance of deposits and borrowings are not officially published. Therefore, the utilization of the RHS is restricted to the analysis of portfolio selections in rural households.

Figure 9.2 Composition of household financial assets since 1992

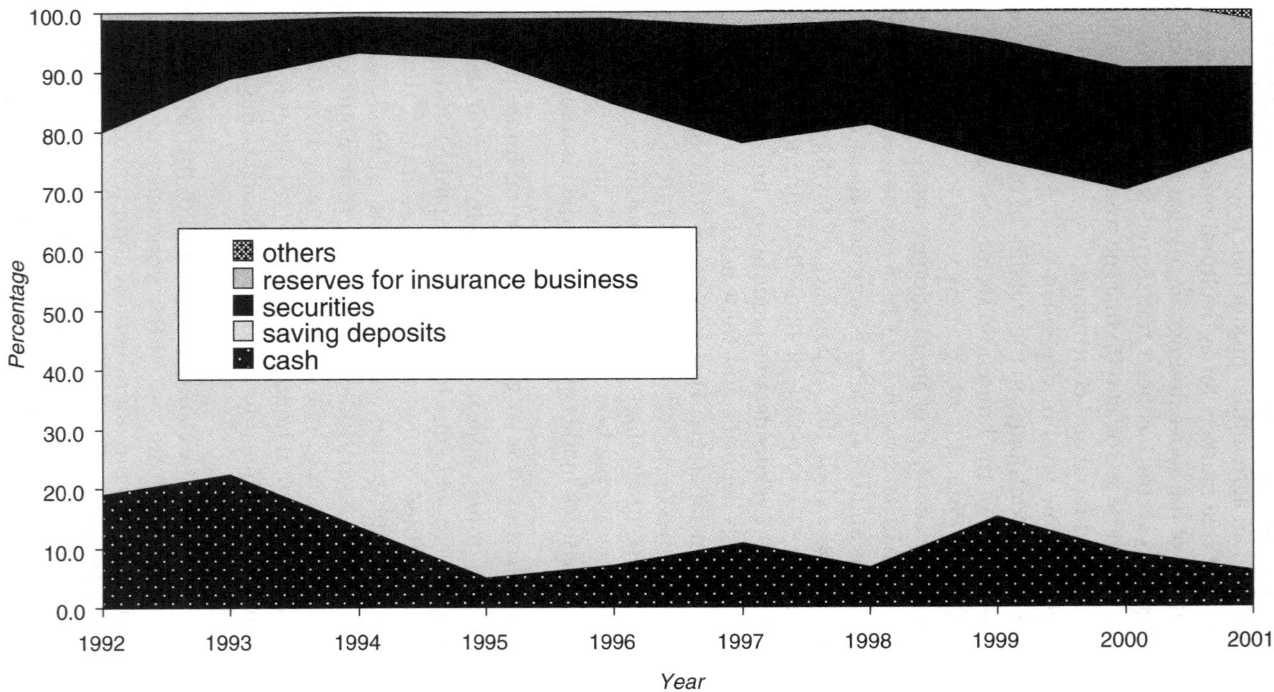

Source: The People's Bank of China, *Quarterly Statistical Bulletin* (various issues).

Figure 9.3 Change of financial asset composition in rural households since 1986

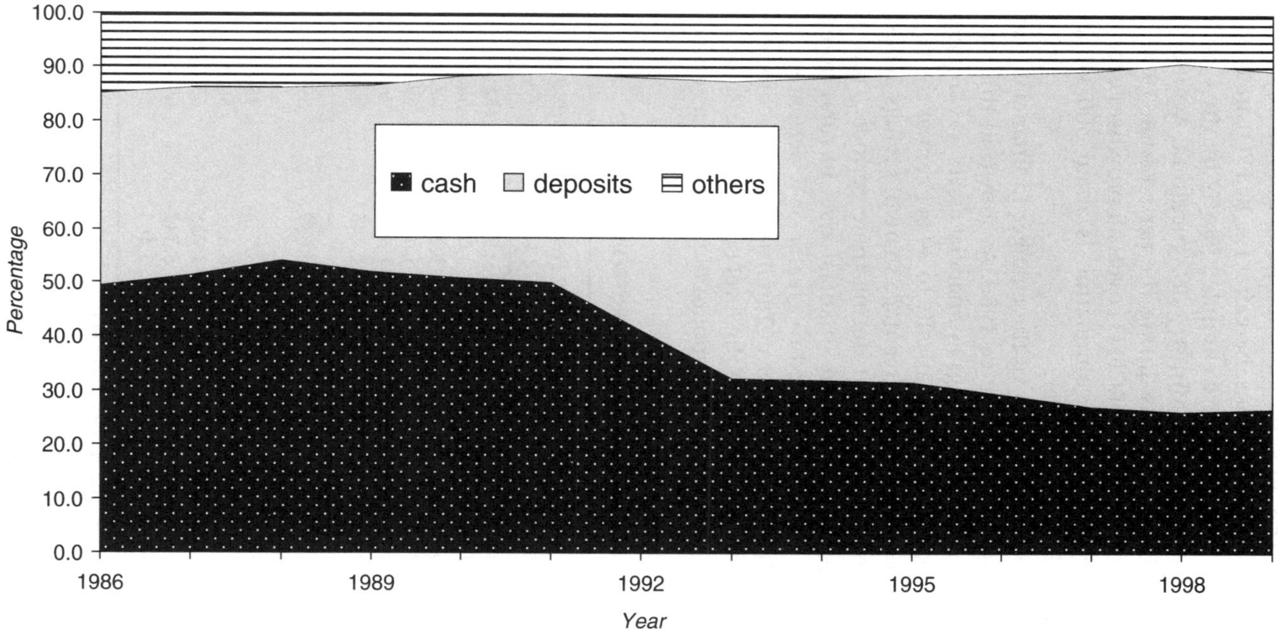

Source: Office for Policy Research of CCP and Office on RCFPO of Ministry of Agriculture (eds) (2001).

Note: Because the household survey was not conducted in 1992 and 1994, the numbers for those years are calculated by averaging the totals of before and after these years.

Instead of the RHS, longitudinal rural household survey data (Rural China Fixed Point Observations, hereafter the RCFPO) are used in this study. These observations were compiled jointly by the China Communist Party (CCP) and the Ministry of Agriculture. Aggregated data on household financial assets during the period from 1986 to 1999 were officially published. The RCFPO covers all provinces except Tibet, and the sample size of this compilation is about 300 villages and 25,000 households for each year.

Figure 9.3 shows a summary of the changes in financial asset composition in rural households since 1986. As shown in this figure, the percentage share of cash holdings in financial assets was around 50 per cent in 1986 and then fell dramatically to 30 per cent at the beginning of the 1990s. In contrast, the percentage share of savings deposits rose from 35 per cent to 60 per cent during these periods. Thus, savings deposits have become the prime financial asset in rural households. These trends have been observed to greater or lesser extent in every area (Eastern, Middle, and Western China) and in all income classes.

Next, consideration is given to the level of financial assets compared with household income and the amount of production assets possessed

Table 9.1 Structure of asset holdings on RCFPO households

	(a) Household income	*(b) Financial assets*	*(c) Production assets*	*(b)/(a) (%)*	*(b)/(c) (%)*
1986	2,444	1,263	941	51.7	134
1987	2,945	1,719	1,070	58.4	161
1988	3,505	2,187	1,292	62.4	169
1989	3,722	2,592	1,421	69.6	182
1990	3,920	2,983	1,502	76.1	199
1991	4,093	3,280	1,745	80.1	188
1992					
1993	5,966	3,524	2,639	59.1	134
1993					
1995	9,840	4,798	3,954	48.8	121
1996	10,214	5,812	4,558	56.9	128
1997	10,576	6,951	4,725	65.7	147
1998	10,232	7,071	5,247	69.1	135
1999	10,256	7,891	5,465	76.9	144

Source: Office for Policy Research of CCP and Office on RCFPO of Ministry of Agriculture (eds) (2001).

Note: Financial assets include cash on hand, deposits and others (lending, securities etc.). Production assets include agricultural assets (agricultural machinery, farm tools and draft animals) and non-agricultural production assets. The production assets are evaluated at book prices.

by rural households. Table 9.1 shows the amount of financial assets and the percentage share of financial assets to rural household income and production assets. Financial assets increased steadily in the period from 1986 to 1999. Although the percentage share of financial assets to household income rose from 50 per cent to around 80 per cent during the period from 1986 to 1991, increases in financial assets grew at a slower rate in the middle of the 1990s, and this share dropped to around 60 per cent. The percentage share of financial to production assets shows the same trends, despite the fact that the amount of financial assets has been more than that of production assets.

From earlier discussions of I–S balances and the composition of financial assets in rural households, it seems evident that the financial assets of the household sector, especially in the form of saving deposits, have been utilized as investment funds in the enterprise sector. These assets have been supporting rapid and steady economic growth in China. Further, the percentage share of deposits in financial assets of rural households increased remarkably at the beginning of the 1990s. A change of portfolio selection in rural households probably took place in this period.

9.3 Analysis of the portfolio selection of rural households using MHTS panel data from Shanxi Province

This section concerns the influences of savings mobilization policies on the financial asset portfolio selection of rural households in China. In order to investigate the characteristics of the portfolio selection, we conduct econometric estimations on the financial portfolio selection using household-level data from four villages. A supplemental field survey of the financial structures in Dingxiang County of Shanxi Province was conducted in November 2002 and July 2004.[3]

Dingxiang County is one of the areas in which econometric estimations are made using household-level data. Information was collected on the activities of financial branch offices at the village level, the incentive mechanisms for workers, and the savings behaviors of rural households.

9.3.1 Financial institutions at the village level

Like other LDCs, China utilizes not only formal finance such as state-owned commercial banks (i.e. Agricultural Bank of China) and cooperative credit unions (i.e. Rural Credit Cooperative (RCC)), but also informal finance such as Rotating Savings and Credit Associations (ROSCAs) and RCFs (Rural Cooperative Funds) to provide rural finance.

ROSCA has developed, especially in the southeast coastal area (Zhejiang, Fujian, etc.), and the funds from ROSCA have functioned as investment and working capital for enterprises and household businesses. In Shanxi, however, the informal finance has been less developed, and formal finance systems have played a central role in deposit collecting and in lending. Although the existence of RCFs is not negligible in Shanxi, this discussion concentrates on the systems of formal finance.

Dingxiang County is located 100 km northeast of Taiyuan, the capital of Shanxi. The presence of RCC has been crucial in villages of Dingxiang County. Branch offices of RCC, which are called "service stations" (*fuwu zhan*) or "savings offices" (*chuxu suo*), began in the 1950s, and the number of such offices increased rapidly throughout the 1980s. In 2004, Dingxiang had 12 branch offices and 255 service stations of RCC. About 80 per cent of the total amount of savings in Dingxiang is deposited in service stations.

Service stations are operated as side jobs, and the individuals who manage these stations are usually educated, having stable income sources. They generally have good accounting and/or store management skills. Customer service at service stations is restricted to the management of deposits and withdrawals; in general, procedures involving remittance and loans are not available. RCC provides service stations with a calculator, a machine for detecting counterfeit bills, and a strongbox. In return, the home or shop of the service station worker is used as a window of the service station. At least three times a month, staff from the branch office visits service stations in order to check the accounts.

Workers in RCC service stations are paid according to the level of deposits made at each station. Dingxiang is uniformly regulated, and 0.85 yuan is paid per 10,000 yuan of total deposits. If the amount of deposits is 3 million yuan, the wage of the worker is 255 yuan a month. Hence, it is in the interest of workers in service stations to make an effort to improve the quality of service in order to attract more deposits. Account records of each household are used for credit inquiries in loan decisions. Thus, the development of service stations has contributed to the mobilization of household savings and the development of finance facilities in rural areas.

9.3.2 Description of sample villages and households

The Minor set of High-quality Time Series (MHTS) panel database is a resampling database of RCFPO. It was developed as an international joint project between the Rural China Research Center (RCRE) in China, Kyoto University, and Hitotsubashi University in the period 1999 to 2002. The MHTS panel dataset covers 14 provinces and 54 villages. Among these, Shanxi Province was selected for the following reasons: (i) Non-sampling errors in Shanxi data are fewer than those in the data of other provinces, and continuity as a fixed-point survey is higher; (ii) because MHTS panel data include data from seven villages in Shanxi, it is suitable for comparing the difference of village structures; (iii) as mentioned, the development of informal finance is limited in Shanxi, so attention can be focused on the formal financial sector.

Shanxi Province is located in the northern middle region of China, and the income level of rural areas is just below that of the average of the whole of rural China. Based on economic structure and the income level, four villages were selected as a sample. These villages are located in different counties – Linqiu, Dingxiang, Taigu and Linyi. Hereafter, in order to maintain anonymity, these four villages will be denoted by their county name. Basic information on these villages is shown in Table 9.2. Linqiu County is located 225 km northeast of Taiyuan. Due to its location in the hilly and cold northern district of Shanxi, the natural conditions around Linqiu village are not suitable for crop production. The major industries of Linqiu are dairy farming and forestry. Manufacturing and non-farm household businesses have not developed and a large part of the labor is migrating to nearby townships. Linqiu village has been officially designated a poor village (*pinkun cun*) since the middle of the 1980s.

Dingxiang village is a relatively large village, comprising about 750 households. From the mid-1980s, individual businesses and private

Table 9.2 Characteristics of sample villages

	Geographical features	*Number of households*		*Per capita income*		*Others*
		1986	*2001*	*1986*	*2001*	
Linqiu	mountain	75	76	215	1,188	officially acknowledged poor village
Dingxiang	plain	755	756	736	2,583	"well-off" village
Taigu	plain	70	76	634	3,018	"well-off" village
Linyi	hill	246	335	362	2,480	

Source: MHTS panel database and village-level survey data.

enterprises developed within the village, and income levels were higher than those in other villages in the same county. However, manufacturing industries have been stagnant since the end of the 1990s. Dingxiang is officially designated as a "well-off village" (*xaiokang cun*). Taigu County is 60 km south from Taiyuan. Because of its mild climate, rich soil and well-developed irrigation system, Taigu County is a model district of agricultural modernization in Shanxi. The major industry of Taigu village is farming. This includes not only crop production, but also the cultivation of cash crops such as vegetables and fruits. Taigu village is also officially designated a "well-off village."

Finally, Linyi County is located in the southwest part of Shanxi near the provincial boundary with Henan and Shaanxi provinces. Linyi is a medium-sized village of around 300 households, and engages in crop production. Except for crop production, cash crops have been flourishing in this village. Although the per capita income of Linyi village in 1986 was relatively low, income has risen dramatically during the 1990s and has now reached the same level as that of Dingxiang village.

Summing up the characteristics of each village, Linqiu faces a severe natural environment, and the average living standards in Linqiu are just above the poverty line. Though the size of each village is different, Taigu and Linyi are similar with regard to their agricultural conditions and types of farming. The development of Dingxiang preceded that of other villages. However, with the exception of Linqiu, agricultural modernization and the development of off-farm works in Taigu and Linyi have reduced the disparity of income levels among these four villages.

9.3.3 Characteristics of portfolio selection in sample villages

Before conducting an econometric analysis on the portfolio selection of rural households, the change of asset holdings on sample villages during the period of 1986 to 2001 must be considered. First, the amount of total assets and the percentage of assets possessed in the form of financial assets to production assets are shown in Table 9.3.[4] The level of assets is increasing steadily in all villages. While the percentage of financial assets is either rising or remaining high in Dingxiang and Taigu, it is decreasing in Linqiu. The percentage of financial assets in Linyi increased until the middle of the 1990s, but a reverse trend has been observed since then. Thus, a distinction in the pattern of asset holdings can be observed, and the pattern of Dingxiang and Taigu is different from that in the other villages.

Secondly, the composition of financial assets is presented in Table 9.4. These assets may be broken down into deposit savings, cash in

Table 9.3 Composition of asset holdings for sample villages

Linqiu	*Total*	*Financial assets (%)*	*Production assets (%)*
1986	919	35.0	65.0
1991	1,208	30.0	70.0
1996	4,118	23.8	76.2
2001	7,930	10.2	89.8

Taigu	*Total*	*Financial assets (%)*	*Production assets (%)*
1986	3,138	37.2	62.8
1991	8,051	67.8	32.2
1996	9,519	62.2	37.8
2001	19,108	66.0	34.0

Ding-xiang	*Total*	*Financial assets (%)*	*Production assets (%)*
1986	3,866	70.3	29.7
1991	8,716	76.5	23.5
1996	13,035	76.0	24.0
2001	20,383	86.9	13.1

Linyi	*Total*	*Financial assets (%)*	*Production assets (%)*
1986	1,673	26.4	73.6
1991	3,355	42.9	57.1
1996	7,549	65.2	34.8
2001	10,519	58.9	41.1

Source: MHTS panel database.

Note: See Table 9.1.

hand, and others. As shown in Table 9.4, except for Dingxiang, the percentage share of cash in hand was over 50 per cent in 1986. This means that cash holdings were a major form of assets in the middle of the 1980s. Since then, the percentage share of deposit savings has grown rapidly in Taigu and Linyi villages, while it has decreased in Linqiu village because of a decline in the standard of living.[5]

Except for Linqiu, the percentage share of deposits increased during the 1990s to a level of about 80 to 90 per cent of the level found in the remaining villages. Thus, there has been a change in portfolio selection from cash to deposit savings holdings in those three villages. By contrast, the trend of financial asset holdings in Linqiu village shows a bewildering change that does not seem to follow a particular pattern. This may be due to missing data on savings deposits in Linqiu. Data are especially lacking for the period after 1997, so estimates for the econometric model of Linqiu households are based on 1986–1996 data in order to reduce bias.

The percentage share of financial assets to household total income is also reported in Table 9.4. In Dingxiang village, the percentage share has been over 100 per cent since 1986 and was over 200 per cent in 2001. A gradual increase in this percentage share can be observed in Taigu and Linyi villages except for 1991. Accordingly, the accumulation

Table 9.4 Change of financial assets for sample villages

Linqiu	*(a) Income*	*(b) Financial assets*	*Deposit (%)*	*Cash*	*Others*	*(b)/(a) (%)*
1986	818	322	22.4	73.2	4.4	39.3
1991	882	363	1.7	98.3	0.0	41.1
1996	2,459	979	52.2	31.7	16.1	39.8
2001	3,880	810	23.8	59.7	16.5	20.9

Dingxiang	*(a) Income*	*(b) Financial assets*	*Deposit (%)*	*Cash*	*Others*	*(b)/(a) (%)*
1986	2,688	2,719	74.2	11.0	14.8	101.2
1991	4,784	6,670	75.0	16.8	8.2	139.4
1996	8,403	9,907	87.3	9.7	3.1	117.9
2001	8,537	17,706	85.5	8.7	5.8	207.4

Taigu	*(a) Income*	*(b) Financial assets*	*Deposit (%)*	*Cash*	*Others*	*(b)/(a) (%)*
1986	2,760	1,166	39.3	55.8	4.9	42.2
1991	3,837	5,461	63.5	32.1	4.5	142.3
1996	7,483	5,926	72.1	18.1	9.8	79.2
2001	10,879	12,613	84.9	14.9	0.2	115.9

Linyi	*(a) Income*	*(b) Financial assets*	*Deposit (%)*	*Cash*	*Others*	*(b)/(a) (%)*
1986	1,738	441	18.9	58.2	22.8	25.4
1991	2,901	1,439	48.4	45.8	5.8	49.6
1996	10,286	4,926	84.0	15.6	0.5	47.9
2001	9,605	6,198	87.6	11.9	0.5	64.5

Source: MHTS panel database.

of household assets in financial form has advanced to a greater or lesser extent in those three villages. On the other hand, in Linqiu, the percentage share has stayed around 20 to 40 per cent, and the accumulation of financial assets has remained at a lower level.

Finally, the situation of financial institutions in sample villages is explored. Table 9.5 shows the number and the year of establishment

Table 9.5 Number of RCC service stations by village

Village	*Service station*	*Year founded*
Linqiu	2	1989,91
Dingxiang	6	1979,85
Taigu	2	1988,90
Linyi	2	1988,92

Notes: 1. Branches of the RCC were funded from 1958 to 1959 in all townships for every village. 2. Three service stations of Dingxiang village were funded in 1979, and another three were funded later by the Joint RCCs, the China Construction Bank, and the Agricultural Bank of China which were reorganized as service stations of the RCC in 2002.

for FCC service stations, tabled by village. With the exception of Dingxiang village, where the founding of service stations preceded other villages, almost all stations were established around 1990. The period in which service stations were founded coincides with a period in which a shift of asset holdings from cash to deposits in Taigu and Linyi villages was occurring. It seems probable that a causal relationship exists between the founding of service stations and changes in the portfolio selection in those villages. Therefore, focusing on service station foundation years, the change of portfolios in rural households is investigated next.

9.3.4 Review of portfolio selection in LDCs; setting econometric models

Since the risks related to income variability are likely to be uninsured in the rural households of LDCs, these households must deal with these risks using a variety of measures. Existing studies have mainly focused on household savings from the viewpoint of liquidity constraints or preliminary savings.[6] Articles that investigate the relationship between income variability and portfolio selection in rural households are limited.

Rosenzweig and Binswanger (1993) measured the risks of farmers' investment portfolios in terms of their sensitivity to weather variation using panel data from the ICRISAT Indian village survey. Using household data from the ICRISAT Burkina Faso survey, Zimmerman and Carter (2003) developed a stochastic dynamic programming model with endogenous asset price risks in order to explore savings and portfolio decisions in poor resource environments as characterized by risk and subsistence constraints. By taking into account differences of income shock across income groups, Alderman (1996) examined differences in marginal rates of financial and physical savings in rural households in Pakistan. With regard to rural households in China, Jalan and Ravallion (2001) studied portfolio and other behavioral responses to idiosyncratic risk using RHS panel data.

These studies have not specifically examined the impact of financial infrastructure development on portfolio selections of rural households. The study presented in this chapter introduces the variable of access to the financial system (as indicated by the foundation of service stations) into portfolio selection models and estimates the effect of this variable numerically. In order to explore the influence of permanent income and transitional income on portfolio selection, a revision of the model adopted in Jalan and Ravallion (2001) is used.

First, permanent income is defined as the predicted value of an income function as follows:

$$Y_{it} = X'_{it}\beta + \varepsilon_{it} \tag{9.1}$$

where Y_{it} is the income of household i in time t, and X_{it} is a vector of exogenous variables. The error structure is assumed as follows:

$$\varepsilon_{it} = \eta_i + \nu_{it} \tag{9.2}$$

where η_i is an individual effect of household i, and ν_{it} is random i.i.d. error. Since a Hausman test of all villages leads to rejection of the null hypothesis that η_i is uncorrelated with X_{it}, Y_{it} can be estimated using a Fixed Effect Model.[7]

In order to divide true income into predicted permanent income and transitional income, transitional income is specified as the difference between true income and predicted permanent income. Predicted income is defined as the sum of the fit value of (9.1) and an individual effect:

$$Y^{p}_{it} = X'_{it}\hat{\beta} + \hat{\eta}_i \tag{9.3}$$

True income does not necessary coincide with predicted permanent income. It is natural that some disparity exists. This spread can be defined as transitional income that means a shock to household income.

$$\hat{Y}^{T} = Y_{it} - \hat{Y}^{P}_{it} \tag{9.4}$$

The effect of transitional income may not be the same on positive and negative shocks. Unlike positive income shocks, negative income shocks usually have a serious impact on rural households. This is because the income level of rural households is generally low, and even slight negative shocks directly influence household behaviors owing to limited formal insurance arrangements in poor households.

Transitional income is therefore divided into two parts: (1) positive income shock ($\hat{Y}_{it}^{+T}$); and (2) negative income shock ($\hat{Y}_{it}^{-T}$). In this formulation, transitional income includes both idiosyncratic shocks and collective shocks. Instruments that do not correlate with household-specific components and represent aggregated (or village-level) shocks (such as regional rainfall data or inflation indices of local areas) are needed to single out idiosyncratic shocks. However, such instruments are difficult to find in village surveys of the RCFPO or in other sources. Although the above formulation of transitional income is not sufficient to represent household-specific risks, aggregated shocks can be controled to some extent by introducing a year dummy variable in the estimation of income function.

In order to test for the portfolio effects of income risk and access to financial institutions, the following equation for estimation may be used:

$$S_{it} = Z_{it}'\theta + \gamma_1 \hat{Y}_{it}^{P} + \theta_1 \hat{Y}_{it}^{+T} + \theta_2 \hat{Y}_{it}^{-T} + D^{SS} + \pi_t + e_{it} \qquad (9.5)$$

where S_{it} is the share of deposit savings to total cash in hand and deposit savings of household i in time t, Z_{it} is a vector of exogenous variables which can influence portfolio selections, π_t is real deposit interest rate, and D^{SS} is a dummy variable which takes a value of 1 after the first foundation of a service station (SS) in each village. However, the foundation of a service station is not necessarily independent of income level or the saving ratio of each village; it must be determined simultaneously. For controling the endogeneity of D^{SS}, first lagged variables of the permanent income and the share of deposit savings are used as instruments for D^{SS}. The village averages of those lagged variables ($\hat{Y}_{it-1}^{P}$ and $\bar{S}_{it-1}$) are utilized for IV estimations.

The effects on service stations cannot be fully shown before and after the year of their foundation. In time, the reliability of rural banking systems generally rises after the establishment of service stations. In order to capture the "vintage effect" of rural banking branches, D^{SS} is replaced with a "vintage index" (which takes on a value of 1 at the

Table 9.6 Basic statistics for sample data

		Linqiu		*Dingxiang*		*Taigu*		*Linyi*	
Variable	*Unit*	*Mean*	*Standard Deviation*	*Mean*	*Standard Deviation*	*Mean*	*Standard Deviation*	*Mean*	*Standard Deviation*
Savings ratio (S_{it})	(deposit savings)/(deposit savings+cash in hand)	0.163	0.289	0.726	0.308	0.564	0.351	0.480	0.380
Real income (Y_{it})	Household income deflated by CPI	775.8	647.3	2827.5	1682.2	2735.5	1538.1	2512.7	1469.1
Income shock(–) (Y_{it}^{-T})	See text	–125.9	191.8	–368.2	531.1	–329.4	521.7	–385.8	559.2
Income shock(+) (Y_{it}^{+T})	See text	125.9	261.4	368.2	664.1	329.4	569.7	385.8	701.5
Permanent income (Y_{it}^{P})	See text	775.8	531.2	2827.5	1354.8	2735.5	1245.7	2512.7	1027.4
Cadre	Dummy variable, 1 if household head is a member of cadre in village or town office, 0 if not	0.098		0.036		0.092		0.036	
Middle school	Dummy variable, 1 if educational level of household head is middle school, 0 if not	0.349		0.304		0.526		0.615	
High school	Dummy variable, 1 if educational level of household head is more than high school, 0 if not	0.121		0.087		0.034		0.107	
Occupational training	Dummy variable, 1 if anyone of household members is taking or has already taken occupational training, 0 if not	0.046		0.066		0.162		0.051	

Table 9.6 Basic statistics for sample data – *continued*

Variable	*Unit*	*Linqiu*		*Dingxiang*		*Taigu*		*Linyi*	
		Mean	*Standard Deviation*	*Mean*	*Standard Deviation*	*Mean*	*Standard Deviation*	*Mean*	*Standard Deviation*
Labors	Number of household labors	1.923	0.823	2.352	0.955	2.388	1.077	2.623	1.061
Type I	Dummy variable of agricultural type, 1 if ratio of off-farm work days to total work days is 10% to 49%, 0 if not	0.349		0.182		0.310		0.269	
Type II	Dummy variable of agricultural type, 1 if ratio of off-farm work days to total work days is over 50%, 0 if not	0.164		0.474		0.235		0.123	
Land area	Total area for cultivation, tree planning and breeding including land of subtenancy	3.549	3.168	11.807	8.629	8.267	3.784	12.922	4.704
Production assets	Total of agricultural and non-agricultural production assets deflated by CPI, and evaluated at	491.6	719.3	587.7	1166.6	1263.0	1496.7	967.2	876.0
Coefficient of dependants	(number of household member)/(number of household labor)	1.916	0.709	1.715	0.532	1.747	0.563	1.882	0.694

Source: MHTS panel database.

year of service station foundation and increases by 1 every year thereafter) and a "vintage squared" which expresses the nonlinear effect of vintage on S_{it}. Table 9.6 summarizes basic statistics for the empirical variables used in estimations.

9.3.5 Results of estimations

Table 9.7 reports the results for estimations of the income function. Exogenous variables of the income function include three types of dummy variables: (1) educational level; (2) occupational training; and (3) cadre. These indicate the accumulation of human capital and networks within the village. In addition to these, land area, number of household laborers, amount of production assets, and the type of farm management are also included as exogenous variables. The definition of a part-time farm household type II is based on the ratio of off-farm workdays to total workdays. When this ratio falls below 10 per cent, these households are defined as "agricultural households". Ratios of 10 per cent to 49 per cent define "part-time farm households type I" and ratios over 50 per cent denote "part-time farm households type II". Since no find prominent distinction in income could be found between agricultural households and part-time farm households type I, only a dummy variable for part-time farm households type II was inserted as an explanatory variable.

Since use of the Hausman test led to rejection of the null hypothesis that individual effects are uncorrelated with the explanatory variables in every village, the income function was estimated by use of a fixed effect model. Table 9.7 shows that income levels are significantly affected by production factors such as household labor and land area. Although some coefficients of dummy variables are statistically significant, those for education and cadre are not. Coefficients of part-time farm households type II are significantly positive in every village, and this indicates that participation in off-farm work leads to an increase in the income level of rural households.

Based on the results obtained from the income function, permanent income and two types of transitional income can be predicted, and the portfolio selection model presented in Equation (9.4) can be estimated. In order to control household characteristics, the number of household laborers, part-time workers of farm households (type I and type II) and a coefficient of dependants (total number of household members divided by number of household laborers) are added as explanatory variables. The real deposit rate (the official deposit rate minus the CPI of rural Shanxi) indicates the profitability of savings deposits, and this

Table 9.7 Result of regression on income

	Linqiu		*Dingxiang*		*Taigu*		*Linyi*	
	Coefficient	*t-statistic*	*Coefficient*	*t-statistic*	*Coefficient*	*t-statistic*	*Coefficient*	*t-statistic*
Cadre	55.7	0.69	152.1	0.54	245.8	1.05	350.7	1.70
Middle school	168.2	2.75***	74.9	0.56	20.1	0.18	–120.4	–1.16
High school	88.5	0.66	–2.0	–0.01	183.5	0.64	–259.7	–1.60
Occupational training	23.0	0.22	–65.8	–0.32	93.3	0.72	1198.8	7.29***
Labors	121.3	3.15***	452.9	7.07***	321.5	6.19***	194.9	4.70***
Land area	632.4	10.30***	594.9	5.47***	868.5	8.17***	591.8	6.53***
Type II	18.9	1.91*	47.0	6.15***	116.4	6.63***	83.6	8.39***
Production assets	0.285	8.13***	–0.009	–0.22	0.247	7.43***	0.077	1.95*
Constant	164.7	1.66	616.7	2.87***	–76.3	–0.37	–246.8	–1.22
Sample Size	634		1,032		936		1,949	
R2. Within	0.427		0.186		0.413		0.338	
Between	0.425		0.232		0.523		0.343	
Overall	0.413		0.209		0.469		0.324	
F test that all $X_1 = 0$	F(91, 526)=4.05***		F(98,912)=7.82***		F(100, 8147)=3.83***		F(163, 1764)=3.21***	

Notes: Owing to reliability of saving data on Linqiu after 1997, data from 1986 to 1996 are used for estimations on Linqiu.
***significant at the 1 per cent level,** at the 5 per cent level, and *at the 10 per cent level.

is introduced as an independent variable. We expect that the coefficient of the real deposit rate would take the positive sign, because the rise in the real deposit rate would increase the return of from the saving deposits. The results are reported in Tables 9.8 and 9.9. The definition of the service station variable is different in these two tables. Table 9.8 includes the dummy variable of service station foundation, and Table 9.9 replaces this dummy variable with the vintage and vintage square of service station establishment.[8]

Table 9.8 shows that, with the exception of Linyi, the coefficient of permanent income is significantly positive. This indicates that an increase of permanent income is likely to induce a shift of financial asset holdings from cash holdings to savings deposits. With the exception of Linqiu, the coefficients for negative income shock are significantly positive in three villages. However, those for positive income shock are not significant in all villages. This implies that unexpected negative income shocks tend to reduce the share of savings. Positive income shocks, however, do not give rise to a change in financial asset holdings. Hence, negative income shocks are a more influential factor on the portfolio selection of rural households than positive income shocks. It is somewhat surprising that neither coefficients of income shock is significant in Linqiu, the poorest village. This may be related to the fact that the percentage share of households in Linqiu that had positive deposit savings was relatively low compared to that in other villages.[9] Since households in Linqiu can not afford deposit savings, the savings ratio is probably unresponsive to variations in income.

Some parameters representing household characteristics – such as the number of household laborers and part-time farm households type II – are significant. With the exception of Linyi, the coefficient for the number of household laborers is significantly negative. The reasons for a negative relationship between household labor and the percentage share of savings deposits are not clear, but factors related to the household lifecycle could be related. In Dingxiang and Taigu, the coefficient of part-time farm households type II is significantly positive relative to the share of savings. This indicates that part-time farm households type II earn considerably more income than agricultural and type I households. Type II households tend to retain their assets in the form of saving deposits. Since the development of part-time farms in Dingxiang and Taigu has precedence, this effect seems particularly striking.

The estimate for the coefficient of the real deposit rate is different among villages. The sign of the coefficients for Dingxiang and Taigu are positive and statistically significant, while the coefficients for

Table 9.8 Estimation results for the portfolio selection model (service station dummy)

	Linqiu (REM)		*Dingxiang (FEM)*		*Taigu (FEM)*		*Linyi (FEM)*	
	Coefficient	*Asym. t-statistic*	*Coefficient*	*Asym. t-statistic*	*Coefficient*	*Asym. t-statistic*	*Coefficient*	*Asym. t-statistic*
Income shock (–)	3.14E-05	0.49	6.05E-05	2.99***	6.04E-05	2.66***	1.35E-04	7.35***
Income shock (+)	–2.16E-05	–0.48	3.96E-06	0.25	2.45E-05	1.19	2.01E-05	1.43
Permanent income (PI)	1.45E-04	3.81***	8.71E-05	2.82***	3.19E-05	1.76*	–8.36E-06	–0.50
Service station	–0.175	–3.37***			0.438	10.77***	0.531	10.13***
Type I	0.005	0.18	0.031	0.97	–0.013	–0.46	–0.037	–1.65
Type II	0.068	1.59	0.071	2.10**	0.090	2.54**	0.020	0.60
Labors	–0.047	–2.02**	–0.063	–2.38**	–0.050	–2.51**	0.006	0.34
Coefficient of dependents	–0.031	–1.58	–0.002	–0.06	–0.038	–1.32	0.026	1.23
Real deposit rate	–1.20E–03	–0.68	4.24E-03	2.66***	1.22E-02	6.24***	–4.10E-04	–0.23
Constant	0.306	3.92***	0.614	6.98***	0.283	2.90***	0.032	0.38
Sample size	614		1,020		921		1,894	
For Wald statistics for zero slope	$\chi^2(9)$ =48.42***		F(8,913) = 5.75***		$\chi^2(9)$ = 3514.0***		$\chi^2(9)$ = 3667.4***	

Notes: 1. Owing to reliability of saving data on Linqiu after 1997, data from 1986 to 1996 are used for estimations on Linqiu.
2. In order to control the endogeneity of the service station dummy, first lag of the permanent income and the share of deposit savings are used for IV of service station dummy. The village averages of those lagged variables are utilized for IV estimations.
***significant at the 1 per cent level, **at the 5 per cent level, and *at the 10 per cent level.

Linqiu and Linyi are negative and not significant. The results for Dingxiang and Taigu are consistent with our expectations. Real deposit ratios for Linqiu and Linyi households were not significant, and this may be attributed to an income effect which offsets the substitution effect of the real deposit rate. It may also be due to the degree of financial market integration, specifically the underdevelopment of financial markets and the failure of financial markets in those villages that affect portfolio selection in rural households.

The coefficient for the service station dummy variable is significant for three villages, but the signs differ. While the foundation of service stations has, as expected, a positive effect on Taigu and Linyi it has a negative effect on Linqiu. The estimated parameters of service stations in Taigu and Linyi are 0.44 and 0.53 respectively. This indicates that the establishment of service stations probably facilitated deposit savings and gave rise to a considerable portfolio shift from cash holdings to deposit savings in Taigu and Linyi. By contrast, it probably created a significant decrease in the share of deposit savings in Linqiu. As mentioned, in Linqiu economic conditions at the end of the 1980s were worsening, and the establishment of service stations may have been an impetus for the withdrawal of money from saving accounts in order to make ends meet. Hence, the establishment of service stations may contribute to the mobilization of rural household savings in developing areas, but may not do so in less developed areas.

The effects of establishing service stations, however, are not fully explained by the service station dummy term, and those effects may change with the passing of time. In order to evaluate the effect of founding service stations in terms of making rural financial systems more reliable, the variable of vintage was substituted for the service station dummy variable. In this formulation, the effect of service stations in Dingxiang, where they were established before 1986, can be estimated. The result is reported in Table 9.9. The coefficient of vintage is significantly positive in Taigu and Linyi and significantly negative in Linqiu. These results are consistent with those observed in Table 9.8. The parameter of vintage squared is significantly positive in Linqiu and Dingxiang, and significantly negative in the case of Linyi. This result shows that the effects of vintage take a positive concave form in Taigu and Linyi, a negative concave form in Linqiu, and a positive convex form in Dingxiang. The sign of the total vintage effect in Linqiu turns positive in 1996, and this indicates that it may take time for the effects of service station establishment to appear in this poor village.

Table 9.9 Estimation results for portfolio selection model (vintage)

	Linqiu (REM)		Dingxiang (REM)		Taigu (FEM)		Linyi (REM)	
	coefficient	t-statistic	coefficient	t-statistic	coefficient	t-statistic	coefficient	t-statistic
Income shock (–)	2.09E-06	0.03	6.20E-05	3.19***	7.73E-05	3.55***	1.26E-04	7.56***
Income shock (+)	–3.47E-06	–0.08	1.92E-06	0.13	8.06E-06	0.41	2.40E-05	1.88*
Permanent Income (PI)	9.48E-05	2.44**	5.61E-05	4.00***	3.44E-06	0.19	8.49E-05	6.69***
Vintage	–4.28E-02	–3.22***	–2.18E-02	–1.47	4.12E-02	4.94***	4.69E-02	7.35***
$(\text{Vintage})^2$	5.64E-03	3.27***	9.75E-04	2.04**	–8.80E-04	–1.42	–2.96E-03	–6.53***
Type I	–2.52E-03	–0.10	1.33E-02	0.44	–1.32E-02	–0.50	–3.91E-03	–0.19
Type II	0.051	1.27	0.017	0.55	0.046	1.30	–0.024	–0.86
Labors	–0.016	–0.76	–0.030	–1.64*	–0.035	–1.81*	–0.026	–2.05**
Coefficient of dependents	–0.028	–1.44	0.020	0.81	–0.014	–0.48	0.005	0.31
Real deposit rate	–1.38E-03	–0.81	2.50E-03	1.52	8.09E-04	0.42	–1.05E-02	–7.05***
Constant	0.190	2.87***	0.698	5.35***	0.460	5.19***	0.251	4.00***
Sample size	614		1,020		921		1,894	
For Wald statistics for zero slope	$\chi^2(10)$= 49.69***		$\chi^2(10)$ = 69.01***		F(10,810) = 20.22***		$\chi^2(10)$ = 270.7***	

Notes: Owing to reliability of saving data on Linqiu after 1997, data from 1986 to 1996 are used for estimation on Linqiu.
***significant at 1% level, **at 5% level, and *at 10% level.

As seen in Table 9.9, the coefficient of PI is significant in Linyi and not significant in Taigu. This is not consistent with the results seen in Table 9.8, which may be due to the correlation between PI and vintage variables. Results for estimates of income shock are virtually the same in Tables 9.8 and 9.9. Except for Linqiu, negative income shock appears to have a significant positive effect on savings deposit holdings. Positive income shock is significantly positive only in Linyi. The results for income shock are relatively robust, regardless of specifications. The coefficient for the real deposit rate is significant only in Linyi, but with a negative sign. This implies that rural households do not necessarily decide to save money based only on considerations of profitability for savings deposits. The profitability of production asset investments also seems to affect the portfolio of financial asset holdings.

9.4 Conclusions

This chapter has included an examination of the relationship between the savings decisions of rural households and the development of rural financial networks in China. To investigate the functions of rural financial systems from the viewpoint of rural households, portfolio selection models on household financial assets were estimated in order to clarify the effects of rural financial infrastructures and income variability. Rural household data of Shanxi province from MHTS panel data were used for sample villages.

The main findings of this chapter are summarized in the following three points. First, using the flow-of-funds table and RCFPO, it can be confirmed that the assets of the household sector, especially in the form of savings deposits, have been used as investment funds by the enterprise sector. These have supported rapid and steady economic growth in China without depending heavily on government spending or foreign capital. The percentage share of deposits in financial assets of rural households increased substantially in the early 1990s, and a change in portfolio selection for rural households probably took place in this period.

Secondly, in the case of the field survey on Dingxiang County in Shanxi, it was found that the number of branch offices of the RCC (called service stations) increased rapidly during the 1980s. These service stations have played important roles in rural finance. Station workers are paid according to the amount of deposits in each service station, and this creates an incentive to collect more deposits from the village people. In turn, this contributes to a mobilization of savings at the village level.

Thirdly, the estimated result of portfolio selection models between cash holdings and savings deposit holdings demonstrated that the foundation of service stations at the village level has contributed to a rise in the percentage share of savings deposit holdings in every village, with the exception of Linqiu, the poorest village. This indicates that the effects of service station establishment are not uniform between villages. The establishment of service stations contributes significantly to the mobilization of rural household savings in middle-level and upper-level villages. Further, the increase of predicted permanent income is likely to induce a shift from cash to savings deposit holdings. Unexpected negative income is likely to impede the mobilization of deposit savings in rural households. However, positive income shock does not necessarily lead to an increase in the savings deposit ratio for financial assets.

From this study, it seems evident that the development of financial infrastructures in rural China has made a strong contribution to the mobilization of household savings in that sector. Combined with the increase of permanent income due to the decentralization and development of the rural economy, the establishment of service stations has made accessibility to formal finance in rural areas much easier, and this has caused a shift of portfolio selection from cash holdings to deposit savings.

It must be remembered that the behaviors of rural households in respect of financial asset selection are not the same among all villages. Especially in poor areas, the development of financial branch offices has not necessarily contributed to the mobilization of savings. This suggests that the indiscriminate development of a financial infrastructure may not lead directly to the mobilization of household savings in less developed areas and may actually impose a heavy economic burden on the formal financial sector. In evaluating the effects of the financial infrastructure at the rural level, differences in the economic structure of each village as well as the efficiency of financial networks as a whole must be taken into consideration.

Notes

1 Tang (2003) has made a more systematic investigation of the structure of I–S balances of each sector.
2 The characteristics of economic transition in Eastern Europe and the CIS are briefly summarized in EBRD (1999) and chapters 1 and 2 in this volume.

3 Field surveys and interviews were conducted with great help from the Department of Agriculture in Shanxi Province and Dingxiang County. Data were gathered in Dingxiang County and Taiyuan November 21–4 2002 and July 12–15 2004.

4 Production assets do not include agricultural land, housing, or consumer durable goods. Further, production assets are evaluated at book prices, not taking depreciation into account.

5 The percentage share of households under the poverty line in Linqiu has risen from 55 per cent in 1986 to 72 per cent in 1991. The poverty ratio in Linqiu villages is calculated based on the official poverty line (per capita household income below 635 yuan (price in 1998)) as defined by the National Bureau of Statistics. The definition of poverty line is briefly described in Rural Survey Organization of National Bureau of Statistics (ed.) (2000).

6 See Deaton (1992) and Besley (1995). Guiso, Jappelli and Terlizzese (1996) and Carroll and Samwick (1997) examine relationships among portfolio selections, changes in permanent income and/or income shocks in developed countries.

7 Jalan and Ravallion (2001) adopted a first-stage autoregressive formulation for ν_{it}, and using white noise ω_{it}, defined "household-specific income uncertainty" as follows:

$$\hat{\sigma}^2_{i,y} = \Sigma(\omega_{it} - \overline{\omega})^2/T \ (T = \text{total survey years})$$

Although the same approach was tried here for estimation of the portfolio selection model, the result of this estimation is neither stable nor robust. Therefore, a more direct definition of income uncertainty, as mentioned in the text, is used in this chapter.

8 Based on the statistical value of the Hausman test, estimation methods have been determined to be significant ($p < .05$). A Random Effect Model (REM) is adopted relative to Linqiu in Table 9.8 and in Linqiu, Dingxiang, and Linyi in Table 9.9. A Fixed Effects Model (FEM) is adopted for Dingxiang, Taigu and Linyi in Table 9.8 and for Taigu in Table 9.9.

9 The percentage share of households that had positive deposit savings in Linqiu drastically decreased from 59 per cent in 1986 to 21 per cent in 1991. This low level has remained consistent since that time, while other villages have maintained a ratio of 70 to 90 per cent during the survey period.

References

Adams, Dale W. (1978) "Mobilizing Household Savings through Rural Financial Markets," *Economic Development and Cultural Change* 26(3), 547–60.

Alderman, Harold (1996) "Saving and Economic Shocks in Rural Pakistan," *Journal of Development Economics* 51(2), 343–65.

Besley, T. (1995) "Saving, Credit and Insurance," in J. Behrman and T.N. Srinivasan (eds), *Handbook of Development Economics*, vol. III. Amsterdam: North-Holland.

Carroll, Christopher and Andrew Samwick (1997) "The Nature of Precautionary Wealth," *Journal of Monetary Economics* 40(1), 41–71.

Deaton, Angus (1992) *Understanding Consumption*. Oxford: Oxford University Press.

EBRD (1999) *Transition Report 1999: Ten Years of Transition*. London: EBRD.

Guiso, Luigi, Tullio Jappelli and Daniele Terlizzese (1996) "Income Risk, Borrowing Constraints, and Portfolio Choice," *American Economic Review*, 86(1), 158–72.

Hellmann, Thomas, Kevin Murdock and Joseph Stiglitz (1997) "Financial Restraint: Towards a New Paradigm," in M. Aoki, H.-K. Kim and M. Okuno-Fujiwara (eds), *The Role of Government in East Asian Economic Development: Comparative Institutional Analysis*. Oxford: Clarendon Press, pp. 163–207.

Hellmann, Thomas, Kevin Murdock and Joseph Stiglitz (1998) "Financial Restraint and the Market Enhancing View," in M. Aoki (ed.), *Proceedings of the IEA Round Table Conference: The Institutional Foundation of Economic Development in East Asia*, pp. 255–84.

Izumida, Yoichi (2003) *Rural Development Finance: Asian Experiences and Economic Growth (Nouson Kaihatu Kinyu Ron: Ajia no Keiken to Keizai Hatten)*. Tokyo: University of Tokyo Press (in Japanese).

Jalan, Jyotsna and Martin Ravallion (2001) "Behavioral Responses to Risk in Rural China," *Journal of Development Economics* 66(1), 23–49.

Office for Policy Research of CCP and Office on RCFPO of Ministry of Agriculture (eds) (2001) *National Rural Social-economic Survey Data Collection 1986–1999*. Beijing: China Agriculture Press.

Rosenzweig, Mark and Hans Binswanger (1993) "Wealth, Weather Risk and the Composition and Profitability of Agricultural Investments," *Economic Journal* 103(416), 56–78.

Rural Survey Organization of National Bureau of Statistics (ed.) (2000) *Poverty Monitoring Report of Rural China 2000*. Beijing: China Statistics Press.

Tang, Cheng (2003) "Analysis on Money Flow in China after the 1990s," METI-RAD Working Paper Series No. 2.

Zimmerman, Frederick and Michael Carter (2003) "Asset Smoothing, Consumption Smoothing and the Reproduction of Inequality under Risk and Subsistence Constraints," *Journal of Development Economics* 71(2), 233–60.

10

Repression of the Banking Sector in the Transition to a Market-based Economy: The Case of Vietnam

Koji Kubo

10.1 Introduction

One of the characteristics of Vietnam's transition from a planned to a market-based economy is that the Communist party-led government directed the process. The government demonstrated leadership in implementing a "shock therapy" stabilization program in 1989–91, which comprised price liberalization and the abolition of central planning. The stabilization program provided the basis for subsequent economic growth.[1] Real GDP recorded an average annual growth rate of 7.3 per cent for the period between 1989 and 2003.[2] In terms of the banking sector, the stabilized macroeconomic environment gave impetus to savings mobilization. The deposit-to-GDP ratio has tripled to over 50 per cent in 15 years in the process of transformation of a mono-bank system to a two-tier banking system.

On the other hand, the government continues to preserve direct controls over the economy. The state-owned enterprises (SOEs) still account for more than 40 per cent of the industrial outputs. The financial sector is dominated by four large state-owned commercial banks (SOCBs). We can view this large presence of the state in the economy as constituting a particular type of transition process. With such a form of transition, there can be a conflict of interests between the roles of the government as the owner of SOEs and the regulator of the banking system. In Vietnam, the banks were repressed to supply funds to the targeted sector, notably SOEs.

The functions of the banking system in a centrally planned economy and a market-based economy differ substantially. In a centrally planned economy, the role of the banking system is to allocate funds according to the planning needs identified by the government. In a market-based economy, its functions are more positive. Following Levine (1997), we can list the following five basic functions: (1) risk diversification and maturity transformation; (2) producing information about investment and allocating resources; (3) monitoring borrowers and enforcing discipline; (4) mobilizing savings; and (5) facilitating transactions. With these functions, financial intermediaries play roles in economic growth. We may argue that among these functions, (2) and (3) are the functions specific to the banks in a market-based economy, whereas in a centrally planned economy, it is the government that performs these functions, albeit imperfectly. In this chapter, we call the ability to perform these two functions the "lending capacity."

In this chapter, we are interested in how the repression affected the development of the lending capacity of the Vietnamese banking system in the course of that transition process. The banking system had to develop lending capacity through its operations. In addition, the development of the lending capacity largely depends upon institutional factors such as accounting practices (for the information production on borrowers) and commercial legislation (for the enforcement of contracts). The preparation of the institutional environment requires an explicit government commitment. However, as the government repressed the banking system by forcing it to supply credit to the targeted sector, the repression might hinder the development of the sector's lending capacity.

Our intention in this chapter is to examine the extent of the financial repression and its effects on the lending capacity of the banking system. While the Vietnamese economy recorded notable levels of economic growth in the 1990s, the lower growth rates in recent years suggests further economic reforms are necessary in order to sustain development. The pressure to allocate credit to the SOEs is one area that requires such reforms. In terms of industrial output, the annual growth rate of the private sector recorded an average of 20 per cent in 2000–02, which is much higher than that recorded in the state sector (12.5 per cent). However, the private sector is reportedly credit constrained. Through an analysis of the financial repression, we shed light on the lending capacity and draw some policy implications for the further banking sector reforms. In particular, we verify whether the financial repression left room for the development of the lending capacity.

The structure of this chapter is as follows. In the next section, we illustrate the conditions of the repression in terms of credit allocation, interest rate controls, and non-performing loans. In section 10.3, we review the recent banking sector reforms from the viewpoint how the reform afforded the banks the scope for sound banking operations. In section 10.4, in order to evaluate the effects of the repressive environment on the lending capacity development, we perform a quantitative analysis on the loan supply behavior of the banking system. Finally, in section 10.5, we summarize the analysis and draw some conclusions.

10.2 Conditions of the repression

The state-owned commercial banks (SOCBs) were the central pillars of the banking sector. At the same time, they were the primary suppliers of credit to the government-targeted sector – namely the SOEs. The interest margins were regulated in favor of the borrowers. A large portion of the policy-directed lending turned into non-performing loans. In this section, we illustrate these repressive conditions of the banking sector.

10.2.1 Dominant state-owned commercial banks

The Vietnamese banking sector has been geared to supply funds to the targeted sector, notably the state-owned enterprises (SOEs), and the four large state-owned commercial banks (SOCBs) dominate the banking sector. In 2004, the banking sector in Vietnam consisted of five state-owned commercial banks (SOCBs), two government financial institutions, 35 joint stock commercial banks (JSBs), four joint-venture banks, and 27 foreign bank branches. According to the World Bank (2002), the banking sector is dominated by four large SOCBs, which accounted for around 70 per cent of domestic lending. The share of the foreign banks is around 15 per cent, and the JSBs and the joint-venture banks have market shares of 12 per cent and 3 per cent, respectively.[3]

The current shape of the SOCBs is largely the result of the transformation of the mono-bank system into a two-tier banking system from 1988. Before the transformation, the Vietnamese banking sector consisted of the State Bank of Vietnam (SBV, the central bank), the Bank for Foreign Trade of Vietnam (Vietcombank), which engaged in foreign exchange transactions, and the Bank for Investment and Development of Vietnam (BIDV), which supplied long-term credit mainly to infrastructure projects. In the transition process, Vietcombank, and later the BIDV, were changed into commercial banks. Short-term commercial lending was divested from the central bank, and moved to two newly launched SOCBs in the late 1980s – the Vietnam Bank for Agricultural and Rural Development (VBARD) and the Industrial and Commercial Bank of Vietnam (Incombank).[4]

Table 10.1 Selected indicators of the deposit money banks in Vietnam, 1990–2003

	1990	*1991*	*1992*	*1993*	*1994*	*1995*	*1996*	*1997*	*1998*	*1999*	*2000*	*2001*	*2002*	*2003*
Real GDP (annual percentage change)	5.1	5.8	8.7	8.1	8.8	9.5	9.3	8.2	5.8	4.8	6.8	6.9	7.1	7.3
GDP deflator (annual percentage change)	42.1	72.8	32.6	17.4	17.0	17.0	8.7	6.6	8.8	5.7	3.4	1.9	4.0	5.4
Total loans (percentage of GDP)	13.9	13.1	13.7	16.5	18.7	18.5	18.7	19.8	20.1	28.2	35.3	39.3	43.1	49.0
Total deposits (percentage of GDP)	17.4	17.7	14.8	12.8	13.6	14.4	15.2	17.9	20.9	29.8	38.7	44.4	47.6	53.1
Lending rate (VND, working capital)	48.0	42.0	32.4	25.2	28.3	28.3	16.1	12.7	14.7	11.7	9.8	8.8	9.9	na.
Deposit rate (VND, 3 month savings-household)	na.	na.	24.0	16.8	18.2	18.2	8.7	8.1	9.7	4.0	4.3	5.9	7.0	na.
Lending rate (foreign currency)	na.	na.	na.	7.5	9.0	9.5	9.5	8.5	7.5	6.5	7.0	4.6	4.3	na.
Deposit rate (6 month, foreign currency)	na.	na.	na.	na.	na.	na.	na.	na.	4.9	4.5	4.8	1.6	1.6	na.

Source: Real GDP, GDP deflator: IMF, *International Financial Statistics*. Total loans, Total deposits: World Bank (1995) and M F Country Report (various issues) for 1990–2001, and IMF, *International Financial Statistics* for 2002–2003.

Note: Interest rates are in per cent per year, end of period.

The entry of non-state banks into the banking industry were liberalized by the Law on the State Bank of Vietnam (central bank) and the Law on Credit Institutions in 1991. By 1996, more than 50 joint stock commercial banks (JSBs) had obtained banking licenses. For JSBs, raising the capital reserve has been a barrier to their growth. The legislation required that, from 1994, at least 10 per cent of the shares must be held by SOEs. Recently, the bulk of JSBs are majority owned by SOEs, SOCBs and the government. With regard to foreign bank branches, their operations were partially liberalized in 1991, while restrictions remained in operations such as local currency deposits.[5] Consequently, these circumstances are advantageous to the SOCBs

The playing field of the banking industry is not level between the SOCBs and other banks, since the branch network of non-state banks have been restricted. For example, VBARD has 1,568 branches, including savings counters, and Incombank has 104 branches, while the Asia Commercial Bank, the largest non-state bank, has only 33 branches. In addition, the regulation on the capital share of JSBs, which necessitates that at least 10 per cent of shares be held by SOEs, effectively hampered efforts by JSBs to raise paid-up capital (Hattori, 1998).

10.2.2 Credit allocations and interest rate controls

The Vietnamese credit market is somewhat segmented. Almost 50 per cent of the loan balance of SOCBs goes to the SOEs, foreign banks serve foreign companies in Vietnam, and the JSBs' target customers are mainly the private sector. Table 10.2 shows the distribution of bank credit. The market share of the four SOCBs has remained around 70 per cent in recent years, while in 1977 credits to the non-state sector surpassed those to the state sector. Not only JSBs and foreign banks, but also the SOCBs increased their supply of credits to the private sector. It should be noted, however, that the bulk of the agricultural sector is included in the private sector, and that the loans of VBARD to farmers and traders account for a large proportion of the SOCBs' loans to the "private sector."[6]

With regard to interest rates, by 1995, the central bank had come to determine both the lending and the deposit rates. In 1996, the direct interest rate control was replaced with: (i) the imposition of a ceiling on the lending rate; and (ii) controls on the maximum spread between lending and deposit rates. These changes effectively allowed banks to lend with a lower lending rate and to collect deposits with a higher deposit rate. In 1998, the controls on the spread were abolished and the deposit rate was fully liberalized, though the ceiling on lending

Table 10.2 Distribution of bank credit, 1989–2002

	1989	*1990*	*1991*	*1992*	*1993*	*1994*	*1995*	*1996*	*1997*	*1998*	*1999*	*2000*	*2001*	*2002*
	Trillions of VND													
Loans to SOEs														
4 SOCBs	3.5	5.2	8.5	11.4	14.4	18.6	20.9	22.0	26.6	34.2	na.	61.3	72.8	81.6
Other banks	—	—	0.5	0.9	1.1	2.4	3.2	4.8	4.6	3.9	na.	8.7	6.9	7.9
Loans to other sectors														
4 SOCBs	0.5	0.6	1.0	2.5	6.6	9.0	12.8	16.3	21.4	24.9	na.	52.9	70.6	93.9
Other banks	—	—	0.0	0.3	1.0	3.3	5.4	7.7	9.6	9.7	na.	32.8	38.8	47.7
	Percentage													
4 SOCBs' share in bank market														
Total	—	—	94.6	91.9	90.7	82.8	79.6	75.5	77.2	81.4	67.9	73.3	75.8	75.9
To SOEs	—	—	94.5	92.3	92.7	88.6	86.6	82.2	85.3	89.9	na.	87.6	91.3	91.2
To other sectors	—	—	95.5	89.9	86.5	73.0	70.3	68.0	69.1	72.0	na.	61.7	64.5	66.3
Exposure to SOEs in bank portfolio														
4 SOCBs	87.6	90.2	89.9	82.2	68.4	67.4	62.0	57.5	55.4	57.9	na.	53.7	50.8	46.5
Other banks	—	—	91.8	77.5	52.3	41.8	37.4	38.5	32.5	28.6	na.	21.0	15.1	14.2

Source: World Bank (1995); IMF Country Report (various issues).

rates remained. Lending rates were first liberalized in foreign currency lending in 2001, followed by the VND lending rate in 2002. The margin between the VND lending and deposit rates was held down to between 5 and 10 per cent until 1998, and it widened to 7.7 per cent in 1999 after the abolition of the interest spread controls.

10.2.3 Non-performing loans

A measure of the negative influences of repressions on the banking system is the level of non-performing loans (NPLs). The policy-directed lending to the SOEs consisted of the bulk of the non-performing loans of the SOCBs. In Table 10.3, we summarize the changes in overdue loans (officially classified NPLs) of the deposit money banks. The NPL ratio, although high, is considered to be significantly underestimated since the definition of overdue loans was vague. The introduction of prudential regulations did not prohibit loose loan classification, such as the rescheduling of overdue loans.

According to IMF (1999), based on international accounting standards (IAS), the NPL ratios of the four SOCBs at the end of 1997 were estimated at 30–35 per cent on average, ranging from 17–25 per cent for BIDV and VBARD, and 40–45 per cent for Vietcombank and Incombank. With regard to JSBs, the estimated size of their NPLs was 30–40 per cent of their total loans in 1998–99 (IMF, 1999). The sharp rise in their NPL ratio in 1997 was largely attributable to the problems of letters of credit in the face of the Asian financial crisis.

10.3 Recent reforms and the lending capatity

In this section, we review the recent reforms of the Vietnamese banking sector in order to consider how far the operational ground was improved for sound lending operations. In particular, we focus on the following two points: (i) insulation of the government interventions on the banking operations; and (ii) preparation of the institutional framework for the transparency and the accountability of the bank management.

10.3.1 Insulation of government influences

First, it has been a problem that the government as the owner of the SOEs exerted influences on the regulation and supervision of the banking sector. Under the Law on the Central Bank legislated in 1997, while the central bank was in charge of the regulation and supervision of the banking system, it enjoyed no independence from the government,

Table 10.3 Overdue loans of deposit money banks, 1989–2002

	1989	*1990*	*1991*	*1992*	*1993*	*1994*	*1995*	*1996*	*1997*	*1998*	*1999*	*2000*	*2001*	*2002*
Overdue loans						(Trillions of VND)								
4 SOCBs	0.5	1.1	1.9	1.9	2.6	3.0	3.1	4.2	5.8	6.5	7.8	10.9	12.0	12.7
Other banks	—	—	0.2	0.2	0.1	0.1	0.3	0.5	1.9	2.2	4.1	4.2	4.1	3.6
Total	—	—	2.0	2.1	4.4	3.2	3.3	4.7	7.7	8.7	11.9	15.1	16.1	16.3
Percentage of NPL to SOEs	86.9	83.9	81.4	81.5	38.2	58.8	49.7	44.2	34.8	34.7	na.	na.	na.	na.
NPL ratio (NPL/total loans)														
4 SOCBs (%)	12.3	18.5	19.7	13.7	12.2	11.1	9.1	11.0	12.0	11.0	10.8	10.0	8.8	7.6
Other banks (%)	—	—	29.1	14.1	6.4	1.7	3.3	4.2	13.5	16.4	28.9	9.0	7.7	5.6

Source: World Bank (1995) and IMF Country Report (various issues).

because the governor of the central bank was given a seat in the cabinet. In this circumstance, the credit supply to the SOEs was given priority over the stability of the banking sector. In fact, as the performance of the SOEs worsened in 1997–98, prudential regulations were relaxed in order to expand credit for them. Although the legislation was revised in 2003, the independence of the central bank is not yet secured.

Another challenge is to divest the SOCBs of policy-directed lending. In this respect, two government financial institutions were launched recently. The first, the Development Assistance Fund (DAF), established in 2000, focuses on the long-term financing of infrastructure projects. The second, the Social Policy Bank, was separated from the VBARD in 2002 in order to concentrate on poverty alleviation. These institutions raise funds mainly through government bonds and borrowing from governmental institutions and the SOCBs. They rapidly expanded lending, but their loan balance amounts to less than 20 per cent of the four large SOCBs.

As suggested earlier, state ownership is considered to make it difficult for the SOCBs to operate independently. This inefficiency arose not only from the interventions of the government to credit allocations, but also from the dependence of the management of the SOCBs on government support. With the intention of improving the accountability of management, the government scheduled the equitization of the SOCBs for 2004, but at the time of writing the plan has not yet been carried out.

10.3.2 Preparation of the institutional framework

The increased transparency of operations and accountability of the management deter outside stakeholders from intervening in banking operations. In this regard, the audits of banks have been adjusted gradually to comply with international accounting standards (IAS). For instance, the loan classification scheme became more compatible with international standards in 2001; the new legislation required banks to file the entire loan balance as overdue if any interest or principal payment became overdue. However, the enforcement of such reforms is still imperfect.

On the other hand, given the impaired assets of the banks under the repression, the consolidation of their balance sheet is necessary to encourage the efforts of the banks for better credit risk management. With regard to the JSBs in particular, the central bank carried out an assessment of the assets of the JSBs in Ho Chi Minh City in the aftermath of the Asian financial crisis. The assessment revealed the undercapitalization of many JSBs,[7] and pushed the government and the central bank to implement a comprehensive reform program for the distressed JSBs in the period 1999–2002. The program required the JSBs to comply with minimum capital requirements within a time schedule, and to strengthen operation skills and management. While relatively less distressed JSBs underwent the temporary capital injection by the SOCBs, others were merged or liquidated. Consequently, the 51 JSBs in 1999 were reorganized into 39 banks by 2002.

The consolidation of the SOCBs has been put off because their reform would involve substantial reform of the SOEs. The government instructed the SOCBs to set targets for NPL resolution. At the same time, it set a recapitalization scheme to make four installments with a total of VND 10.39 trillion in 2002–04, which was equivalent to about 2 per cent of GDP in 2002.[8] A phased recapitalization was essentially made conditional on meeting the targets, so that the capital injection would provide incentives for them to promptly resolve their NPLs. However, resolution has been slow, especially of the loans to SOEs.

10.4 Credit supply behavior under the repression

We consider that one of the obstacles to the development of lending capacity in the Vietnamese banking sector might be the policy-directed lending and implicit interventions of the stakeholders to the bank's lending decisions. In addition to the SOCBs, the JSBs may be subject to such repression as their large shareholders, including the SOEs and the SOCBs. In this section, we attempt to evaluate quantitatively the repression by focusing on the loan supply behavior of the banking system in the period when the lending rate ceiling was in operation. The baseline hypothesis is as follows: in the absence of repression, bank's lending decisions are commercially based, and we would observe an upward-sloping loan supply curve. With the repression, the loan supply would not always react to the ceiling rate.

The regulations on the lending rate may allow us to identify the supply behavior of the banking system. In a liberalized credit market with no ceiling on the lending rate, the volume of loans is determined by both demand and supply factors. Thus, we cannot identify the loan supply curve from the observed loan volume. In contrast, as far as the interest controls as in Vietnam are concerned, they kept the lending rate artificially low. We may assume that the low lending rate brought about excess demand for loans, and that demand factors did not affect the loan volume *ex post*. With such an assumption, we estimate the loan supply behavior of the banking system from the observed loan volume.

10.4.1 Data and estimation strategy

We have collected the annual financial data of commercial banks in Vietnam for the period 1996–2002 from *Bankscope*, and macro-economic data from the *IMF Country Report Statistical Appendix*. The balanced panel data comprise the four state-owned commercial banks (SOCBs), nine joint stock commercial banks (JSBs), and two joint-venture banks. The list of banks with their total asset sizes and profits (deficits) after taxation is provided in Table A10.1 in the Appendix.

Employing panel data of the banks' financial data, we first estimate the following credit supply function with a fixed effect model:

$$\ln B_{i,t} = \alpha_i \cdot Dummy_i + \beta_1 \cdot r_t + \beta_2 \cdot r_t^T + u_{i,t} \tag{10.1}$$

The dependent variable is the logarithm of the loan balance of each bank. The explanatory variables are r, the ceiling rate, and r^T, the Treasury bond rate. We are interested in the coefficient of the ceiling rate, β_1. A positive and significant β_1 implies commercial-based credit supply behavior. In contrast, $\beta_1 < 0$ indicates the possibility of a backward-bending credit supply curve. Alternatively, the coefficient can be insignificant if the credit supply of banks is influenced by other factors such as government interventions. Treasury bonds are substitutes for loans in a bank's portfolio, so that the coefficient on the Treasury bond rate is expected to be negative.

Estimations with level variables appear spurious. For the estimation result of (10.1), $\beta_1 = -0.131$, and the result is significant at the one per cent confidence level. However, the Durbin–Watson statistic is 1.038, which implies the autocorrelation of error terms. To cope with the problem, we take the first difference of the variables as follows:

$$\Delta \ln B_{i,t} = \alpha_i \cdot Dummy_t + \beta_1 \cdot \Delta r_t + \beta_2 \cdot \Delta r_t^T + X_{i,t} \cdot \gamma + v_{i,t} \tag{10.2}$$

where the symbol Δ indicates the first difference.

In equation (10.2), the dependent variable can be interpreted as the growth rate of loans. We add $\boldsymbol{X}$, a matrix of control variables. For the control variables, we include the first lag of the equity-to-loans ratio, the deposit growth rate of individual banks, and the GDP growth rate. The equity-to-loans ratio is used as a proxy for the capital adequacy ratio. A low capital adequacy ratio bank is considered to be

Figure 10.1 Plots of the loan growth rates (SOCBs)

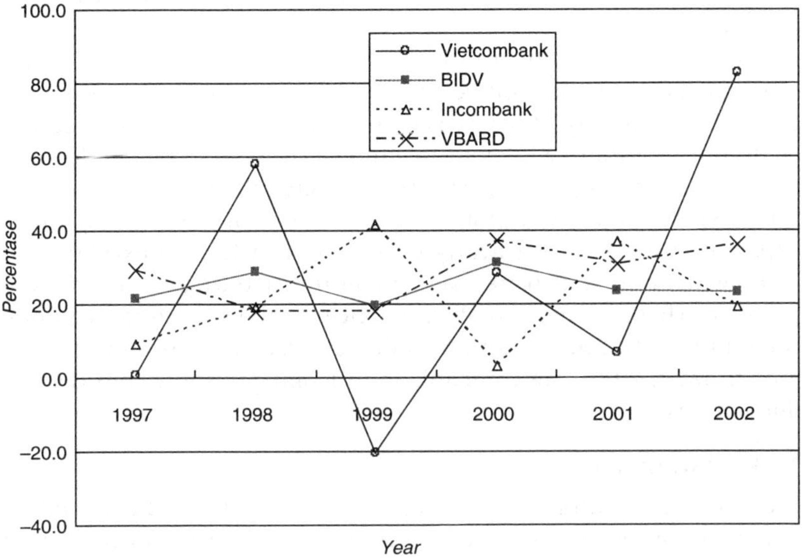

Source: *Bankscope*.

Figure 10.2 Plots of the loan growth rates (JSBs and joint-venture banks)

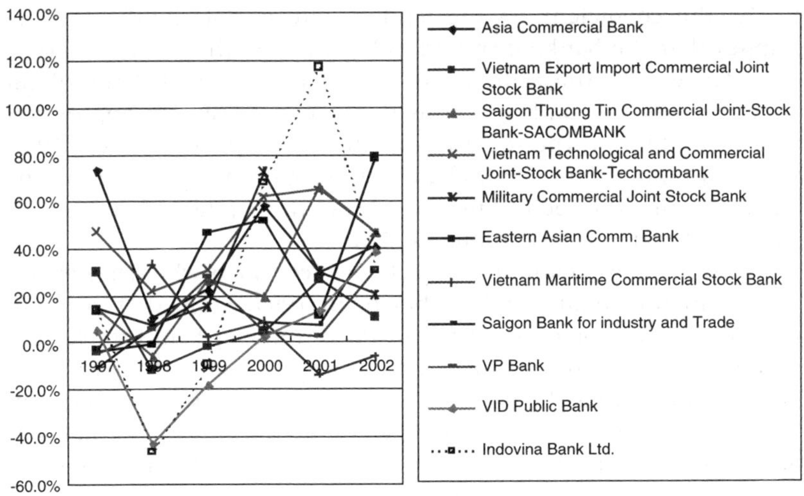

Source: *Bankscope*.

inhibited from expanding its loans by prudential regulations. The sign of the coefficient on this ratio is expected to be positive. The GDP growth rate is expected to capture changes in technology, which in turn improve the creditworthiness of borrowers. The sign of the coefficient is expected to be positive. Finally, the growth rate of deposit captures the availability of funds available for loans. When banks ration credit due to a shortage of loanable funds, the growth rate of deposits may be positively correlated with the loan growth rate.

Figures 10.1 and 10.2 plot the growth rates of loans. Most banks expanded their loans in nearly every period, with the exception of 1998, when non-state banks were under restructuring due to the NPL problem. There are remarkable differences in the growth rates among the four SOCBs. BIDV and VBARD demonstrate generally steady loan growth rates, while Vietcombank and Incombank show considerable fluctuations.

10.4.2 Estimation results

We estimate equation (10.2) using the Pooled Ordinary Least Squares (OLS) estimation and the fixed effect model estimation for the period 1997–2002.[9] Table 10.4 summarizes the estimation results. With regard to the pooled OLS estimations, the intercept dummy for SOCBs is not significant. We cannot detect a systematic difference in the credit supply behavior between SOCBs and other banks (Models 1 to 3)

Regarding estimations using the fixed effect method (Models 4 to 7), firstly, the coefficient on the lending rate is not significant. This implies that the banking system did not adjust the credit supply in accordance with the ceiling rate. Secondly, the coefficients of the Treasury bond rate and GDP growth rate do not have the appropriate signs. In addition, the inclusion of the intercept dummy for 1998, which is highly significant, changes the significance of these coefficients. Finally, the coefficient of the lag of the capital to loans ratio is significant and has the appropriate sign.

We estimate two additional models. One considers whether there is a change in the credit supply behavior in 1999. From that year, the deposit mobilization of the aggregate deposit money banks accelerated, and the deposits-to-GDP ratio surpassed the loans-to-GDP ratio. There is a possibility that the banking sector as a whole relied less on the refinancing facilities of the central bank from this point, and that their autonomy on lending decisions increased. To test this behavioral change, we add an intercept dummy and a slope dummy on the lending rate change for the period 1999–2002. These dummy variables

Table 10.4 Estimation results

	(1)	(2)	(3)	(4)	(5)	(6)	(7)	(8)	(9)
	Pooled OLS	*Pooled OLS*	*Pooled OLS*	*Fixed effect*	*Fixed effect*	*Fixed effect*	*Fixed effect*	*Fixed effect*	*Fixed effect*
Dependent variable					*f* ¢lnB				
Explanatory variables	0.167***	0.618***	0.646***						
constant	(5.406)	(4.408)	(4.536)						
f ¢r	–0.003	–0.010	–0.010	–0.004	–0.010	–0.009	0.030	–0.023	0.001
	(–0.223)	(–0.710)	(–0.751)	(–0.250)	(–0.768)	(0.676)	(1.573)	(–1.690)	(0.010)
f ¢ TB rate	0.003	0.018*	0.017*	0.003	0.018*	0.091*	0.011	0.015	
	(0.257)	(1.708)	(1.665)	(0.271)	(1.802)	(1.973)	(1.180)	(1.127)	
f ¢ Nominal GDP		–4.005***	–3.978***	–3.998***	–4.070***	–1.143	0.198		
		(–3.290)	(–3.270)		(–3.462)	(–3.578)	(–0.743)	(0.054)	
C/B ratio (–1)			–0.111			0.347*	0.406**	0.399**	
			(–1.077)			(1.814)	(2.196)	(2.135)	
SOCB	0.038	0.040	0.018						
	(0.696)	(0.761)	(0.324)						
f ¢D/D									0.619***
									(5.743)
DU98							–0.287***		
							(2.697)		
DU9902								0.045	
								(1.527)	
DU9902* *f* ¢r								0.243	
			(1.439)						
Durbin–Watson stat.	1.517	1.707	1.758	1.920	2.233	2.259	2.256	2.254	2.017
Adjusted Rsqd	–0.028	0.077	0.079	0.045	0.170	0.195	0.261	0.252	0.341

Source: Author.

Note: ***denotes statistical significance at the 1 per cent confidence level, **at the 5 per cent level, and *at the 10 per cent level.

are, however, insignificant (Model 8). The Wald test fails to reject the null hypothesis that the sum of the coefficients of the lending rate and the slope dummy is zero.

The other model is to test if the banks may have faced shortages of loanable funds so that the credit supply growth was constrained by deposit growth (Model 9). The coefficient of the deposit growth rate is highly significant, supporting the hypothesis of a shortage in loanable funds. However, this may be a biased estimation due to the endogeneity of this explanatory variable. If we replace this variable with its lag, it is no longer significant.[10]

10.4.3 Interpretation of the results

The preliminary analysis implies that the lending decisions of banks were not always commercially based during the sample period; the credit supply of banks did not respond to changes in the ceiling rate. One of the possible reasons for this relationship between the ceiling rate and the credit supply is that banks might have intervened to supply credit at a lending rate lower than the ceiling rate. In fact, the lending rate of the policy-directed loans was reportedly lower than the ceiling rate.

Secondly, the estimation result of Model 9 suggests that credit growth has been constrained by the growth in deposits. Given the endogeneity of the explanatory variable, we have to be careful in interpreting this result.

Thirdly, while the implementation of prudential regulations on capital adequacy appears to be imperfect, the results imply that undercapitalization may have constrained credit growth.[11] Given the weak capitalization of many banks, the bank capital must be strengthened to ensure the sustained growth of the credit supply.

10.5 Concluding remarks

Among the characteristics of the transition process in Vietnam are that the Communist party-led government directed the transition process, and that there is still a large state presence in both the real and financial sectors. This combination of a transition process with a large state sector resembles the Chinese experience. In such a transition process, there can be a conflict of interests between the government roles as both the owner of the state-owned enterprises (SOEs) and also the regulator of the banking system. In Vietnam, the banks were repressed in order to secure adequate funding for the targeted sector, notably SOEs. The concentrated lending on the SOEs, the interest rate controls and the high NPL ratios all indicate that the government prioritized the credit supply to the SOEs.

In general, in order to try and ensure a smooth transition to a market-based economy, the banking system has to take over from the government the functions of producing information about investment and allocating resources, and of monitoring borrowers and enforcing discipline. It is through the market-based lending operations that the banking system develops the capacity for these functions. However, the preliminary econometric analysis indicates that the lending decisions of the banks may not yet be commercially based in Vietnam. We may assert that the repression might hinder the development of the lending capacity.

The recent deceleration in the rate of economic growth suggests further economic reforms are necessary for sustained development. Given the substantial presence of the state sector in the economy, a continued reform in the banking sector will be necessary to insulate the interventions of the outside stakeholders and to prepare the institutional framework for sound banking operations.

Notes

1 Fforde and de Vylder (1996) provide a comprehensive summary of the early phase of the transition process in Vietnam.

2 Calculated from data of IMF, *International Financial Statistics*.

3 These market shares are as of December 2000. World Bank (2002) also shows the distribution of loans by borrowers; Agricultural, forestry and fishery sector (25 per cent), industrial sector (16 per cent), commerce (22 per cent), construction (13 per cent), and others (22 per cent).

4 The other state-owned commercial bank is the Housing Bank of Mekong Delta.

5 For local currency deposits, foreign banks can only offer demand deposits. Time deposits are not permitted. In addition, the amount of local currency deposits is tightly controlled in proportion with the equity of the bank.

6 In 2000, VBARD's loan balance to such categories was VND18.9 trillion, amounting to 46 per cent of its loan balance, or 35 per cent of loans by the SOCBs to the private sector.

7 We can trace the weak capital position of many of these banks back to their establishment as commercial banks in the early 1990s. Many were created through twinning of distressed credit cooperatives for the purpose of rescuing them. Thus, the initial regulations on the entry of JSBs were not very strict. The minimum capital was VND10 billion for rural JSBs, and VND50 billion for JSBs incorporated in Ho Chi Minh City. In addition,

these banks inherited bad loans from the former institutions (Hattori, 1998).

8 For the capital injection, the government transferred the special recapitalization bond with a term of 20 years that carries an annual coupon of 3.3 per cent. Therefore, the net present value of the SOCB recapitalization cost amounts to more than that described as above.

9 Taking differences reduces one observation.

10 The Two-stage Least Squares (2SLS) method can be used to evade the problem with endogeneity. However, we could not find any appropriate variables which could be used as an instrument variable for the deposit growth rate. For instance, the deposit interest rate, which is a candidate in this case, was negatively correlated with the deposit growth rate.

11 Fries and Taci (2002) performed a similar analysis on the banks in the transition economies in the East Europe. In their analysis, the equity to total assets ratio is significantly related with the growth in credit.

References

Fforde, A. and S. de Vylder (1996) *From Plan to Market: the Economic Transition in Vietnam*. Boulder: Westview Press.

Fries, S. and A. Taci (2002) "Banking Reform and Development in Transition Economies," EBRD Working paper No. 71.

Hattori, R. (1998) "Financial Reforms and Banking Crises in Vietnam," in S. Watanabe (ed.), *Financial Crises and Regulations*, IDE Research Series No. 485 (in Japanese)

Hellmann, T., K. Murdock and J. Stiglitz (1996) "Financial Restraint: Toward a New Paradigm," in M. Aoki, M. Okuno-Fujiwara and H. Kim (eds), *The Role of Government in East Asian Economic Development: Comparative Institutional Analysis*. Oxford: Clarendon Press, pp. 163–207.

International Monetary Fund (IMF) (various issues) *IMF Country Report* No. 03/382, 03/381, 03/380, 02/151, 02/5, 02/4, 99/56, 99/55, 98/30.

Levine, R. (1997) "Financial Development and Economic Growth: View and Agenda," *Journal of Economic Literature* 35, 688–726.

Li, D.D. (2001) "Beating the Trap of Financial Repression in China," *Cato Journal*, 21(1), 77–90.

Watanabe, S. (2000) "Bad Loan Problem in Vietnam: Ad Hoc Measures and Long-term Reform Policies," in K. Kunimune (ed.), *Financial Restructuring and Corporate Restructuring: Asian Experience*. IDE Research Series No. 510 (in Japanese).

World Bank (2002) *Banking Sector Review: Vietnam*. Washington, DC: World Bank.

World Bank (1995) *Vietnam Financial Sector Review: An Agenda for Financial Sector Development*, Report No. 13135-VN. Washington, DC: World Bank.

Appendix

Table A10.1 List of Banks

	Ownership	*Total assets (Dec. 02)*	*Income after tax (Dec. 02)*
		billions of VND	
Vietnam Bank for Agriculture and Rural Development (VBARD)	SOCB	91,359	–1,449.9
Bank for Foreign Trade of Vietnam (Vietcom bank) BIDV	SOCB	81,535	223.4
Bank for Investment and Development of Vietnam (BIDV)	SOCB	70,835	27.7
Industrial and Commercial Bank of Vietnam (Incom bank)	SOCB	68,012	175.7
Asia Commercial Bank	JSB	9,368	123.3
Vietnam Export Import Commercial Joint Stock Bank	JSB	4,773	na.
Saigon Thuong Tin Commercial Joint–Stock Bank (SACOM BANK)	JSB	4,336	55.5
Vietnam Technological and Commercial Joint-Stock Bank (Techcom bank)	JSB	4,062	4.6
Military Commercial Joint Stock Bank	JSB	3,969	61.6
Eastern Asian Commercial Bank	JSB	3,126	57.0
VID Public Bank	Joint-venture bank	2,028	15.4
Vietnam Maritime Commercial Stock Bank	JSB	1,921	na.
Indovina Bank	Joint-venture bank	1,888	35.4
Saigon Bank for Industry and Trade	JSB	1,584	35.4
Vietnam Joint Stock Commercial Bank for Private Enterprises (VP Bank)	JSB	1,478	na.

Source: *Bankscope*.

Corporate Governance Under State Dominant Ownership

11

Improving Corporate Governance and Regulations of Power Abuse by the Controling Shareholder in China

Jianlong Zhou

11.1 Introduction

One of the most important agendas of the transition from a planned economy to a market-based economy is the separation of the company from the state. In this respect it must be said that the process in China is still ongoing. As mentioned in the Preface to this book, a slow and gradual positive transformation of institutions has been seen to date. However, those aspects of state that remain continue to have a negative impact on the corporate sector. The power abuse by the state as concentrated owner is a common phenomenon in China and is seen as a serious problem by researchers in both law and economics. This chapter and chapter 6 both approach this problem with legal and economic theories.

Company Law of the People's Republic of China (hereafter referred to merely as "company law")[1] was enacted in December 1993 to advance the reform that a state-owned enterprise would be changed into a stock company. Company law is completely different from traditional enterprise legislation that is based on ownership form. It recognizes two kinds of company forms: (i) the stock company; and (ii) a limited liability company based on the investor's responsibility. Under company law, when the state invests in the stock company or the limited liability company, it becomes a shareholder along with other investors.

Because the state is the controling shareholder in most companies, it is in a position to abuse its position, for example, by forcing the company to provide security for its controling shareholder's debt, appropriating company's funds, and so on. These kinds of abuses occur frequently, and are often the subject of severe criticism. Therefore, in present-day China, company law enforcement must take strict measures in order to restrain power abuse by the controling shareholder and thus improve corporate governance.

The principles of corporate governance of listed companies (hereafter referred to as the "Principles") were enacted by the China Securities Regulatory Commission (CSRC) in January 2002. Relative to the previous discussion, regulations related to the behaviors of the controling shareholder have already been established. The purpose of this chapter is: (i) to explain the meaning of the status of the state shareholder in a company; (ii) to clarify what the shareholders' rights are in Chinese company law and who enforces the shareholders' rights in reality; and (iii) to show the new developments in restraining the abuse of power by the controling shareholder in China.

11.2 The legislation of corporate property rights and the establishment of the status of the state shareholder

As is widely known, the reform of state-owned enterprises has been occurring in Chinese cities since 1979. The purpose of this reform is to determine how to make state-owned enterprises survive in the private sector. In the first stage of reforms, the Chinese government performed measures such as "Fang Quan Ran Li" (the expansion of independent management rights to the state-owned enterprises, and the execution of an economic responsibility system) and "Li Gai Sui" (in which enterprises are required to pay taxes to the state instead of giving all of their profits to the state). In order to achieve these aims some administrative regulations, such as those "regarding the expansion of independent management rights of state-owned enterprises," "regarding the execution of the profits reservation of state-owned enterprises," and "regulation relating to the Li Gai Sui" and others were enacted.

Obviously, an incentive for undertaking business was given to the management of enterprises, and this led to competitive relations arising between enterprises and between employee and employee within an enterprise. This gradually led to the development of an active atmosphere in the enterprise. When the nature of state-owned enterprises are considered, it is apparent that enterprises are not dynamic, and many still reflect their administrative origins. Therefore, further reforms are necessary to completely change state-owned enterprises into relatively independent economic entities driven by the pursuit of profits.

The practice of the separation of company ownership and company management that is common in advanced capitalist countries, the legal theory of separation between company ownership and company management, and the experience of a management responsibility system that had been enforced in some small and middle state-owned enterprises lead to the argument that company management should be separated from company ownership in state-owned enterprises.

This argument is based on the maintenance of the state ownership of enterprises, and it recognizes enterprises to have collective management rights, including those related to production, marketing, personal resource and so on. Chinese legislators have adopted this theory in the "general provisions for civil law" which were enacted in April 1986. This is fundamental to Chinese civil law, and it recognizes the management right of state-owned enterprises to deal sensitively with the realities of economic reform. According to the "general provisions for civil law," under the law, state-owned enterprises have an authorized management right related to the assets of an enterprise, and this management right is protected from the state (§82). Furthermore, state-owned enterprises themselves must undertake responsibility in civil cases with all business assets that are authorized by the state (§48). Following the "general provisions for civil law," an "all peoples' ownership system industry enterprise law" (hereafter referred as to "enterprise law") was enacted in April 1988. This asserts again that all of the business assets of an enterprise belong to the state, but that the state trusts the management rights to the enterprise according to the principle of separation between ownership right and management right. The enterprises have a right to occupy, use, and to legally dispose of all state-owned assets that they have been authorized to operate. As a result, the management rights have become more concrete. The management rights of the enterprise were also reconfirmed in "the state-owned enterprise management mechanism conversion regulation" (hereafter referred as to "the mechanism regulation") that was enacted in 1992. However, relative to where the administrative organ belongs, there has been no fundamental change in the status of state-owned enterprises.

One major problem in China is that enterprises still do not enjoy access to independent assets. Certainly, China has accepted a legal personal system in the "general provisions for civil law," and has recognized that the state-owned enterprises are legal entities. Further, providing certain legal procedures are followed, state-owned enterprises can acquire certification for business as a corporation just like other kinds of enterprises. But state-owned enterprises only have the name of a legal person – they do not have substantial content.[2] Another problem is that state-owned enterprises still cannot undertake independent responsibility for civil cases. Certainly, as mentioned earlier, the enterprise law specifies that state-owned enterprises are responsible for civil cases. However, many enterprises are unable to undertake responsibility for civil cases because they carry excess repayment debts; many need almost daily subsidies from the state. It seems clear that the only way to solve such problems would be to introduce a modern company system in which the stock company is central. Given all of this, the company law was enacted in December 1993.

To make state-owned enterprises become real corporations in both name and reality, company law first requires that a stock company and a limited liability company are legal persons of enterprise. It also includes some regulations to which we should pay considerable attention. First, the new general idea of corporate property rights was introduced, and the company has corporate property rights formed by the investment of the shareholder. It also has rights and responsibilities in civil cases as a result of the law (§4(2)). Secondly, company law states clearly that shareholders have a right to gain profits, to make important management decisions, to elect management officers and to carry out other matters depending upon their invested capital stock (§4(1)). Thirdly, shareholders are responsible for the company to limit of their invested capital stock, and the company assumes responsibility for the debts of the company with all its assets (§3). As a result of these regulations, the company has independent property and is a separate entity from the state; in turn, the state assumes a legal position as a shareholder in the company.

Much attention has been given to corporate property rights, and the concept itself has been controversial since the enactment of the company law.[3] There are three basic positions: In the first, corporate property rights are viewed as corporate ownership rights. The second position views the corporate property rights as neither corporate ownership rights nor management rights; rather, there are new special rights. The third sees corporate property rights as the usual management rights that are recognized in the "general provisions for civil law." There is considerable support for the first position because it is based on the legal theory of traditional civil law and the corporate property rights are seen as rights which include real rights, credit and intellectual property rights. Major aspects of corporate property rights and how company law recognizes them may be more precisely determined by taking the first position. The existence of a company implies that the company has an individual legal personality that is persistently different from all investors, including the state. Under company law, as a shareholder the state should exercise its rights against the company within the range of the law and the articles of incorporation just like other investors.

11.3 Rights that shareholders have in the company

11.3.1 Shareholders' rights in a stock company

To a company, shareholders' rights is a generic term for various rights that shareholders have according to the position they have attained through the acquisition of stock. After state-owned enterprises are changed into stock companies, the state should be concerned with the company only as a shareholder and by exercising shareholders' rights that company law prescribes. According to company law, shareholders have the right to gain profits, to make important decisions about management, to elect or dismiss management officials and so on depending on each shareholders' investment of capital stock (§4(1)). Chinese legal theory also divides shareholders' rights into the "rights for self-profits" and the "rights for company profits" in accordance with classifications in the traditional theory of civil law. The rights for company profits mean rights that are exercised for the purpose of a shareholder participating in company management. For example, there are injunction rights (§111), question and proposal rights (§110), rights for calling temporary shareholder's meetings (§104(3)), voting rights (§106) and others enacted by Chinese company law. The rights for self-profits mean rights that are exercised for getting economic benefits from the company. For example, this includes the right to distribute profits (§103(7)), the right to distribute remainder property (§195(3)) and others enacted by Chinese company law.

The so-called separation between company ownership and company management simply means that the everyday business executions are entrusted to the directors or the management officers of the company. It does not mean that shareholders have no involvement in the management of the company. Participation of shareholders in company management is realized mainly by exercising voting rights as prescribed in company law. The place exercising this right is only at shareholders' meetings.

Under the principle that the shareholders' meetings are at the center of company decision-making, some countries such as Japan and Germany have allowed shareholders to be involved in every aspect of company affairs. Though the legal position of shareholders' meetings as the highest point of organizational power remains unchanged now, their authority is limited to matters that the law and the articles of incorporation prescribe. Chinese company law is similar to Japanese commercial law in respect of the authority of shareholders' meetings. According to company law, shareholders' meetings are composed of shareholders, and shareholders' meetings follow company law exercising their own authority as the highest power point in the organs of company (§102). Company law recognizes the following authorities: (i) to decide the management policy and investment plans of the company; (ii) to decide matters of election and dismissal of directors as well as rewards for directors; (iii) to decide matter of election and dismissal of supervisors as representatives of shareholders, as well as rewards for supervisors; (iv) to deliberate and to reach consensus about the report of board of directors; (v) to deliberate and to reach consensus about the report of the board of supervisors; (vi) to deliberate and reach consensus about the yearly financial budget bill and the official settlement plan; (vii) to deliberate and to reach consensus about plans for profit appropriation and management of loss for the company; (viii) to decide whether to increase or decrease the registration capital stock of the company; (ix) to decide on the issuing of corporate bonds; (x) to decide matters related to the combination, division, dissolution and liquidation of the company; and, finally, (xi) to change the articles of incorporation.

11.3.2 Shareholders' rights in a limited liability company

The limited liability company is a company in which the shareholders are responsible for the company within the limitation of invested capital stock, the company is responsible for its debts with all assets (§3(2) in company law). Unlike the form of a stock company that is suitable for a large company, the limited liability company is suitable for small and medium-sized companies. Thus, Chinese company law sets the legally fixed number of shareholders as being between 2 and 50 (§19). It seems that many state-owned enterprises have been changed into limited liability companies because stock companies are mostly limited to listed companies in the securities exchange and the over-the-counter market in China.

Similar to shareholders in stock companies, shareholders in limited liability companies have the right to gain profits, to make important decisions on management, to elect or dismiss management and other rights depending on their invested capital stock (§4(1) in company law). Shareholders' meetings are the highest decision-making organ in a limited liability company, and shareholders are able to participate in management mainly through shareholders' meetings. Rights which shareholders can exercise in the shareholders' meetings are clearly specified by company law as follows (§38): (i) to decide the management policy of the company and its investment plans; (ii) to decide matters relating to the election and dismissal of directors and their rewards; (iii) to decide matters relating to the election and dismissal of the supervisors as representatives of the shareholders and their rewards; (iv) to deliberate and reach consensus about the reports of board of directors; (v) to deliberate and reach the reports of board of supervisors or supervisor; (vi) to deliberate and reach consensus about the yearly financial budget bill and official settlement plans; (vii) to deliberate and reach consensus regarding company plans for appropriation of profits and management loss; (viii) to decide whether to increase or decrease the registration capital stock of the company; (ix) to decide issues relative to corporate bonds; (x) to decide whether or not shareholders can transfer investments to persons other than shareholders; (xi) to decide matters related to the combination, division, dissolution and liquidation of the company; and (xii) to change the articles of incorporation.

11.4 Executor of the state shareholder's right

11.4.1 Administrative system of state-owned assets

Although there were various opinions regarding the subject (representative) of state-owned assets property rights at the beginning of the economic reforms,[4] the policy of "state unification ownership and the administration by various levels of the government" was clearly formulated in the 3rd General Meeting, the 14th Term Central Committee of the Chinese Communist Party, in November 1993. With regard to state unification ownership, the "mechanism regulation" enacted in 1992 clearly indicates that assets in state-owned enterprises belong to all of the people, and the State Council directly exercises the state-owned enterprise property rights on behalf of the state. Following that, "state-owned enterprise assets supervision and administration regulation" enacted in 1994, emphasized this again.

"Supervision and administration by various levels of the government" means that each level of government (from central government to local government) has certain rights to occupy, to use, to gain profits, and to deal with state-owned assets that they controled directly.[5] Today, state-owned assets are administrated by three levels of government in China. The first is the central government – in other words, the State Council. The second is the peoples' government of provinces, ethnic autonomic districts (*min zu zi zhi qi*) and directly controled cities (*zhi xia shi*). The third is the peoples' government of cities and counties. Concretely, the authority for administrating state-owned assets is concentrated in state-owned assets supervision and administration commission.

11.4.2 Executor of the state shareholders' rights

When the state acquires stock in a stock company or share in a limited liability company, it becomes a shareholder. However, the state is not actually able to participate in shareholders' meetings in order to exercise its voting right. There are essentially five opinions regarding how the state may exercise its voting rights as follows.[6]

First, the state-owned assets administration bureau (which changed to the state-owned assets supervision and administration commission from March 2003) may actually exercise voting rights as a shareholder. Secondly the former administrative organs of enterprises that were changed into stock companies or limited liability companies may actually exercise voting rights. Thirdly, the state financial organs may actually exercise voting rights. Fourthly, a state-owned assets investment company or a state-owned assets operation company may actually exercise voting rights as holding company on behalf of the state. Fifthly, the stock company or the limited liability company itself may actually exercise voting rights on behalf of the state. The fourth position seems most suitable when considering these positions according to "the principle of the separation between the government and the enterprise function" which is one of the goals of economic reform in China. It is necessary to establish an economic entity such as a holding company that lies between the government and the enterprise and to make this economic entity be the investor of state-owned assets. The fifth position implies agreement with the acquisition of so-called "treasure stock." But the only exceptional cases are applied for acquisition of such "treasure stock" within present-day Chinese company law.[7] Obviously, this position goes against present company law.

There is much agreement relative to the fourth opinion, and it is also accepted by the Chinese government. Many attempts have been made to realize aspects of this opinion. The concept of an "investment institution authorized by the state" introduced into Chinese company law is thought to be equivalent to a state-owned assets investment company or a state-owned assets operation company. Under present conditions, most investment institutions authorized by the state are established in the form of holding companies. These include not only pure assets investment companies or pure assets operation companies, but also operating holding companies. Some cities, such as Shanghai, have experimented with the establishment of investment operation companies, changing from specialized governmental sections, or specialized total enterprises to holding companies, or investment operation companies. Since 1993, the State-Owned Assets Administration Bureau in the State Council has experimented with the authorized operation of state-owned assets in eight huge corporate groups such as the First Automobile Work Company and the Dong Feng Mobile Company. The intentions of these arrangements are as follows: to change the usual relationship between the enterprises into a relationship between a parent and a subsidiary company combined by capital tie-up through making the center company in the corporate group hold shares of related companies.

Through the use of these experiments, the Chinese government is expanding the state-owned assets investor system in which "the investment institution authorized by the state" exists between the state and the company. Under this system, this institution actually exercises rights that the state has as a shareholder.

11.5 Suggestions for measures preventing power abuse by the controling shareholder

From a legal viewpoint, a stock company in which investors are pluralistic is substantially different to the usual state-owned enterprise. However, if the state continues to hold a majority of capital stock and continues to intervene in company management, the stock company is "the same" as the usual state-owned enterprise. With regard to related persons dealings as seen in the listed companies of China, a quantitative analysis may be seen in Chapter 6 of this volume regarding who may abuse and how much they abuse. To prevent power abuse by the state as the controling shareholder, it is necessary to adopt measures that can adjust the structure of company control based on the principle of decision by majority capital stock and requests for securing economic justice in which the main point is to protect minority shareholders. Chinese company law has adopted the following measures to protect minority shareholders.

First, each shareholder has the right to inspect the articles of incorporation, records of the proceedings of the shareholders' meetings and financial accounting reports, and to propose and question management of the company according to company law (§110). Secondly, when resolutions of shareholders' meetings and the board of directors violate law or administrative regulations and infringe on the legal rights and profits of shareholders, they may institute suits in a peoples' court to prohibit these illegal or infringement acts according to the company law (§111). In relation to the number of stocks and others relating to usage of these rights, company law no longer make regulations. All of these rights are independent shareholders' rights. In the Chinese stock company, the minority shareholders are in a very weak position, but it is expected that these rights will become a strong weapon for minority shareholders to supervise the state as the controling shareholder and to protect their rights and profits.

However, when we review Chinese company law generally, we can conclude that there are few measures protecting minority shareholders and restraining power abuse by the controling shareholder. There are strong assertions for the following measures that will strengthen protections of minority shareholders in China.

11.5.1 The legal recognition of the duty of fiduciary of the controling shareholder

Often, a controling shareholder may have a tendency to work for self-profits by abusing this position at the cost of company profits and minority shareholders. A legal theory that may break this behavioral pattern is that of the duty of fiduciary, in which the controling shareholder has a duty not to infringe on the rights and profits of the company and minority shareholders, and not to work for self-profits through abusing their special position. Because present-day Chinese company law does not have such regulations, it seems of little use for the regulation of power abuse of the controling shareholder. Thus, the establishment of the duty of fiduciary of the controling shareholder seems mandatory.

11.5.2 Introduction of the cumulative voting system

Cumulative voting means that when more than two directors are elected in the shareholders' meetings, the election of all directors is carried out collectively at one time, and each shareholder has the same number of votes as the number of directors on each stock (For example, when 3 directors are elected, 3 voting rights are given to each stock.) Under this system, each shareholder can place all of his votes on one candidate or separate votes for several candidates. This system is derived from American company law. In China, the state shareholder is in the position of the controling shareholder, and the state can determine all directors of company and control the management of the company through the principle of decision by majority of capital stock. Conversely, minority shareholders can have little or no impact on company management. Thus, the cumulative voting system should be introduced into Chinese company law in order to make the board of directors reflect the opinions of minority shareholders and allow the representatives of minority shareholders supervise the activity of directors elected by the state shareholder.[8]

11.5.3 Introduction of the shareholder derivative suit

A shareholder derivative suit can be very powerful as a supervisor for company management. It is an important measure of corporate governance in America, Japan and other countries. Chinese company law has no regulations regarding the shareholder derivative suit. In a shareholder derivative suit, a shareholder can sue the directors or the controling shareholder who has damaged the company instead of the company itself when the company itself fails to deal with such misconduct. From the viewpoint of corporate governance, it is no doubt important to introduce the shareholder derivative suit into Chinese company law.[9]

11.6 Regulations in the "Principles of Corporate Governance of Listed Companies"

The "principles"[10] enacted by CSRC acknowledge the problem of the controling shareholder abusing power and infringing on the rights and profits of company and minority shareholders as being a very serious problem, and it includes the following regulations to prevent power abuse by the controling shareholder.

11.6.1 Transactions between related persons

So-called related persons of the listed companies are shareholders (especially, the controling shareholder), directors, and supervisors and others. Attention must be given to the problem of how to protect the profits of listed companies when we focus on transactions between listed companies and the controling shareholder (or controling company), or related companies inside the same corporate group. The "principles" require listed companies to adopt some effective measures to prevent related persons from intervening in company management using a way of exclusive transaction to infringe on profits of listed companies (§13). Transactions between related persons should be conducted in accordance with the principle of: (i) market transactions; (ii) price decisions that are based on the marketing price with a third party who is a independent; and (iii) disclosure of the decision criteria of the marketing price and others, are thought to be effective measures.

Listed companies are required to conclude a written agreement with related persons at the time of transaction, to observe principles of equality, freedom, equivalent price and payment, and to disclose items such as conclusion, changes, end and conditions of fulfillment for contract (§12 in the "Principles"). The "Principles" also clearly regulate that listed companies should not provide security for the debts of shareholders and related persons (§14).

11.6.2 Standards for acts of the controling shareholder

The "Principles" include the following regulations on standards for acts of the controling shareholder.

First, the controling shareholder is required to introduce a stock system into any state-owned enterprises that is planned to restructure itself into a stock company. The controling shareholder must observe the principles related to the company going public, and establish a reasonable checks and balance system by shareholders when the state-owned enterprise is reformed into a stock company (§15 in the "Principles").

Secondly, the "Principles" certainly requires that the controling shareholder has the duty of fiduciary to listed companies and other shareholders (§16). In other words, the controling shareholder must exercise investors' rights to listed companies that it controls in strict accordance with the law, and it cannot infringe on the legally fixed rights and profits of listed companies and other shareholders by methods such as the reorganization of property. Further, the controling shareholder should not make unreasonable profits by using its special position in listed companies (§19).

Thirdly the "Principles" regulate the relationship between the controling shareholder and the management of listed companies as follows (§20, 21). A controling shareholder must strictly observe the requirements and procedures that law, administrative regulations and the articles of incorporation prescribe about candidate nomination of director and supervisor. Candidates of director and supervisor nominated by the controling shareholder need to have special knowledge, the ability to make decisions and competent supervision related to their work. The controling shareholder must not perform any illegal permissive procedure regarding the personnel resolutions passed by the shareholders' meetings and personnel appointment resolutions of the board of directors in advance. Further, the controling shareholder must not ignore the shareholders' meetings and the board of directors in appointing or dismissing senior executives of listed companies. Important decisions of listed companies must be made in the shareholders' meetings or by the board of directors in accordance with the law. The controling shareholder must not directly or indirectly intervene in company's production and management activities based on legal and company decisions, and violate the rights and profits of the company and other shareholders.

11.6.3 The independence of listed companies

While the "Principles" set out standards for the acts of the controling shareholder, it also placed an emphasis on the independence of listed companies from the controling shareholder.

With regard to personnel independence, according to the "Principles," executives such as the person in charge of financial affairs, the person in charge of marketing and the secretary of the board of directors at the controling companies, as the controling shareholder, must not take charge of posts other than that of the director at listed companies. When the senior executives of the company, as the controling shareholder, serve as the director of the listed company, they must put sufficient time and energy into the business of the listed company (§23).

Regarding the independence of assets, the "Principles" requires that assets in listed companies in which the controling shareholder has invested must have independence from owner relations. The controling shareholder must change the title of assets when the controling shareholder has investment, and clearly decide the range of the assets concerned. For the assets concerned, listed companies must register with its individual title, make a commercial account book, make settlements and manage assets (§24).

The controling shareholder must respect the independence of the financial affairs for listed companies, and must not intervene in the financial accounting of the companies (§25).

In addition, relations such as those between the top and the bottom must not exist between the controling shareholder, its functional section, and listed companies, functional sections in listed companies. The controling shareholder and the subordinate organization must not take business opportunities from listed companies (§26, §27).

11.7 Conclusion

This chapter has included discussion of: (i) the establishment of the status of the state shareholder as the controling shareholder; (ii) the problem of the abuse of power by the controling shareholder; and (iii) suggestions for the implementation of measures preventing power abuse by the controling shareholder. The "Principles" have established regulations to prevent abuse of power by the controling shareholder. In order to reform the state-owned enterprises and establish a modern corporation system, the Chinese government should introduce a stock system along the lines usually accepted in advanced capitalist countries. There were particular historical reasons for the process through which the state became the controling shareholder in China. Whether or not the stock system is successful depends upon the successful solutions to the problem of abuse of power by the controling shareholder. To control this abuse effectively, it is proposed that Chinese company law, which is currently in line to have the first important revision since it was enacted in 1993, must accept the mentioned suggestions.

Notes

1 For a commentary on the contents of Chinese company law, see Zhou, Jianlong (1994). Even after the People's Republic of China was formed in 1949, the stock company was recognized as one of the forms of business companies in the early 1950s according to the "temporary regulations on private enterprises" enacted in 1950. However, the stock system was completely excluded from Chinese economic society because of the establishment of planned economy by centralization tape, and the transition from an enterprise form that has more than one investor to an enterprise form that has a sole investor.

2 See Wang, Baoshu (1995).

3 For details on this controversy, see Zhou, Jianlong (1997).

4 For example, the "Draft on the Establishment of the State-Owned Assets Administration Bureau" written in 1988, requires the State-Owned Assets Administration Bureau as the representative of state-owned assets. The "Notice on the Strengthening of the State-Owned Assets Administration" enacted in 1990, indicates that both the State-Owned Assets Administration Bureau and the Department of Finance are representatives of the state-owned assets. See Kawai (1996).
5 See Xie, Cichang (1996).
6 See Wang, Baoshu, note 2 above, p. 60.
7 Only in cases where the amount of the corporate capital is decreased or the company combined another company whose stocks are owned by the former company, may the company be permitted to acquire its own stock under present Chinese company law (§149). Within the Chinese economic and law world in the late 1980s, there was a great dispute about whether or not accumulated earnings of companies could be made treasury stock when state-owned enterprises are changed into stock companies. For details on this depute, see Zhou, Jianlong (1990).
8 See Liu, Junhai (1997).
9 See Zhou, Jianlong (1995).
10 For comment on the "Principles," see Zhou, Jianlong (2002).

References

Kawai, Shin'ichi (1996) "A Recent Trend and Subjects of the Transit from the State-Owned Enterprise to the Stock Company in China" (kokuyu kigyo no kaishasei he no tenkan – saikin no doukou to kadai), *Journal of the Japan–China Economy Association* (*Nicchukeikyo Journal*) 4, 3 (in Japanese).

Liu, Junhai and Zhang, Xinbao (1997) "Comments on the Research of the Commercial Law," *Cass Journal of Law* (*Faxue yanjiu*) 1, 48 (in Chinese).

Wang, Baoshu (1995) "The Difficult Points of the Transit from the State-Owned Enterprise to the Stock Company and the Legal Thinking" (Guoyouqiye zouxiang gongsi de nandian jiqi falu sikao), *Cass Journal of Law* (*Faxue yanjiu*) 1, 58 (in Chinese).

Xie, Cichang (1996) "Exercise and Development of the State Property Right Theory in Practice" (Guojia suoyouquan lilung zai shijiang zhong de yunyong he fazhang), *China Legal Science* (*Zhongguo faxue*) 6, 37 (in Chinese).

Zhou, Jianlong (1990) "A Legislative Looking at the Acquisition of the Treasury Stock in the Chinese Stock Company" (Chugoku no kabusikigaisha ni kansuru ripporon teki kosatu), *Ikkyoronso* 103(1), 121 (in Japanese).

Zhou, Jianlong (2002) "Comments on the Principles of Corporate Governance in China" (Chugokugata corporate governance no doko)," 30(5–6), *Journal of the Japanese Institute of International Business Law* 654 and 796 (in Japanese).

Zhou, Jianlong (1997) "Study on the Concept of the Corporate Property Right in Chinese Company Law" (Chugoku kaishahou ni okeru hojinzaisanken no gainen wo megutte), *Comparative Law* (*Hikaku hougaku*, Waseda University), 32(1), 267 (in Japanese).

Zhou, Jianlong (1995) "Study on the Self-Control Mechanism in the Stock Company Management" (Lung gufeng youxian gongsi jingying de neibu jiandu jizhi), *Law Review* (*Faxue pinglun,* Wuhan University), 1, 11 (in Chinese).

Zhou, Jianlong (1994) "The Reform of the State-Owned Enterprise and Law – On Common Company Law of the People's Republic of China" (Chugoku kokuyukigyou no kaizou to hou), *Case Law Times* (*Hanrei Times*), 850, 50 (in Japanese).

12

The State as an "Expropriating" Concentrated Owner in China*

Mariko Watanabe

12.1 Introduction

Under the gradualist transition process in Asian post-planned economies, the state sector still retains its control over economic activity. It may be the case that this helped to prevent a collapse of institutions which has facilitated a secure economic transition to date. However, whether this state-owned market economy will be sustainable in the future is another question. These economies, particularly in China which has the longest history of transition and has not yet completed its reforms, are encountering another problem: when and how will the state withdraw from economic life? So far, whether the state should exit or not has not been seriously addressed in the context of evaluating the gradual/shock transition process. It is this question that we will consider here.

The gradualist transition process has been highly evaluated as it has accomplished a "Pareto-maintaining process", which has generated no losers in the society (McMillan and Naughton, 1992; Lau and Qian, Roland, 2000). As predicted in the research, China, Vietnam and Myanmar have enjoyed steady levels of macroeconomic growth during the era of gradual reform. Despite slogans of marketization and privatization, however, the share of the state sector in the economy has still remained substantial over the whole course of reform to date. China and Vietnam illustrate this phenomenon, at least in terms of the ownership of firms (see the Preface to this book), and it has become controversial among local academics.

* I would like to thank for comments from all the members of this project, and Hidenobu Okuda (Hitotsubashi University), Akira Kohsaka (Osaka University), Liu Deqiang (Tokyo Education University) and Hiroshi Ohashi, Yun-chul, Choi (both University of Tokyo) for helpful comments.

Based on arguments in corporate governance literature, the purpose of this chapter is to address whether or not the corporate governance system in China – in which even listed companies are still owned and governed by the state and governments – generates a negative impact on the value maximization.

The structure of this chapter is as follows: section 12.2 introduces the institutional and structural status of China's equity market and corporate governance issues affecting listed companies. Here, the story of Jinan Qingqi Motorcycle collapse will be given as a typical case of the ultimate owner's expropriating behavior. Section 12.3 will give an intuitive illustration of theoretical arguments on the concentrated owner's agency problem and application. Sections 12.4 and 12.5 will address an empirical model and estimation strategies. Finally, the results are presented in section 12.6.

12.2 Ownership and governance structure in China

12.2.1 "State-owned listed companies"

In China, listed companies are still ultimately owned by central and local governments (Tables 12.1–12.3). About 80 per cent of listed companies are ultimately owned by the state sector (Table 12.1).

Table 12.1 Characteristics of ultimate controlers of all listed companies in China

	1999		*2000*		*2001*		*2002*	
	Freq.	*%*	*Freq.*	*%*	*Freq.*	*%*	*Freq.*	*%*
0 State	763	83.1	864	82.0	920	81.4	940	78.9
1 Collective	31	3.4	33	3.1	33	2.9	29	2.4
2 Union	7	0.8	8	0.8	8	0.7	8	0.7
3 NPO	8	0.9	7	0.7	6	0.5	5	0.4
4 Foreign Owner	9	1.0	9	0.9	10	0.9	12	1.0
5 Private Owner	67	7.3	96	9.1	119	10.5	163	13.7
6 No classification	33	3.6	37	3.5	34	3.0	35	2.9
Total	918	100	1,054	100	1,130	100	1,192	100

Ratio of controler's share of all listed companies, 1998–2002

minimum	average	maximum	standard error
0.39	44.54	88.58	17.78493

Source: Center for China Economic Research, Sino Fin China Financial Statement Database.

Table 12.2 Characteristics of ownership structure: international comparison

	Year	*Bank*	*Insurance company and pension fund*	*Investment fund*	*Non-financial enterprise*	*Individuals*	*Public authorities*	*Foreigner*	*Total*
P.R. China	–	0	0	1	25	31	39	3	100
UK	1994	10	50	8	1	21	1	9	100
US	1996	7	28	12	0	49	0	5	100
Japan	2001	30	10	0	22	20	1	18	100
Germany	1996	10	12	8	42	15	4	9	100
France	1994	4	2	2	58	19	4	11	100
Italy	1994	5	3	0	25	50	8	9	100
Korea	1996	12	6	8	21	34	7	12	100
Sweden	1996	1	14	15	11	19	8	32	100
Australia	1996	4	25	8	11	20	0	32	100
India	—		3	2	11	76	1	8	100

Source: China data on listed companies based on Table 12.2, India; CMIE, Prowess. Others; OECD, Survey of Corporate Governance Development in OECD countries, 2004.

Table 12.3 Performance of all listed companies in China

	1995	*1998*	*1999*	*2000*	*2001*	*2002*	*2003*
GDP growth (%)	10.5	7.8	7.1	8	7.5	8.3	9.1
Nominal GDP growth (%)	23.2	4.7	9.5	8.5	8.6	11.8	11.8
Per company							
Total profit (bil. Rmb)	0.79	0.73	0.84	1.02	0.88	1.09	1.40
Income tax (bil. Rmb)	0.12	0.15	0.16	0.18	0.23	0.31	0.37
Minority interest(bil. Rmb)	0.03	0.03	0.04	0.05	0.06	0.10	0.11
Net profit(bil. Rmb)	0.64	0.55	0.66	0.78	0.60	0.68	0.94
Per company: growth							
Total profit (%)	–11	–5	16	21	–14	24	36
Income tax (%)	6	18	6	11	28	36	27
Minority interest (%)	–23	16	38	13	15	76	10
Net profit (%)	–13	–11	19	19	–23	14	44
No. of listed companies	307	821	920	1,057	1,134	1,198	1,252

Source: Center for China Economic Research, Sino Fin China Financial Statement Database.

Usually, this stake is not directly owned by the governments, but rather by "holding companies" (or *jituan gongsi*), who are themselves wholly owned by the government. The share of this ultimate shareholder is 44.5 per cent on average. In the international comparison shown in Table 12.2, this proportion of the state share is substantially higher than not only OECD countries, but also India, which is renowned for having the largest number of listed companies in the world, with its wide coverage of state ownership.

In China, the state sector comprises both central and local governments. Each province or city-level municipal government has an enormous influence over local companies and local economic resources. Furthermore, these governments and state sectors seem not to function to redistribute assets or income between the regions, which is usually expected in the market economy. Figure 12.1 shows that the richer the region, the greater the level of assets available to local governments, where most of the state assets are management assets, that is, that of companies. Weak sign of inter-regional redistribution of economic resources indicated in this figure.

12.2.2 Deteriorating performance record of listed companies

When we consider the performance of a listed company, we can see that it does not reflect China's macroeconomic performance. The performance of listed companies has been sluggish since the late 1990s,

Figure 12.1 The richer the region, the wealthier the government

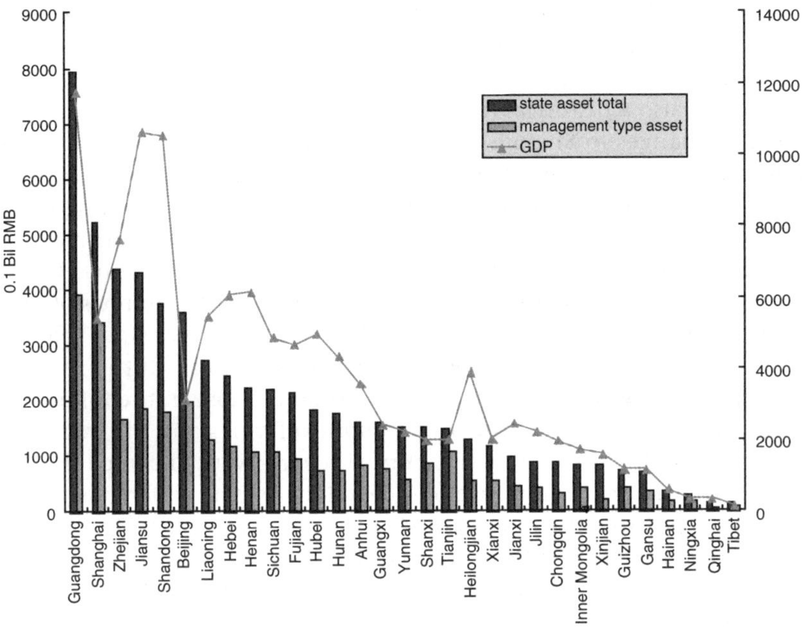

Source: State Committee of State Asset Management HP.

though the number of listed companies has increased steadily and the macro economy has maintained a steady rate of high growth – around 8 per cent per annum. In 2001, the total profits and net profits of listed companies averaged a recorded negative growth in 2001 (Table 12.3).

This poor performance is the result of three main factors: (1) the strict implementation of accounting; (2) the market conditions of most industries in China; and (3) the problems in the corporate governance system. Negative profits of all listed companies on the stock market in both 1998 and 2001 are the direct results of a strict implementation of accounting and disclosure in the respective years. This policy revealed the hidden problems of listed companies. The second factor is product market competition for listed companies; this competitive environment is intensifying alongside the deepening "marketization" throughout China.

The third is a problem of corporate governance, which is the focus of this chapter. As we have seen so far, most of the listed companies have a "concentrated shareholder" or an "absolute controling sole owner" (*yi gu du da* in Chinese). Furthermore, this concentrated owner is the state sector, that is, central or local government. This structure induced an agency problem between the "concentrated owner" and the "minority shareholder."

There is also a historical reason for this phenomenon. In China, two stock exchanges in Shanghai and Shenzhen were established in 1990 and 1991 respectively. The establishment of a stock market was intended to relieve state-owned enterprises (SOEs) by expanding their financing channel. Thus, application of listing has been controled by the government, and has been preferred to the SOE structure. Every year to 2001, the State Council allocated quotas on the number of listings for each provincial government. As a result, China's stock market has been derided as a lifesaver or wallet of the SOEs. All too often a well-performing company in one year would collapse in the following year. False disclosures on the initial public offerings and the increases in new capital, or in every year's annual reports were to come into the open, following the emergence of independent media which have been actively reporting business scandals since the late 1990s.[1] The public paid more attention on these scandals in the listed company The story of Jinan Qingqi Motorcycle, discussed below, offers illustrates an extreme but characteristic example of negative intervention by the state via holding companies.

12.2.3 The case of Jinan Qingqi Motorcycle

In 2001, after an audit by an accounting firm, Jinan Qingqi Motorcycle announced a huge "non-performing" account receivable which caused much concern to their management. Their account receivable single to the holding company reached as much as 2.7 billion, which was far beyond their net worth or even their sales. This news shocked every stock market in China.

Jinan Qingqi Motorcycle, headquartered in Jinan City, Shandong Province, was a leading company in its sector. In the early 1990s, thanks to challenging management reforms, cost saving and marketing by the manager of this period, the company experienced rapid growth. It chased out a rival company located in Sichuan, which had been run in a traditional SOE way, then assumed a leading position in the motorcycle market. However, its success stopped abruptly in the late 1990s as its sales shrank drastically in 1999 (see Table 12.4). This change in company fortunes was partly because of market competition and partly because of the "empire building" of their holding company.

Table 12.4 Financial status of Jinan Qingqi Motorcycle, 1998–2003

					Account payable							
	Financial expense (%)	*Current borrowing (%)*	*Long-term borrowing*	*Account receivable (%)*	*To holding company and group (%)*	*To holding company and groups (including accumulated) (%)*	*To holding company and group (%)*	*Non performed (%)*	*Guarantee to holding company*	*Profit*	*Sales (mil. RMB)*	*Total assets (mil. RMB)*
1998	–0.7	2.1	0	53.4	n.a.	n.a.	3.6	n.a.	n.a.	14.5	1,950	3,290
1999	–1.1	3.4	0	61.0	16.9	58.1	16.2	2.4	n.a.	0.9	902	3,850
2000	0.3	12.3	0	62.7	31.6	61.6	17.5	1.7	n.a.	–6.6	534	4,150
2001	1.1	16.7	0	71.4	35.9	77.2	19.1	2.0	13.6	–20.7	643	3,460
2002	5.1	76.9	0	14.9	64.4	316.7	76.4	4.0	75.5	–357.1	661	954
2003	0.4	15.0	0	16.4	30.8	105.8	43.6	1.5	0.0	0.9	983	2,029

Source: Sino Fin Database for 1998–2002, Annual Report of Jinan Qingqi Motorcycle Co. Ltd.

Notes:

*normalized by total asset other than notice. *ultimate owners share remained 40.9 per cent during whole period in the table.

In recent years, the motorcycle market in China has been very active and very competitive. However, the distress of the company can also be attributed to the fact that the company committed to excess investments such as the establishment of a marketing branch in Japan or investing equity in a security trading company located in Jinan via its Japanese branch.

This "Japan project" in total accounted for around 0.1 billion Japanese Yen in 2000 (the company's annual report 2000). The function of this branch was marketing and procurement, but it cannot be expected to be profitable. Regarding marketing, the Japanese market is occupied by Japanese local giants, such as Suzuki, Honda and Kawasaki. Qingqi seems not to have implemented any marketing research or test sales. Procurement itself cannot make an actual profit, as its main sales are directed to their parent or group company. Furthermore, diversifying into a local security company has nothing to do with implementing a corporate strategy as a motorcycle manufacturer. The suspicion must be that the Jinan local government utilized the listed company's resources to boost the earnings of other failing companies in Jinan City. Likewise, a substantial part of their resource is "expropriated" by the ultimate owner's irrational decision, via a holding company, China Qingqi Motorcycle.

In the 2001 annual report, the listed company reported that it is "expropriated" via two channels: the first is via account receivables of the listed company: the unlisted holding company took charge of the sales function of the listed company, income from sales should be paid to the listed company, but not due to some reason such as utilizing them for another purpose, and documented as the account receivables on the balance sheet, which amounted to 2.7 billion or 77 per cent of total assets (the company's annual report 2001).

Another channel is the bank loan guarantee for the holding company. The balance sheet revealed that the listed company provided a massive amount of bank loan guarantees for the holding company, which amounted to another 16 per cent in 2001.[2] The company itself has no long-term borrowing from the bank, thus their financial expenses are very small. However, due to massive account receivables of non-performing assets, the company fell deeply into debt.

As deficits were recorded in two consecutive years, the company was moved onto the Special Treatment list. The company started to dispose of these non-performing assets, by removing the account receivables at once and reducing the total assets to around one-quarter of their 2001 level. Thus, its deficit reached a negative 350 per cent of total assets.

In August 2003, the Jinan government finally declared their commitment to this disposal procedure. The government committed to work out the debt with the holding company as follows: (i) repayment of 0.8 billion of account receivables; (ii) to make the bank loan guarantee provided by the listed company void; and (iii) to initiate the holding company's bankruptcy procedure and inviting new investors to the listed company.

Jinan Qingqi presents a most extreme case. However, "expropriation" by the holding company and related companies is a prevalent phenomenon, thus the Committee of Security Regulation China provided "a guideline on related trading" after this scandal.

12.3 Mechanisms of "expropriation": agency problems in concentrated ownership

12.3.1 Literature on the agency problem of "concentrated ownership"

The "expropriating" behavior of the concentrated owner is becoming an increasingly popular topic in theoretical analysis on corporate governance literature. Standard literature on corporate governance and ownership, such as Jensen and Meckling (1976), analyzed agency problems between management and owners. Recent literature focuses on the structure among owners and conflicts of interests between owners. The distribution of ownership differs from economy to economy. In the United States or Japan, most of the share is diversified and it is rare to recognize a concentrated owner in a listed company. By contrast, in most developing economies, each listed company has (usually) one concentrated owner/block shareholder, who can exercise control over the management, and other minority shareholders. Agency problems among shareholders will emerge in the latter case; concentrated shareholders vs minority shareholders. In this structure, actual power over the management is no more equal to their shareholding, though as it is provided by the law.

If the interests of concentrated and minority shareholders coincide, there will be no conflict of interests between them. However, such conflicts often occur in the real world. Recent theoretical literature on corporate governance argues that this happens if the private (non-monetary) benefit of the controling shareholder is sufficiently large. Under this circumstances, he/she will be able to exert stronger controling power (= controling right) over the management than he/she are attributed due to number of their shares (= cash flow right) in their hand. The literature calls this phenomenon the "separation of cash flow right and decision right." Theory predicts that an agency problem between the controling shareholder and the minority shareholder emerges from the separation of controling rights and cash flow rights (Bebchuk, 1999; Bebchuk *et al.*, 2000; Claessen *et al.*, 2000; Faccio *et al.*, 2001). Furthermore, theory predicts that this separation possibly emerges via the following three kinds of corporate structure (Bebchuk *et al.*, 2000):

(a) *Pyramiding*: forming a corporate group by investing vertically, such as the holding company investing in its subsidiary, then the subsidiary investing in its own subsidiary, and so on.

(b) *Cross-holding*: the share is cross-held between member companies of a group, by which the controling right of a core or holding company in the group might be increased at each share.

(c) *Dual-class share*: when heterogeneous shares such as common stock and preferred stock coexist, the controling company may gain a stronger controling right than the share they hold directly.

12.3.2 Separation of controling rights and cash flow rights in China

Are any of these three cases cited above applicable in the case of China? First, the cross-holding seems unlikely. Table 12.5 shows that 24.8 per cent (legal person and private placement) is invested by other corporates. The common perception in China is that it is only invested in one direction. Furthermore, banks have been prohibited from investing in the companies since around 1997. Thus, cross-holding only happens very rarely in China.

However, pyramiding and the dual-class share are both prevalent phenomena. As referred to already, pyramiding under a "holding company" or "*jituan gongsi*" is very prevalent in China. Most of the listed companies have been established so as to be listed as a financing channel, particularly for the companies listed in the early period. In this structure, we must identify who is the ultimate owner located at the top of the pyramid, and who can exert controling power over the management. Table 12.1 depicts this distribution of listed companies in China.

The dual-class share also exists by allowing the circulating share and non-circulating share to coexist (Table 12.5). In China, it is often criticized that the prices of non-circulating shares are said to be substantially lower than the circulating ones. Thus, they claim that the shareholders of circulating ones and non-circulating ones effectively

Table 12.5 Dual-class ownership

Share structure on IPO	
Total number of shares	
438,961,064,425	
Non-negotiable shares (%)	70.7
State share (%)	39.2
Legal person share (%)	17.9
Foreign share (%)	1.3
Private placement (%)	6.9
Staff share (%)	4.2
Negotiable (circulating) shares	29.3
A share (domestic denominated)	27.1
B share (foreign denominated)	1.3
H share (listed abroad)	0.8
Number of shareholders	
1,531,758,067	
Average number of shareholders	
1,575,883	

Source: Center for China Economic Research, Sino Fin Financial Statement Database.

hold different shares. For the holder of non-circulated shares, the cost of voting rights is substantially higher than for the holder of non-circulating ones. Non-circulated shares, which can be presumed to enjoy preference, account for 70 per cent of total listed capital in China. However, strictly speaking, there is no good documentation about whether or not this difference really exists. Thus, in this chapter, we will argue that the separation of cash flow rights and controling rights happens due to the pyramiding structure, not due to the dual-class shares. We find that it is sufficient that the pyramiding structure is clear enough for us to presume there are agency problems between concentrated and minority shareholders.

With regard to the separation between controling rights and cash flow rights, Teneve *et al.* (2000) documented the degree of this separation as a deviation in the share and ratio of directors who are appointed by the shareholders. Based on the survey of 257 listed companies in the Shanghai Exchange, Tables 12.4.6 and 4.7 of Teneve *et al.* (2000) show that non-circulating shareholders, state, legal person and employee accounted for 72 of 76 directors (95 per cent) contrary to their shareholding of 70 per cent. 36 and 44 per cent of managing directors are dispatched from state shareholder and state-owned legal shareholders, 93 per cent are from non-circulating shareholders, 3 per cent from employee shareholders, and 5 per cent from circulating shareholders. Regarding auditors, 81 per cent represent non-circulating shareholders and 11 and 7 per cent represent employee shareholders and circulating shares.

The limit of these studies, based on descriptive data, is that the number of dispatched directors is only a proxy for control rights. It does not precisely measure the actual size of their influential power – that is, how much assets are destroyed or consumed by the ultimate concentrated owner. As we will show later, aim of this chapter is to measure this.

12.3.3 Channels of "expropriation"

In this chapter, we take some accounting items on a balance sheet of the company as showing channels of "expropriation." On the liability side of the balance sheet a conflict of interests between the company and debt stakeholder is an issue. Current borrowing or long-term borrowing from financial institutions, account payables to the trading firm, payable to labor, such as wage or welfare, are observable in Chinese financial statements. These items, on the liability side of the balance sheet, can become a channel of expropriation of resources of debt stakeholders by the company.

On the asset side of the balance sheet, account receivables can become a channel of expropriation to the company by the concentrated owner, as we saw in the case of Jinan Qingqi Motorcycle. In the

Figure 12.2 Channels of "expropriation"

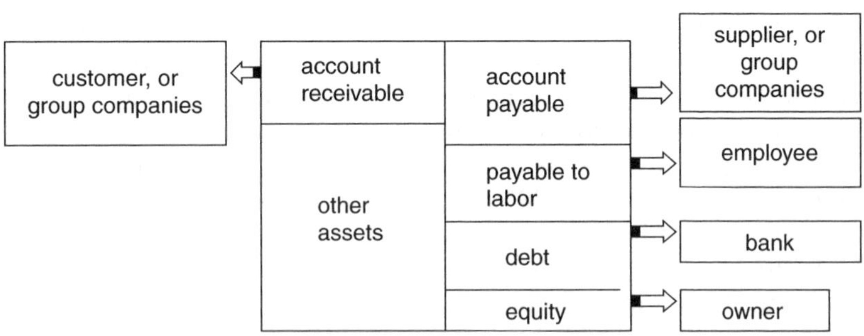

Source: Author.

particular case of China, direct lending between firms was legally prohibited even in 2004. Trade credit has been functioning as an alternative to inter-firm lending, and has become a channel of "asset expropriation," which we need to take into consideration.

We assume here that the concentrated controling owners of listed companies in China are provided with the following channels to receive resources from listed companies: (i) share dividends; (ii) expropriation channels above, that is account receivables, account payables and debt, furthermore, in the case the owner is the government. We see the following three items on the balance sheet as potential channels of "expropriation": (i) account receivables; (ii) account payables; (iii) payments to labor (wage and welfare). Items (i) to (iii) are so-called trade credits, on which no interest usually is charged.

Account receivable is an item on the asset side of the listed company. Expropriation via this item implies that the concentrated owner appropriates the assets of a listed company. Account payable is a liability to a procurement partner, payments to labor are liabilities to employees on the listed company. Expropriation via these items means that the listed company is occupying the resources of a procurement partner, or employee, so as to finance consumption of either the company themselves or the concentrated owner. As a whole, the asset-side items are more convincing as channels of "expropriation," because, strictly speaking, liability-side items imply only "expropriation by listed company" to relating stakeholders. However, here we assume that resources expropriated were used only for the usage of concentrated owners.

In the next section, we will outline a strategy to estimate this degree.

12.4 Empirical framework

12.4.1 Target: to directly estimate the "degree of expropriation"

The problem with empirical studies in this literature is how to define control rights. The definition of cash flow rights is clear: share of equity. However, how to define the control rights is controversial; most empirical literature defines size of control rights in an ad hoc fashion (Lang, Classens, and Djankov, 2000; Faccio, Lang and Yong, 2001; and so on). It would be more informative to estimate degree of separations directly by the structural model. This paper aims at this.

12.4.2 Model: ultimate controling owner's decision

Here, we present a behavioral model of this empirical study. An ultimate controling owner will solve the following constraint profit maximization problem. Here, we assume that even if the ultimate owner invested in several listed companies, the choice of asset size for each individual company is unaffected.

Here, the controling owner will decide the level of assets, by solving the following constraint maximization problem. The objective function consists of the sum of monetary benefits from shareholding and private benefit via expropriation. The former represents in the first term – dividend from owner's shares – the latter shows in the second term – private benefit obtained via "expropriation." The first constraint is budget constraint for "expropriation," that is, expropriation is only feasible within the current profit of the company in eq. (12.1a). The current profit is defined as eq. (12.1b). The last constraint shows the opportunity cost for the ultimate owner to invest this company. This is assumed as eq. (12.1c), which is assumed to measure the actual disbursement of interest payments to debtors and dividends to shareholders.[4]

$$\underset{k}{Max} \quad \varphi[f(K) - rK - ex(K)] + P[ex(K)] \tag{12.1}$$

$$\text{s.t. } ex(K) \leq \pi \tag{12.1a}$$

$$\pi = f(K) - rK \tag{12.1b}$$

$$rK = qD + sE \tag{12.1c}$$

where φ: shares of the controling owner. ex: expropriation–asset ratio (EX/K: both EX and K are the amounts of each item on the balance sheet.) ex are following channels for "expropriation." e.g., ar: account receivable–total asset ratio (AR/K), ap: account payable–total assets ratio (AP/K), paytolaborta: payable to labor–to total asset ratio (Payable to labor/K). All variables are measured in nominal terms. K is the capital or total assets of the company, Y is total sales, r is the opportunity cost for the investors. $f(K)$ is the production function. We assume this takes the forms of a Cobb–Douglas function, $Y = f(K) \equiv AK^a$ ($A>0$, $0 \leq a \leq 1$) its derivative is aY/K, where a is the distribution ratio to capital K. ex(K) is an "expropriation" function, which is also assumed to take the following form, $EX = ex(K) \equiv BK^b$ ($B>0, -\infty<b<\infty$), and its derivative is bEX/K. $P(X) \equiv X$ is the private benefit function.

The first order condition for this problem is derived as follows;

$$f'(K) = r + ex'(K) - \frac{1}{\varphi + \lambda} ex'(K) \tag{12.2}$$

In forming Lagrangian, we combined constraints (12.1a) and (12.1b). Thus, here, λ is the Lagrangian multiplier for the combined constraints of (12.1a) and (12.1b). Constraint (12.1c) is omitted because it does only identify factors of capital cost, or opportunity cost of all investors in this company.

Taking (12.2) as a function of λ and doing Taylor approximation on λ at λ = 0, the FOC above becomes as follows;

$$f'(K) = r + ex'(K) - \frac{1}{\varphi}\, ex'(K) + \frac{1}{\varphi^2}\, ex'(K) \qquad (12.2a).$$

The first order condition implies as follows: (i) If the second to fourth terms are confirmed statistically insignificant, in other words, only the coefficient of r is significant, the size of total assets of the company is at the socially efficient level, which is free from any waste for private benefit of the ultimate owner; (ii) If the second and/or third and fourth terms are confirmed statistically significant and the predicted deviation of the investor's opportunity cost is negative, expropriation by the controling owner happens at the expense of violating minority shareholders' interests. Excess investment happens in this case; (iii) If the predicted deviation of the investor's opportunity cost – that is, sum of size of the second to the fourth terms is positive – the size of asset K or the investment of the company is smaller than efficient and socially optimal size.

12.4.3 Test equation

Here we assume the following error terms; it consists of time-invariant unobservable factor and residual error, the latter is assumed to be independent to other variables.

$$\varepsilon_{it} = c_i u_t + \xi_{it} \qquad (12.3)$$

Production function is assumed to be Cobb–Douglas form, and its derivative on K is aY/K. A derivative of $ex(K)$ on K is $b^*EX/K \equiv b^*ex$. Plugging (12.3) and derivatives of $f(K)$ and $ex(k)$ into (12.2), a testable equation is derived as follows:

$$a\frac{Y}{K} = r + b^*ex - b\frac{ex}{\varphi} + \lambda b\frac{ex}{\varphi^2} + c_i u_t + \xi_{it} \qquad (12.4)$$

or

$$\frac{Y}{K} = \beta_0 r + \beta_1 ex + \beta_2\frac{ex}{\varphi} + \beta_3\frac{ex}{\varphi^2} + c_i u_t + \xi_{it} \qquad (12.4a)$$

where, $\beta_0 = \frac{1}{a}$, $\beta_1 = \frac{b}{a}$, $\beta_2 = \frac{b}{a}$, $\beta_3 = \lambda\frac{b}{a}$.

12.5 Data and estimation

12.5.1 Data

In this chapter, we used a database of the financial statements of all listed companies in China, compiled by Sinofin Information Services, China Centre for Economic Research, Beijing University. The database has supplied data since 1994, we used the period from 1998 to 2002 on financial statements of all listed companies in China. Information on ownership and corporate governance characteristics were available for the author during the period 1998 to 2002.

The data we used to estimate the model previously described consists of the following variables; total assets (K), opportunity cost of investment for the owner (r). As channels for "expropriation," it is ideal if we can utilize exact values of account receivable or account receivable to the holding company. These figures are reported in the financial statement for all the listed companies at least since 2001. However, the figures for different years often contradict one another. Thus we give up using these here.

As a proxy of expropriation, we use the total asset–gross account receivable ratio (ar), the total asset–gross account payable ratio (ap), or the payable wage or welfare–asset ratio. In order to substitute these proxies for the omitted information, we add the following variables on business: basic information (total sales, total assets, number of employed, total wage payments) and characteristics of ownership (% share of state sponsor, % share of legal person sponsor, % share of foreign sponsor, % share of private placement sponsor share, % share of alter right share, % share of negotiable share, % share of preferred share, % share of other shares, % share of employed staff, % share of ultimate controling owner). The ultimate owner types are classified as follows: 0: state owned, 1: collective ownership 2: labor union control, 3: social organization control, 4: foreign entity control, 5: private individual control, 6: unclassified. The information can be obtained from the database. Descriptive statistics are summarized in the Appendix at the end of this chapter.

12.5.2 Sources of endogeneity and estimation strategy

The motivation in this chapter is to test whether or not the owner's decision deviates from the profit maximization principle of the listed company, and, furthermore, to measure directly the degree of the "strength of control right" or the "separation of control and ownership right." The econometric problem here is how to estimate this degree precisely.

There are several potential sources of inconsistency or biases in our estimation. The endogeneity problem in our problem here can be summarized as follows. The first comes from unobservable time-invariant factors for each of the individual companies. If there exist unobservable individual effects as described in (12.3), the error term ε_{it} and independent variables will be positively correlated. In this situation, if we perform the OLS estimator, the coefficients of interest will be upwardly biased because the error term (12.3) will be positively correlated. In order to eliminate this problem, we do use fixed effect estimator and random effect estimator (see Wooldridge 2002, Chapter 11).

The second problem arises because of endogeneity between opportunity cost, *r*, and variables of "expropriation" channels, such as ratios of account receivable, account payables or other channels to total assets. The decision maker, the controling owner, will choose the level of expropriation according to formal financial costs such as interest rate payments against borrowing, payout to equity shares, etc. Thus, the level of opportunity cost and the ratio of "expropriation channel" is endogenously determined. The use of appropriate instruments variables with fixed effect estimator will offer a method to eliminate this endogeneity problem.

The third, serial correlation of errors also needs to be cured. This is done by employing a first differenced estimator with instrument variables. If this endogeneity exists, more poorly managed companies are listed and the degree of "expropriation" – that is coefficients on expropriation channels – are upwardly biased.[5]

12.5.3 Instruments

We need appropriate instruments to solve the problem of endogeneity between opportunity costs for the owner (*r*). Instruments should be variables that are correlated with opportunity cost *r* but not correlated with expropriation channels (*ex*), or vice versa. Here, we tested three instruments: one-period and two-period lags for each "expropriating" channel, and the "controling owner's share." Information related to ownership characteristics and business basics related to the controling owner explained above in section 12.5.1 were included.

When we address autocorrelation in the error term, two-period lag is a preferable instrument for each "expropriating channel." Other than this, we use a percentage ratio of controling owner share (controller ratio), which is relatively correlated with opportunity cost (correlation .12), but not with expropriation via account receivables (.08). However, these instruments are far from ideal.[6] The results of the estimation are poor. Thus, we will assume that the plain fixed effect estimator or random effect estimator is preferable to the fixed effect estimator or first difference estimator with instruments, as the latter may fail to secure a consistent estimator because of the poor instruments.

12.6 Results

12.6.1 Which estimator is preferable in this instance?

First, we tested several estimators taking account receivable as an expropriating channel; ordinary least squares (OLS) (1), Two Step Least Squares (2SLS, or IV) (2), fixed effect estimators (3) and random effect estimators (4), fixed effect estimator with instruments (5) and first differenced estimator with instruments (6) in Table 12.6.

Table 12.6 shows the results of various estimators on "expropriation" via account receivables. As we suspected, the time-invariant unobservable factor biased the OLS estimator. The OLS estimator shows a much larger coefficient to fixed and random effect estimators. Two step least square with instruments, "2 periods lag of opportunity cost," "controler's share ratio" and other basic business information and ownership characteristics. We found here that coefficients of r (opportunity cost for investors) become insignificant and coefficients for 2SLS estimator is much smaller than OLS and fixed effect estimators. We should doubt that variances are exaggerated by inappropriate instruments.

The fixed effect estimator shows smaller coefficients for both opportunity cost (*r*) and "account receivable" (*ar*) than the OLS estimator. This is presumed to happen thanks to the elimination of unobservable factors. The random effect estimator reports very similar coefficients here. A Hausman test does not reject a hypothesis that coefficients of fixed effect estimator and random effect estimator are not dramatically different from one another. Thus, in this instance we will take random effect estimator as a reference in terms of gains in efficiency.

Further, we use the instruments with fixed effect estimator and first differenced estimators in order to eliminate the endogeneity between opportunity cost (*r*) and expropriation channel (*ar*). When we are going to use instruments, first difference estimator is preferable when autocorrelation is uncertain.[7] However, the results in columns (5) and (6) are unsatisfactory. Fixed effect estimator with instruments shows both coefficients of opportunity cost and account receivables to be insignificant. The first differenced estimator yields confusing results. The coefficient of opportunity cost shows more or less the same results as the plain fixed effect estimator. However, the coefficient of account receivables is ten times smaller than the fixed effect estima-

Table 12.6 Expropriation via account receivables

		OLS	*2SLS(IV)*	*Fixed effect*	*Random effect*	*FE with IV*	*FD with IV*
		(1)	*(2)*	*(3)*	*(4)*	*(5)*	*(6)*
r	Coef.	**0.0429**	0.0117	**0.0206**	**0.0239**	0.045034	**0.029652**
	Std.	**0.0087968**	0.0354306	**0.0054033**	**0.0054507**	0.0352114	**0.0138739**
	t/z value	**4.88**	0.33	**3.81**	**4.38**	1.28	**2.14**
	P>|t| or |z|	**0**	0.742	**0**	**0**	0.201	**0.033**
ar average	Coef.	**–0.14794**	–0.43809	**–0.07639**	**–0.08812**	–1.6586	**–0.8564**
	Std.	**0.039**	0.313	**0.035**	**0.034**	0.9124854	**0.3787446**
	t/z value	**–3.79**	–1.4	**–2.16**	**–2.62**	–1.82	**–2.26**
	P>|t| or |z|	**0**	0.161	**0.031**	**0.009**	0.069	**0.024**
arsc average	Coef.	–0.00171	**–0.19261**	0.000685	0.000654	0.063358	0.019486
	Std.	0.00101	**0.05620**	0.00055	0.00057	0.0407745	0.0108782
	t/z value	**–1.7**	**–3.43**	1.25	1.16	1.55	1.79
	P>|t| or |z|	0.09	**0.001**	0.211	0.248	0.12	0.073
arsc2 average	Coef.	7.94E-07	**0.000144**	–8.23E-07	–7.36E-07	–9.6E-05	–2.1E-05
	Std.	8.58E-07	**0.0000541**	4.60E-07	4.77E-07	0.0000682	0.0000135
	t/z value	0.92	**2.66**	–1.79	–1.54	–1.41	–1.54
	P>|t| or |z|	0.355	**0.008**	0.074	0.123	0.159	0.124
R square	Within	—	—	0.2822	0.2244	—	0.0042
	Between	—	—	0.0604	0.1327	0.0002	0.0084
	All	0.2327	—	0.1004	0.2161	0	0

Table 12.6 Expropriation via account receivables – *continued*

	OLS	*2SLS(IV)*	*Fixed effect*	*Random effect*	*FE with IV*	*FD with IV*
	(1)	*(2)*	*(3)*	*(4)*	*(5)*	*(6)*
Chi2 or F	—	4.36	55.4	235	1131.22	9.78
Prob>chi	—		0	0	0	0
Obs	4322	2728	4322	4322	2728	1667
No. of group:	—	—	1200	1200	1050	1050

Source: Author.

Notes: 1 Bold is the case z value is under .05. Following tables follow this expression.
2 All equations are estimated with variables related with basic business conditions: total sales, total asset, number of employed, total wage payment; and variables on ownership characteristics: % share of state sponsor, % share of legal person sponsor, % share of foreign sponsor, % share of private placement sponsor share, % share of alter right share, % share of negotiable share, % share of preferred share, % share of other share, % share of employed staff, % share of ultimate controling owner.
3 Hausman test does not reject a hypothesis that coefficients of fixed effect estimator and random effect estimator is not different, with chi2 value 11.03 for 17 variables, and probability > chi2 .8552. Thus, random effect estimator is the reference estimator here.

tors. The Chi-squared value is low. To date, we have been unable to explain these result.

Thus, we decided to take plain the fixed effect estimator or random effect estimator our preferred variable in this chapter for the following reasons: (i) it seems to effectively eliminate time-invariant unobservable effect in each of the firms; (ii) even if there is some serial correlation, it is known that bias in the fixed effect estimator is sizable and limited (Wooldridge, 2002, 203). However, as we can see already, the fixed effect estimator might have failed to eliminate endogeneity between opportunity cost (r) and expropriation channels. This is a limitation in terms of the econometric techniques employed in this chapter.

12.6.2 "Expropriation" via various channels

Next, we will test the existence of expropriation via the following channels: (i) account receivable on the asset side of the balance sheet; (ii) account payable; (iii) payable to labor. Table 12.7 shows the results on these potential "channels of expropriation" of fixed effect estimators. Comparing three "channels," account receivables clearly shows the existence of expropriation, as coefficients of significant terms in the test equation are negative, that means the predicted deviation of investor's opportunity cost is negative. On the contrary, coefficients on payable to labor, account payable show positive and significant signs. Account receivable is the item on the asset side, and the other two are those on the liability side of balance sheet. This nature may be related with this result.

As we saw in section 12.3.3, account receivable on the asset side is the item that directly captures a possibility of expropriation. Thus, hereafter, we will take account receivables as the expropriation channel. The estimation with product of account receivable and time dummy confirms that there was expropriation via account receivables in 1999 and 2000.

12.6.3 By types of ultimate owner and by municipal governments = ultimate owner

Next, we test the impact of the type of ultimate ownership, and, individual ultimate owner, who is the municipal government in most cases. Table 12.8 shows the estimated coefficients of the linear combination of account receivables and products terms of type of ownership dummy, year dummy and account receivables. Here, the random effect estimator is a reference estimator from the Hausman test. We can see here that the ultimate owner is the state sector, foreigner and union, and the

Table 12.7 "Expropriation" channels

		Average	**99*	**00*	**01*	**02*			
Account receivable									
r	Coef.	**0.022071**							
	Std.	**0.0054687**					R square	Within	0.2863
	t/z value	**4.04**						Between	0.0591
	P>|t| or |z|	0						All	0.0982
ex	Coef.	–0.06745	**–0.12594**	**–0.08825**	–0.09707	–0.00113	Chi(2)		36.43
	Std.	0.121	**0.0509909**	**0.0428821**	0.0555884	0.0536777			0
	t/z value	–0.56	**–2.47**	**–2.06**	–1.75	–0.02	Obs		4322
	P>|t| or |z|	0.57	**0.014**	**0.04**	0.081	0.983	No. of		1200
		7					Groups		
exsc	Coef.	–0.00045	–0.00169	0.006494	0.000108	–0.00289			
	Std.	0.0245948	0.002826	0.0041785	0.0013863	0.001514			
	t/z value	–0.02	–0.6	1.55	0.08	–1.91			
	P>|t| or |z|	0.985	0.551	0.12	0.938	0.057			
exsc2	Coef.	0.000428	5.39E-06	–8.28E-06	–4.07E-06	1.26E-06			
	Std.	0.0016057	8.86E-06	0.0000466	2.08E-06	8.79E-07			
	t/z value	0.27	0.61	–0.18	–1.95	1.43			
	P>|t| or |z|	0.79	0.543	0.859	0.051	0.153			
Account payable									
r	Coef.	**0.021939**							
	Std.	**0.0053023**					R square	Within	0.3087
	t/z value	**4.14**						Between	0.0816
	P>[t] or |z|	0						All	0.1371

Table 12.7 "Expropriation" channels – *continued*

		Average	**99*	**00*	**01*	**02*			
ex	Coef.	0.270019	**0.537432**	**0.4097**	**0.440795**	**0.529928**	Chi(2)		40.56
	Std.	0.2257513	**0.1006419**	**0.0912401**	**0.0824938**	**0.0726593**			0
	t/z value	**1.2**	**5.34**	**4.49**	**5.34**	**7.29**	Obs		4322
	P>|t| or |z|	0.232	**0**	**0**	**0**	**0**	No. of Groups		1200
exsc	Coef.	–6.14E-13	–0.0035	**0.027025**	0.006389	**–0.00919**			
	Std.	7.37E-13	0.0042241	**0.0093296**	0.0053611	**0.0037253**			
	t/z value	–0.83	–0.83	**2.9**	1.19	**–2.47**			
	P>|t| or |z|	0.405	0.407	**0.004**	0.233	**0.014**			
exsc2	Coef.	–2.60E-15	**4.28E-05**	–0.00015	**8.79E-06**	5.15E-06			
	Std.	1.45E-15	**0.0000182**	0.0000915	**2.68E-06**	2.10E-06			
	t/z value	–1.79	**2.35**	**–1.67**	**3.28**	2.45			
	P>|t| or |z|	0.074	**0.019**	0.095	**0.001**	0.014			
Payable to labor									
r	Coef.	**0.021089**							
	Std.	**0.0054137**					R square	Within	0.287
	t/z value	**3.9**						Between	0.0631
	P>|t| or |z|	0						All	0.1045
ex	Coef.	–0.23476	1.041633	1.212169	**1.956118**	**1.93964**	Chi(2)		36.55
	Std.	2.439697	0.9697154	0.0957732	**0.8838276**	**0.8805899**			0
	t/z value	–0.1	1.07	1.27	**2.21**	**2.2**	Obs		4322
	P>|t| or |z|	0.923	0.283	0.206	**0.027**	**0.028**	No. of Groups		1200

Table 12.7 "Expropriation" channels – *continued*

		Average	**99*	**00*	**01*	**02*
exsc	Coef.	–0.35642	0.130526	**0.415119**	0.046585	–0.04844
	Std.	0.8836935	0.1490265	**0.209633**	0.0965087	0.0615537
	t/z value	–0.4	0.88	**1.98**	**0.48**	–0.79
	$P>\lvert t\rvert$ or $\lvert z\rvert$	0.687	0.381	**0.048**	0.629	0.431
exsc2	Coef.	–0.01765	–0.00054	–0.00284	**–0.00151**	1.88E-05
	Std.	0.0963534	0.0006119	0.002018	**0.0004516**	0.0000299
	t/z value	–0.18	–0.89	–1.41	**–3.34**	0.63
	$P>\lvert t\rvert$ or $\lvert z\rvert$	0.855	0.374	0.16	**0.001**	0.53

Source: Author.

Notes: 1 Bold is the case z value is under .05.
2 Fixed effect estimators with the same specification in Table 12.6.

Table 12.8 Ultimate owner's type: via account receivable

		Average	**SOE*	*Private*	**Collective*	**NPO*	**Union*	**Foreign*			
OLS											
r	Coef.	**0.040256**							R square	Within	—
	Std.	**0.0088307**								Between	—
	t/z value	**4.56**							All	0.2493	
	P>|t| or |z|	**0**							Chi(2)		—
ar	Coef.	–0.17656	**–0.12378**	–0.0329	**–0.53701**	–0.74356	–0.48385	**–0.92534**			—
	Std.	0.1848616	**0.0442069**	0.1053677	**0.1785167**	0.7131283	0.4326429	**0.468937**	Obs		4328
	t/z value	–0.96	**–2.8**	–0.31	–3.01	–1.04	–1.12	**–1.97**	No. of Groups		—
	P>|t| or |z|	0.34	**0.005**	0.755	**0.003**	0.297	0.263	**0.049**			
arsc	Coef.	0.000303	**–0.00246**	0.002234	0.028048	0.078216	–0.02199	0.117181			
	Std.	0.0133064	**0.0011298**	0.0033267	0.0296775	0.148356	0.1423152	0.1736727			
	t/z value	0.02	**–2.18**	0.67	0.95	0.53	–0.15	0.67			
	P>|t| or |z|	0.982	**0.03**	0.502	0.345	0.598	0.877	0.5			
arsc2	Coef.	8.75E-06	9.77E–07	–3.60E–06	0.000548	0.005126	**0.029292**	–0.00718			
	Std.	0.0001796	8.64E–07	5.66E–06	0.0010609	0.0165179	**0.0097004**	0.006957			
	t/z value	0.05	1.13	–0.64	0.52	0.31	**3.02**	–1.03			
	P>|t| or |z|	0.961	**0.258**	0.525	0.606	0.756	**0.003**	0.302			
FE											
r	Coef.	**0.01761**									
	Std.	**0.0054507**							R square	Within	0.3012
	t/z value	**3.23**								Between	0.0588
	P>|t| or |z|	**0.001**								All	0.0992
ar	Coef.	–0.03858	–0.06155	–0.0311	–0.07423	–0.7208	–0.09929	**–0.69593**	Chi(2)		28.82
	Std.	0.133832	0.0400401	0.0782604	0.1474631	0.6301319	0.4590922	**0.3436454**			0
	t/z value	–0.29	–1.54	–0.4	–0.5	–1.14	–0.22	**–2.03**	Obs		4322
	P>|t| or |z|	0.773	0.124	0.691	0.615	0.253	**0.829**	**0.043**	No. of Groups		1200

Table 12.8 Ultimate owner's type: via account receivable – *continued*

		Average	**SOE*	*Private*	**Collective*	**NPO*	**Union*	**Foreign*			
arsc2	Coef.	–0.00482	0.000972	0.000155	0.016764	0.004568	**0.214946**	0.092508			
	Std.	0.0069487	0.0006153	0.0017652	0.0161621	0.0854618	**0.10667**	0.1164114			
	t/z value	–0.69	1.58	0.09	1.04	0.05	**2.02**	0.79			
	P>|t| or |z|	0.488	0.114	0.93	0.3	0.957	**0.044**	0.427			
arsc2	Coef.	-2E–05	-7.86E–07	-2.25E–06	0.000462	0.002693	0.009552	–0.00455			
	Std.	0.000094	4.62E–07	3.00E–06	0.0006104	0.0089372	0.0080664	0.0046625			
	t/z value	–0.22	-1.7	–0.75	0.76	0.3	1.18	–0.98			
	P>|t| or |z|	0.828	0.089	0.454	0.449	0.763	0.236	0.329			
RE											
r	Coef.	**0.020233**									
	Std.	**0.0054982**							R square	Within	0.2412
	t/z value	**3.68**								Between	0.1364
	P>|t| or |z|	**0**								All	0.2226
ar	Coef.	–0.03473	**–0.07782**	–0.01755	–0.20171	–0.68541	0.12928	**–0.72427**	Chi(2)		324.5
	Std.	0.1326175	**0.038119**	0.0775755	0.1425166	0.5904046	0.4181715	**0.3399252**			0
	t/z value	–0.26	**-2.04**	–0.23	-1.42	-1.16	0.31	**-2.13**	Obs		4322
	P>|t| or |z|	0.793	**0.041**	0.821	0.157	0.246	0.757	**0.033**	No. of Groups		1200
arsc	Coef.	–0.00416	0.000879	0.000312	0.017777	0.033682	**0.257742**	0.067478			
	Std.	0.0072023	0.0006367	0.0018294	0.0167485	0.0875164	**0.1000796**	0.1167049			
	t/z value	–0.58	1.38	0.17	1.06	0.38	2.58	0.58			
	P>|t| or |z|	0.563	0.167	0.864	0.289	0.7	**0.01**	0.563			
arsc2	Coef.	-1.1E–05	–6.85E–07	–2.09E–06	0.000437	0.006518	0.008675	–0.00374			
	Std.	0.0000972	4.80E–07	3.11E–06	0.0006227	0.0091879	0.0069489	0.004698			
	t/z value	–0.11	-1.43	–0.67	0.7	0.71	1.25	–0.8			
	P>|t| or |z|	0.913	0.154	0.501	0.483	0.478	0.212	0.427			

Source: Author.

Note: 1 About specifications, see Table 12.6. Hausman test does not reject the coefficients of FE estimator and RE estimator is not different, where chi 2 value is 29.41 for 38 variables and probability >chi2 is .8398. Thus, here the random effect estimator is the reference estimator.

coefficients of interest are statistically significant. At least for the state sector and foreign owner, account receivables are used as an expropriation channel as its coefficients are estimated as negative.

Table 12.9 shows the results of specification with coefficients dummy by individual ultimate owner, who is municipal government or private investor, and invested in more than two listed companies. Interestingly, coefficients of most of the regions' dummies are insignificant, and the regions which show results which are consistent with the existence of expropriation are Shanghai and Tianjin. These regions are part of the richest regions, and the governments are the richest, as seen in Figure 12.1. The result here shows that it is the governments in the richest regions who do more expropriating of the listed company's resources. However, not all the governments in the rich area show expropriation (the main exceptions being Guangdong or Beijing). In addition to the economic level, the political culture of these regions may have some influence on this expropriating behavior.

12.7 Conclusion

The empirical econometric test in this chapter documents that "expropriation" via account receivables existed, for the companies whose ultimate owner is the state sector or foreigner. A striking result is that it is the richer municipal governments such as Shanghai, Tianjin who are expropriating, rather than those in the poorer area. This was seen clearly in the case of Qingqi Motorcycles.

Under China's gradual transition process, the state continues to have a substantial share of listed companies, and direct controling power over their economic resources. Even among listed companies, which are supposed to be the most fragmented in terms of ownership compared to unlisted smaller companies, the state is still the ultimate controling owner of about 80 per cent of listed companies. Under this "concentrated and state ownership," listed companies have been derided as the "wallet of state owner enterprises or governments." This chapter, motivated to test this conjecture empirically, confirmed that this occurs.

The state ownership of listed companies can be justified as long as it does not hinder economic efficiency. The results of this chapter confirm that state ownership does, in fact, affect the economic efficiency of listed companies. The privatization of this state ownership, and the resolution of "pyramiding via holding company" that facilitates "expropriation," are the necessary remedies for this.

Table 12.9 By municipal governments (as ultimate owner): via account receivables

		Fixed effect estimator	*Random effect estimator*			*Fixed effect estimator*	*Random effect estimator*
r	Coef.	**0.019819**	**0.0255486**	Changchun	Coef.	–0.595837	–0.4937119
	Std.er	**0.005504**	**0.0056966**		Std.	0.6356219	0.6255369
	t/z value	**3.6**	**4.48**		t/z value	–0.94	–0.79
	P>|t| or |z|	**0**	**0**		P>|t| or |z|	0.349	0.43
ar average	Coef.	**–0.07688**	**–0.0956921**	Gansu	Coef.	0.3088535	0.3080886
	Std.	**0.041099**	**0.039569**		Std.	0.8186057	0.6694139
	t/z value	**–1.87**	**–2.42**		t/z value	0.38	0.46
	P>|t| or |z|	**0.062**	**0.016**		P>|t| or |z|	0.706	0.645
arsc	Coef.	**0.003074**	**0.0035156**	Guangzhou	Coef.	0.1385536	0.1183291
	Std.	**0.000622**	**0.0006459**		Std.	0.42465	0.4263103
	t/z value	**4.94**	**5.44**		t/z value	0.33	0.28
	P>|t| or |z|	**0**	**0**		P>|t| or |z|	0.744	0.781
arsc2	Coef.	**–1.02E–07**	**–1.17E–07**	Hainan	Coef.	–0.539659	–0.3959529
	Std.	**2.07E–08**	**2.15E–08**		Std.	0.5790426	0.5685843
	t/z value	**–4.94**	**–5.44**		t/z value	–0.93	–0.7
	P>|t| or |z|	**0**	**0**		P>|t| or |z|	0.351	0.486
Anhui	Coef.	–0.220316	–0.1680141	Henan	Coef.	0.7393236	–0.0036704
	Std.	0.43876	0.428774		Std.	0.6669471	0.5253912
	t/z value	–0.5	–0.39		t/z value	1.11	–0.01
	P>|t| or |z|	0.616	0.695		P>|t| or |z|	0.268	0.994
Beijing	Coef.	–0.266857	–0.0121926	Hubei	Coef.	–0.798653	–0.6839221
	Std.	0.2401751	0.2255307		Std.	0.4415936	0.4116538
	t/z value	–1.11	–0.05		t/z value	–1.81	–1.66
	P>|t| or |z|	0.267	0.957		P>|t| or |z|	0.071	0.097

Table 12.9 By municipal governments (as ultimate owner): via account receivables – *continued*

		Fixed effect estimator	*Random effect estimator*			*Fixed effect estimator*	*Random effect estimator*
Hunan	Coef.	0.3681754	0.2200002	Shanghai	Coef.	**–0.34542**	**–0.2608115**
	Std.	0.4117435	0.3934762		Std.	**0.111459**	**0.1085067**
	t/z value	0.89	0.56		t/z value	**–3.1**	**–2.4**
	P>|t| or |z|	0.371	0.576		P>|t| or |z|	**0.002**	**0.016**
Jiansu	Coef.	–0.083571	–0.1807932	Shenyang	Coef.	–0.103134	–0.2591204
	Std.	0.4874935	0.4652744		Std.	0.7406587	0.5802647
	t/z value	–0.17	–0.39		t/z value	–0.14	–0.45
	P>|t| or |z|	0.864	0.698		P>|t| or |z|	0.889	0.655
Jilin	Coef.	–0.052881	–0.0895465	Shenzhen	Coef.	0.0379145	0.0221709
	Std.	0.460378	0.4512693		Std.	0.1547288	0.1544715
	t/z value	–0.11	–0.2		t/z value	0.25	0.14
	P>|t| or |z|	0.909	0.843		P>|t| or |z|	0.806	0.886
Jinan	Coef.	–0.590859	–0.5810498	Sichuan	Coef.	0.3750361	0.3136701
	Std.	0.3478447	0.3474954		Std.	0.2390714	0.233577
	t/z value	–1.7	–1.67		t/z value	1.57	1.34
	P>|t| or |z|	0.089	0.095		P>|t| or |z|	0.117	0.179
Qingdao	Coef.	0.5304746	–0.1985288	Tianjin	Coef.	**–0.99839**	–0.6239414
	Std.	0.613754	0.6008398		Std.	**0.49979**	0.3721414
	t/z value	0.86	–0.33		t/z value	**–2**	–1.68
	P>|t| or |z|	0.387	0.741		P>|t| or |z|	**0.046**	0.094
Shandong	Coef.	–0.465883	–0.205089	Xianxi	Coef.	0.367302	0.5118092
	Std.	0.4223118	0.3960013		Std.	0.8232179	0.65655
	t/z value	–1.1	–0.52		t/z value	0.45	0.78
	P>|t| or |z|	0.27	0.605		P>|t| or |z|	0.656	0.436

Table 12.9 By municipal governments (as ultimate owner): via account receivables – *continued*

		Fixed effect estimator	*Random effect estimator*			*Fixed effect estimator*	*Random effect estimator*
Yunnan	Coef.	0.0405344	–0.0665547	China	Coef.	0.367302	–0.1057231
	Std.	0.5025492	0.5063273		Std.	0.8232179	0.1025847
	t/z value	0.08	–0.13		t/z value	0.45	–1.03
	P>|t| or |z|	0.936	0.895		P>|t| or |z|	0.656	0.303
Zhuhai	Coef.	–0.078831	–0.0110863	R square		0.3014	0.2358
	Std.	0.5652385	0.5785684			0.0613	0.1373
	t/z value	–0.14	–0.02			0.1008	0.2162
	P>|t| or |z|	0.889	0.985	Chi(2)		18.85	287.61
Delong	Coef.	–0.211588	–0.5344746	Obs		4328	4328
	Std.	0.7083948	0.5584166	No. of Groups		1200	1200
	t/z value	–0.3	–0.96				
	P>|t| or |z|	0.765	0.339				

Notes:
1 Name of area reports linear combined coefficients of account receivables plus products of account receivables and area dummy.
2 Name of area represents municipal governments or ultimate investors who own multiple listed companies. Areas which are not reported here were not included in the estimation because author could not identify more than one listed company for each. If invest only one company, we could not identify coefficients.
3 Delong is a private company who invested several listed companies.
4 This estimation is only done for reported city/provinces government dummies plus year dummy.
5 Hausman test rejects the coefficients of FE estimator and RE estimator is not different. with chi2 value 367.0 for 64 variables, probability > chi2 0. Thus, here fixed effect estimator is the reference estimator.

Source: Author.

Notes

1 There is an ironic description of the life of a listed company in China that "on the IPO, the company cheated huge money, the performance is excellent in the first year, average in the second year, then refinancing, the performance is no good anymore in the third year, and will fall on to a danger list, or Special Treatment (ST) in the fourth year, again fall into delisting list, Particular Treatment (PT) in the fifth year, then will been merged or acquired and revitalize at Nirvana in the sixth year."
2 Furthermore, the company reported a more striking story: "the holding company and the listed company made bank loan 800 million RMB, in 1998, but it was all used up by the holding company. The company does not know for what purpose the holding company used the loan" (the annual report of the company 2001 page 13).
3 The opportunity cost for the ultimate owner should be captured as market prevailing opportunity. However, due to limitation of data availability, we assume that actual payment to financing source as the opportunity cost.
4 Treatment on this problem has not been attempted in this chapter.
5 Lag variables of opportunity cost of investor (r) are not only correlated with current opportunity cost (.495 for lag1, and.316 for lag 2), but they are also substantially correlated with current account receivables (–.175 for lag1, and –.125 for lag2). It does not satisfy conditions of ideal instruments.
6 The model we estimate $y_{it} = x_{it}\beta + c_i u_t + \xi_{it}$ here. To do get consistent estimator, if the assumption $E(\xi_{it} | x_{it}, x_{it-1}, \ldots, x_{i1}c_i) = 0$ t = 1,2,... T satisfies, which is weaker than strict exogeneity $E(\xi_{it} | x_{iT}, x_{iT-1}, \ldots, x_{it}, \ldots, x_{i1}c_i) = 0$ t=1,2,....T, we can use $\Delta x_{i,t-1}$ as instrument for $\Delta x_{i,t}$, as $E(\Delta x_{it-1}{}' \Delta\xi_{it}) = 0$. In this situation, our model can be estimated in the first difference transformation $\Delta y_{it} = \Delta x_{it}\beta + \Delta\xi_{it}$ by 2SLS using instrument $\Delta x_{i,t-1}$ (Wooldridge, 2002, 302–3.) Thus, we can easily find appropriate instruments here. However, the results seems to implies that our data does not satisfies with exogeneity assumption above.

References

Bebchuk, L. A. (1999) "A Rent-Protection Theory of Corporate Ownership and Control" Working Paper 7203. NBER.

Bebchuk, L.A. *et al.* (2000) "Stock Pyramids, Cross-Ownership and Dual Class Equity: The Mechanisms and Agency Costs of Separating Control from Cash-Flow Right," in R.K. Morck (ed.), *Concentrated Corporate Ownership*. Chicago: University of Chicago Press.

Classens, S., S. Djankov and L. Lang (2000) "The Separation of Ownership and Control in East Asian Corporations," *Journal of Financial Economics* 58, 81–112.

Faccio, M., L.P.H. Lang and L. Young (2001) "Dividends and Expropriation," *American Economic Review* 91(1), 54–78.

Hart, O. (2001) "Financial Contracting," *Journal of Economic Literature* 39(4), 1079–1100.

Jensen, M. and W. Meckling (1976) "Theory of the Firm: Managerial Behavior, Agency Costs and Ownership Structure," *Journal of Financial Economics* 3(4), 305–60.

Lau, Lawrence, Yingyi Qian and Gerald Roland (2000) ''Reform without Losers: An Interpretation of China's Dual Track Approach to Transition,'' *Journal of Political Economy* 108(1), 120–43.

McMillan J. and B. Naughton (1992) "How to Reform a Planned Economy: Lessons from China," *Oxford Review of Economic Policy* 8 (1), 130–42.

Qian, Y. (2003) "How Reform Worked in China," in D. Rodrik (ed.), *Search of Prosperity: Analytic Narratives on Economic Growth*. Princeton, NJ: Princeton University Press.

Tenev, S., C. Zhang and L. Brefort (2002) *Corporate Governance and Enterprise Reform in China: Building the Institutions of Modern Markets*. Washington, DC: World Bank and IFC.

Wooldridge, J.M. (2002) *Econometric Analysis of Cross Section and Panel Data*. Cambridge, MA: MIT Press.

Appendix

Table A12.1 Summary of descriptive statistics

Variable	*Remarks*	*Obs.*	*Mean*	*Std. Dev.*	*Min.*	*Max.*
f′(K)	YK=sales/total asset	5112	0.512177	0.406619	–0.0830648	4.909283
r	opportunity cost for investor=(interest	5115	0.013421	0.597748	–19.045	0.5369708
r (lag1)	1 period lag for r	3912	0.045864	0.306471	–10.28205	0.5369708
r (lag2)	2 periods lag for r	2779	0.066479	0.181994	–3.034977	0.5369708
ar	Account receivable/total asset	5115	0.20797	0.15343	0.0002215	2.694946
arsc	ar/controller's share	5103	0.516819	5.758903	–181.4241	191.3207
arsc2	ar/(controller's share) ^2	5103	174.6113	6.70E+03	3.79E–08	435352.8
ap	Account payable/total asset	5115	0.10431	0.087132	0	0.7671066
apsc	ap/controller's share	5103	4.40E+08	1.14E+10	–5.99E+11	4.61E+11
apsc2	ap/(controller's share) ^2	5103	1.77E+11	7.34E+12	0	4.82E+14
paytolabor	payable wage+payable to welfare/total asset	5115	0.007563	0.009965	–0.0150208	0.1385956
paytolabor	paytolabor/controller's share	5103	0.020118	0.155412	–0.5395186	8.628631
paytolabor	paytolabor/(controller's share) ^2	5103	4.960852	277.8434	–26.32555	19634.56
year99	year dummy for 1999	5115	0.179472	0.383785	0	1
year00	year dummy for 2000	5115	0.206061	0.404514	0	1
year01	year dummy for 2001	5115	0.220919	0.414907	0	1
year02	year dummy for 2002	5115	0.23304	0.422809	0	1
total sales		5112	1.13E+09	6.50E+09	–5.24E+07	3.24E+1
total asset		5115	1.96E+09	7.94E+09	3.57E+07	3.68E+11
number of employed			4336	2966.595	10015.99	10
443808						
total wage payment		5115	6.55E+07	2.76E+08	0.00E+00	1.30E+10
% share of state sponsor		5108	33.15749	26.93096	0	88.58187
% share of legal person sponsor		5108	17.76199	23.8886	0	84.96716

Appendix

Table A12.1 Summary of descriptive statistics – *continued*

Variable	*Remarks*	*Obs.*	*Mean*	*Std. Dev.*	*Min.*	*Max.*
% share of foreign sponsor,		5108	1.023009	5.005032	0	46.16156
% share of private placement sponsor share		5108	8.357258	14.06918	0	74.33992
% share of alter right share		5108	0.464745	2.253012	0	25.18523
% share of negotiable share		5108	37.53235	12.32543	3.596547	100
% share of preferred		5108	0.01624	0.488228	0	15.51997
% share of other share		5108	0.420984	3.936542	0	66.18984
% share of employed staff		5108	1.23937	4.351809	0	48.4767
% share of ultimate controlling owner		5115	44.6489	17.73395	0.39	88.58
Anhui	if ultimate owner is Anhui=1, otherwise=0	5115	0.012317	0.110306	0	1
Beijing	if ultimate owner is Beijing govern't=1, otherwise=0	5115	0.023656	0.15199	0	1
Changchun	if ultimate owner is Changchun govern't=1, otherwise=0	5115	0.005279	0.072469	0	1
China	if ultimate owner is central govern't=1, otherwise=0	5115	0.11437	0.318291	0	1
Delong	if ultimate owner is Delong=1, otherwise=0	5115	0.003324	0.05756	0	1
Gansu	if ultimate owner is Gansu govern't=1, otherwise=0	5115	0.006256	0.078856	0	1
Guangzhou	if ultimate owner is Guangzhou govern't=1, otherwise=0	5115	0.008211	0.090251	0	1
Hainan	if ultimate owner is Hainan govern't=1,	5115	0.005279	0.072469	0	1
Henan	if ultimate owner is Henan govern't=1, otherwise=0	5115	0.006452	0.08007	0	1
Hubei	if ultimate owner is Hubei govern't=1, otherwise=0	5115	0.008016	0.089179	0	1
Hunan	if ultimate owner is Hunan govern't=1, otherwise=0	5115	0.012512	0.111167	0	1
Jiansu	if ultimate owner is Jiansu govern't=1, otherwise=0	5115	0.008211	0.090251	0	1
Jilin	if ultimate owner is Jilin govern't=1, otherwise=0	5115	0.004692	0.068345	0	1
Jinan	if ultimate owner is Jinan govern't=1,	5115	0.005279	0.072469	0	1
Qingdao	if ultimate owner is Qingdao govern't=1, otherwise=0	5115	0.007038	0.083606	0	1
Shandong	if ultimate owner is Shenyang govern't=1, otherwise=0	5115	0.009189	0.095425	0	1
Shanghai	if ultimate owner is Shanghai govern't=1, otherwise=0	5115	0.072336	0.259069	0	1
Shenyang	if ultimate owner is Shenyang govern't=1, otherwise=0	5115	0.006843	0.082445	0	1

Table A12.1 Summary of descriptive statistics – *continued*

Variable	*Remarks*	*Obs.*	*Mean*	*Std. Dev.*	*Min.*	*Max.*
Shenzhen	if ultimate owner is Shenzhen govern't=1, otherwise=0	5115	0.038123	0.191512	0	1
Sichuan	if ultimate owner is Sichuan govern't=1, otherwise=0	5115	0.016031	0.125608	0	1
Tianjin	if ultimate owner is Tianjin govern't=1, otherwise=0	5115	0.012903	0.112868	0	1
Xianxi	if ultimate owner is Xianxi govern't=1, otherwise=0	5115	0.004301	0.065448	0	1
Yunnan	if ultimate owner is Yunnan govern't=1, otherwise=0	5115	0.008016	0.089179	0	1
Zhuhai	if ultimate owner is Zhuhai govern't=1, otherwise=0	5115	0.002542	0.050355	0	1
SOE	if ultimate owner is registered as state sector=1,	5115	0.816031	0.387497	0	1
private	if ultimate owner is registered as private person=1,	5115	0.097752	0.297008	0	1
union	if ultimate owner is registered as union=1, otherwise=0	5115	0.007234	0.084751	0	1
NPO	if ultimate owner is registered as NPO=1, otherwise=0	5115	0.006061	0.077621	0	1
collective	if ultimate owner is registered as collective=1,	5115	0.029521	0.169278	0	1
foreign	if ultimate owner is registered as foreign person=1,	5115	0.009384	0.096426	0	1

Source: Author.

Index